F 2183 .I67 2004

Introduction to the
Pan-Caribbean /
32355003122850

DATE DUE			

Introduction to the Pan-Caribbean

Introduction to the
Pan-Caribbean

Edited by Tracey Skelton

A member of the Hodder Headline Group
LONDON

Distributed in the United States of America by Oxford
University Press Inc., New York

First published in Great Britain in 2004 by
Arnold, a member of the Hodder Headline Group,
338 Euston Road, London NW1 3BH

Http://www.arnoldpublishers.com

Distributed in the United States of America by
Oxford University Press Inc.
198 Madison Avenue, New York, NY 10016

The advice and information in this book are believed to be true and
accurate at the date of going to press, but neither the editor not the publisher
can accept any legal responsibility or liability for any errors or omissions.

British Library Cataloguing in Publication Data
A catalogue record for this book is available from the British Library

Library of Congress Cataloging-in-Publication Data
A catalog record for this book is available from the Library of Congress

ISBN 0 340 70580 9

1 2 3 4 5 6 7 8 9 10

Typeset in 10/14 pt Gillsans Light by Pantek Arts Ltd, Maidstone, Kent.
Printed and bound in Malta.

What do you think about this book? Or any other Arnold title?
Please send your comments to feedback.arnold@hodder.co.uk

For my sisters, Tania and Janina, who have shared the
Caribbean with me, and my nieces, Mia and Freya,
who I hope will do so in the future.

Tracey Skelton

Contents

List of maps

List of plates

List of boxes

List of tables

Notes on contributors

Laurence Brown is Assistant Professor in the Department of History and Social Sciences at the American University of Paris. He has taught courses on Caribbean migration at the University of the West Indies, Cave Hill and has recently published an article on 'The Three Faces of Post-Emancipation Migration in Martinique, 1848–1865', *The Journal of Caribbean History*, 32, 2, 2002.

Jessica Byron studied at the UWI Cave Hill and St. Augustine campuses before doing her Ph.D. in International Relations at the Institut Universitaire de Hautes Etudes Internationales, University of Geneva, Switzerland. Before joining the Department of Government at the University of the West Indies (Mona Campus) in 1994, she lectured in The Hague at the Institute of Social Studies, and worked as a Foreign Service Officer for the Government of St. Kitts and Nevis, and for the Organisation of Eastern Caribbean States. Her research interests and publications are in the areas of Caribbean – European relations, Caribbean – Latin American relations, small states in the multilateral system and gender and International Relations. She currently lectures in International Relations and Latin American politics and development.

Lennox Honychurch is Staff Tutor, Heritage Studies, based at the UWI School of Continuing Studies, Dominica. Born and educated in Dominica, he studied anthropology at St. Hugh's College, University of Oxford. He has published history textbooks for Caribbean schools as well as numerous books on Dominican history and culture.

David Howard is a lecturer in Human Geography at the University of Edinburgh. His main research interests centre on migration and racism in Caribbean societies, with a specific focus on the Dominican Republic, Jamaica and Belize. Recent publications include *Coloring the Nation: Race and Ethnicity in the Dominican Republic* (Lynne Reiner, 2001) and *Kingston: Cities of the Imagination* (Signal Books, 2003.)

Beverley Mullings is Assistant Professor in the Department of Geography at Syracuse University. Her research focuses on the political economy of globalisation, economic restructuring and transformations in the relationship between women and work. She has written more specifically on the impact of new service-based exports on the economic development of the Caribbean, and the transformations in gender relations that these new forms of work have brought. She is the author of a number of articles on the gendered nature of the restructuring of tourism, information technology, finance and banking services in the region.

Cleve McD. Scott is from St. Vincent and the Grenadines. He obtained his Ph.D. entitled, *The Politics of Crown Colony Government: Land, Labour and Politics in a Colonial State, St. Vincent and the Grenadines, 1883 to 1937* from the University of the West Indies,

Cave Hill, Barbados in 2003. Other writings include 'The UNIA in St. Vincent and The Grenadines', *UNIA and Marcus Garvey Papers* (forthcoming from UCLA); ' "Antigua", a review of the economy of Antigua and Barbuda'. In S. Pendergast and T. Pendergast (eds.) *The Worldmark Encyclopedia of National Economies* Detroit: The Gale Group, 2002. He works full-time with Oxfam GB as a project officer responsible for trade and advocacy work in the English-speaking Caribbean. He teaches part-time on History of the Atlantic World and Caribbean Civilisation at UWI, Cave Hill. Otherwise, he is a sound and recording engineer and record producer.

Tracey Skelton is senior lecturer in Human Geography at Loughborough University where she teaches courses on gender and development, culture and development and geographies of social and political difference. Her Caribbean related work has focused on the gender and sexual politics of Jamaican ragga music, racism and representation of Jamaica in the media and the clash between local and global conceptualisations of land. Her main focus in the Caribbean has been on the island of Montserrat, initially the structure of gender relations, and currently the social and cultural impacts of the volcanic crisis. She is the co-editor of *Culture and Global Change* (Routledge, 1998). Tracey has been a very active member of the UK based Society for Caribbean Studies for the past 10 years.

Acknowledgements

With a book project of this kind there are always people who help in small and yet important ways, especially in the final stages. I was fortunate enough to receive many such little gems. They ranged from; advice on formatting given over the phone when a chapter just would not conform, to offers of cups of tea; being replaced at a meeting to give me a 'free' afternoon for the book, and a cooked meal and glass of wine waiting for me at home no matter how late I stayed at work. There were also regular utterances of encouragement to carry on with 'it', the provision of resources, and patience.

To begin with the latter I would like to thank the publishers, Hodder Arnold, and the various commissioning editors I have worked with, who have remained enthusiastic about the book, despite the long wait for it to develop and materialise. I'd also like to express gratitude to all of the chapter authors in the text who responded to my often less than adequate and late editorial comments and pleas for alterations or extra information. I hope you are all pleased with the end product, any errors herein are of course my responsibility.

Friends and work colleagues provided the supportive jewels mentioned above, emotional, technical and social. I am particularly grateful to Jo Bullard, Sarah Holloway, Sue Loveridge, Steve Rice, Mark Szegner and Gill Valentine. I hope to be able to return the favours when they are needed.

Special mention should go to David Howard, Cleve Scott, Clive Cartwright and Mark Szegner. David and Cleve both did a stirling job of providing wonderful images for the book and Clive formatted them all. Mark Szegner showed great patience with my requests, as always, and drew all of the maps for chapter one with great care and accuracy.

Teacher and calypso writer, Rowan Seon, very kindly gave his permission for reprinting of some of his winning St Lucian song lyrics in Chapter five.

Much of the thinking, planning, reading and writing for my parts of this book took place in two places and at two different times. Initially the inception and early thoughts had the time and space to emerge when I was on a Visiting Fellowship at All Souls College, Oxford in 2000–2001. More recently, I was the guest of Dr. Nina Laurie, Visiting Research Fellow in the Center for Latin American and Caribbean Research at the University of Champagne-Urbana, Illinois. I spent an enjoyable and highly productive week as a guest reader of the excellent library there and had access to wonderful materials on the Caribbean. Both institutions (and Nina with her own special and generous brand of hospitality, in particular her BBQ skills) afforded me thinking and reading time just when I most needed it.

Acknowledgements

1
The Pan-Caribbean: diversity and semblance

Tracey Skelton

I have thought about what I would write about the Pan-Caribbean for this introductory chapter for the duration of this whole book project, which can be measured in years rather than months. Each time I feel confident that I have grasped something tangible and meaningful to say about the diversity and semblance in the region, other possibilities crowd in upon me and I lose my grip both of the concept and the words to reflect the intense complexity which constitutes the Pan-Caribbean. The more one learns about, and experiences, the Caribbean, the more one realises it is ever-changing, infinitely varied and yet has a resonance of meaning that lets you know you are 'in' the Caribbean either physically, or tangentially through reading about it.

Working on this book I began to recognise even more the validity (even sanity!) of researchers and authors focusing on one sub-section of the region. Examples include, the English-speaking Commonwealth Caribbean (Payne and Sutton 2001), the Hispanic Caribbean (James and Perivolaris 2000) or the French Caribbean (Aud-Buscher and Ormerod Noakes 2003; Burton and Reno 1995). In this way the subject area is at least geographically and linguistically defined. Another way to 'contain' the complexity of the Caribbean is to focus on a particular theme; tourism (Pattullo 1996), development (McAfee 1991), economics (Alonso 2002), or ethnicity (Oostindie 1996). All of the above are scholarly works and contribute a great deal to our knowledge of the region. In addition there are books which provide highly readable overviews. They are rich in anecdotes and stories which serve to capture the depth of Caribbean pasts and presents (Ferguson 1999; Gilmore 2000). However, a central goal of this book is to provide a range of perspectives from different authors, each focusing on a specific theme, but located within the Pan-Caribbean region. It is therefore an introduction to the Pan-Caribbean through which readers will learn of the diversity across and within the region and the semblances through time and space.

Defining the Pan-Caribbean

Anyone who is familiar with the Caribbean itself or the scholarship about it will realise that defining the region is extremely difficult and also highly varied, and at times contested. In this book alone you will note different interpretations of the Pan-Caribbean;

for some it is the greater Caribbean which includes parts of the Americas; for others it is largely defined as the island Caribbean; and for yet others it is the islands and selected countries on the mainland which have traditionally identified themselves as Caribbean rather than Latin American, for example Belize and Guyana[1]. This means that within one book, we examine a wide definition of the region but always maintain a Pan-Caribbean perspective. This representation includes, among other things: an articulation of Pan-Caribbean pre-history; an examination of European colonialism; a consideration of the development factors of the contemporary independent and dependent/colonial Caribbean; an analysis of the migratory patterns and social transformations throughout and beyond the region; and a scrutiny of the region's role in respect of globalisation and tourism. The Pan-Caribbean is represented through time and space but always from the perspective of an inclusive definition.

This movement towards inclusiveness is reflected in some of the most recent political structures and institutions of the region. The Association of Caribbean States (ACS) boasts 28 members including France, Mexico, Nicaragua and others in Latin America. It is a clear reflection of the way in which the Caribbean is forging, both from its own choice and through 'encouragement' from the European Union and the USA, a regional identity that brings it closer to the Americas. The Caribbean Community (CARICOM) has traditionally comprised the English-speaking independent territories (although Montserrat belongs through its membership of the Organisation of Eastern Caribbean States). Recently though CARICOM has diversified and Dutch-speaking Suriname and French/Creole-speaking Haiti have joined the previous thirteen members. The home page of the web site displays individual country's flags with the CARICOM flag waving in the centre (www.caricom.org). For many in the region this reorientation away from the past colonising powers is a painful and risky process. Old economic securities, however partial, are slipping away or being formally challenged by the hegemonic power in the region, the USA, through international institutions such as the World Trade Organisation. New markets, allies and trade connections must be established, but alongside this, cultural exchanges and a widening of educational curricula will contribute to felt and lived interconnections much more so than the economic linkages will be able to.

There are recent texts that adopt a Pan-Caribbean context for their subject focus. Irma Alonso's edited collection *Caribbean Economies in the Twenty-First Century* (2002) examines whether the Caribbean *island* nations are prepared for the challenges of the new century. The book focuses on 24 islands from The Bahamas to Trinidad and Tobago and, although they are called 'nations', even the dependent territories and départments are included. Holge Henke's and Fred Reno's edited collection *Modern Political Culture in the Caribbean* (2003) focuses on the regional differences among the English, French, Dutch and Spanish Caribbean. These texts combined with our *Introduction* to the region (which does not have dedicated chapters focusing on economics and politics but rather intertwines these subjects within other topics) provide an excellent framework for an awareness and comprehension of the Pan-Caribbean.

Mapping the Caribbean

As a geographer I find maps fascinating. They are an intriguing representation of place and often, until I have seen a place on a map I cannot orientate myself; I don't feel as though I know where I am. However, it is essential to remember that maps are not neutral and 'true' representations of a place, but are often translations of bias, political constructions or cultural superiority (Massey 1995). Nevertheless they have always been, and will continue to be, important factors in our 'seeing' of places.

When I first went to the beautiful, small island of Montserrat for my Ph.D. research (Skelton, 1989) one of the first things I did was purchase a map. It was not a tourist map, which often show partial and commercially oriented information, but something akin to the detailed maps of the Ordnance Survey. I studied the map closely, traced the roads and rivers, rehearsed the names of villages: Kinsale, Gerralds, Long Ground, Molyneaux and tried to conceptualise the physical reality of the heights of mountains such as Chances Peak and the Silver Hills. During the year I spent on the island, conducting my research, I met and worked with people from all over the island and so the map changed in meaning. Now the villages were the homes of people I knew. I learned each curve and twist of the Harris-Plymouth road which I drove almost daily. I had real and vivid three-dimensional images of the island from the top of Chances Peak which I climbed one day. All of these reconstructed what the map meant and brought it to life. At this moment in time, this particular map is an important cultural and historical document. Much of what is shown on that map no longer exists. The volcanic eruption, which began in 1995 and still continues, has totally destroyed large sections of the south, the east and the central parts of the island. Suddenly the places of the north have become important as places of refuge and new home building. The map needs changing in the light of the natural disaster but the original map of Montserrat remains an important representation of memory, place and 'home'. It is a precious artefact which shows what Montserrat once was and indicates what it can re-become in the future.

In a similar way maps of the Pan-Caribbean tell us different stories. They let us see visually which places are included and which left out. They demonstrate geographical and spatial relations between places – which nations are neighbours (Jamaica and Cuba), which share borders (Haiti and the Dominican Republic, Saint Martin and Sint Maarten, Guyana and Suriname[2]), which appear isolated either geographically or culturally (Barbados, Belize). In this section of the book I draw your attention to different representations of the Pan-Caribbean in cartographic form. You will find each of these mappings evident in different parts of the book.

Map 1.1, *The Pan-Caribbean*, is the base map which includes all the islands and mainland countries which form the majority understanding of the Pan-Caribbean for the purposes of this book. Hence the Caribbean coastlines of countries in the Americas and all of the islands are represented here. The Pan-Caribbean is therefore defined as the land masses which meet the Caribbean Sea (although not all the Central American coastlines can be visible in their entirety).

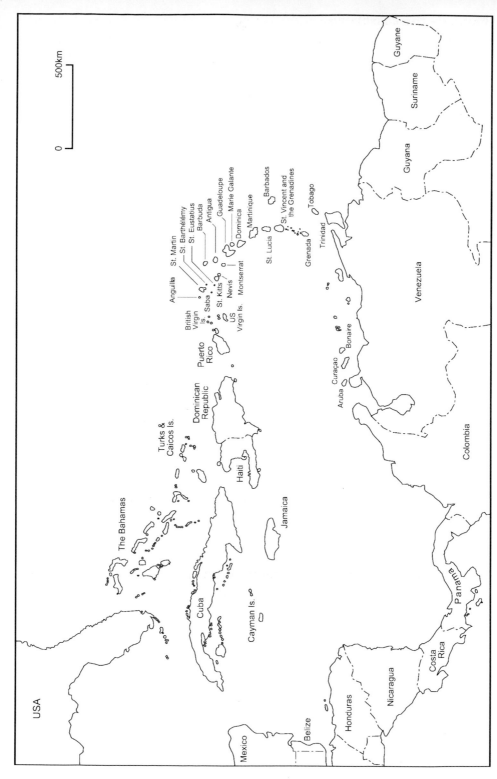

Map 1.1 *The Pan-Caribbean*

From this base map there are thence a multitude of ways in which sub-definitions of the region can be cartographically laid down. It is possible to layer different groupings, clusters and collections of places in the region to show diversities and semblances. For the purpose of this book three layerings have been selected: economic, political and socio-cultural. There could be many more, and each map would represent subtly different information. However, this is not a book of maps but rather of scholarly analysis and discussion of key themes at play in the Pan-Caribbean. The particular maps drawn for this book will help us visualise the region, but they necessarily construct it in a particular way.

Map 1.2 *The Caribbean Community (CARICOM): an economic definition* shows the largest economic clustering of nations in the Pan-Caribbean. It is important to bear in mind that CARICOM also has a political purpose (see Chapter Four). Caribbean economic structures show obvious similarities. Agriculture for the majority remains an important source of employment and foreign exchange earnings. Small-scale farming and gardening is a common feature of rural Caribbean people's lives and provides an important base for household economics and survival. The various attempts at industrialisation are evident in the presence of factories and the lists of export commodities produced in the region. Tourism is ever present and plays a significant and highly visible role in economic structures. Services in the form of offshore banking and data processing are extremely important aspects of the economy for some of the smaller, non-independent islands. The necessity and urgency of diversification is a substantial part of the region's current economic discourse. In addition, when we consider economic structures we can see a striking difference between one country and the rest. Cuba has a socialist state-run economy and is blockaded by a US embargo[3]. The other countries are now all constructed as open economies following the neo-liberal economic models.

Map 1.3 *A political interpretation of the Pan-Caribbean,* illustrates one of the most politically interesting aspects of the region. The Caribbean is the site of the largest number of non-independent/colonised states in the world. There are 12 non-independent[4] and 16 independent 'nations' constituting this particular definition of Pan-Caribbean. This political anachronism contributes profoundly to the diversity of economic and political structures as well as to the social and cultural development status of the different 'states' (see Chapter Three). The non-independent territories face complex political dilemmas in similar ways to their neighbouring independent states but their continued colonial status creates a very specific dimension (see Gamaliel Ramos and Israel Rivera 2001).

A partial representation of social and cultural heritages of the islands is demonstrated in Map 1.4 *A map to show the linguistic diversity of the Pan-Caribbean.* This map shows the remaining legacies of European colonialism. However, it also shows the linguistic heritage that was interlaced with that of the dominant power, that of African languages. In Haiti the Creole spoken and written is a complex merging of French and

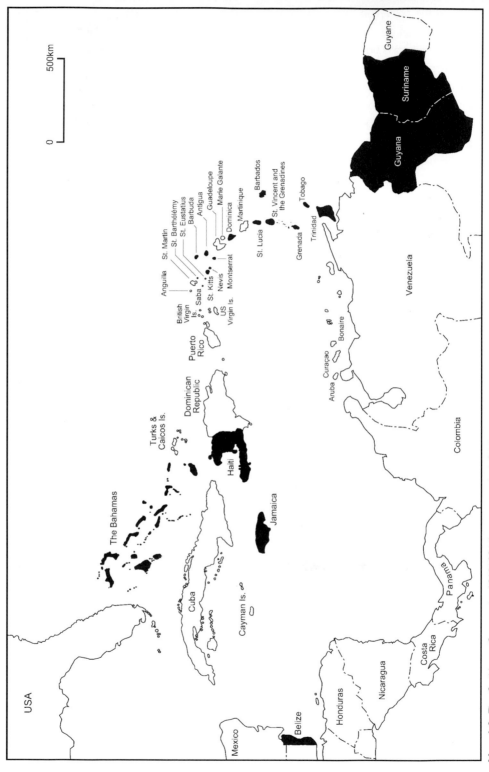

Map 1.2 *The Caribbean Community (CARICOM): an economic definition*

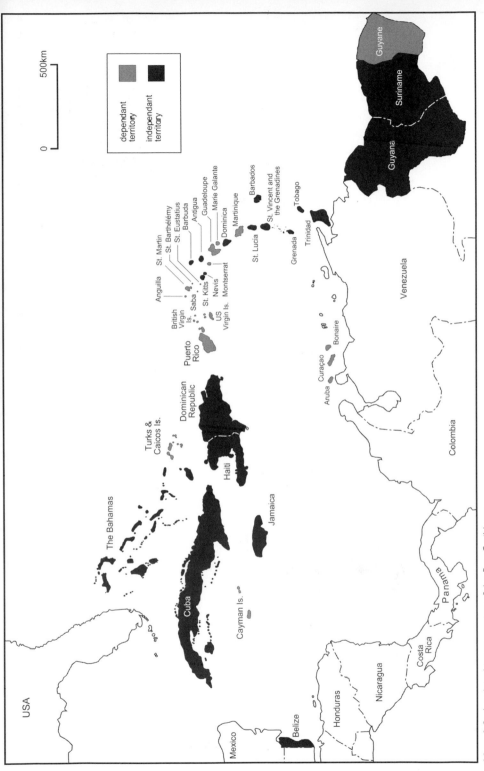

500km

0

dependant territory

independant territory

USA

Mexico

The Bahamas

Turks & Caicos Is.

Cuba

Cayman Is.

Jamaica

Haiti

Dominican Republic

Belize

Honduras

Nicaragua

Costa Rica

Panama

Colombia

Venezuela

Puerto Rico

British Virgin Is.

US Virgin Is.

Anguilla

St. Martin

St. Barthélémy

St. Eustatius

Saba

St. Kitts

Nevis

Barbuda

Antigua

Montserrat

Guadeloupe

Marie Galante

Dominica

Martinique

St. Lucia

Barbados

St. Vincent and the Grenadines

Grenada

Tobago

Trinidad

Aruba

Curaçao

Bonaire

Guyana

Suriname

Guyane

Map 1.3 *A political interpretation of the Pan-Caribbean*

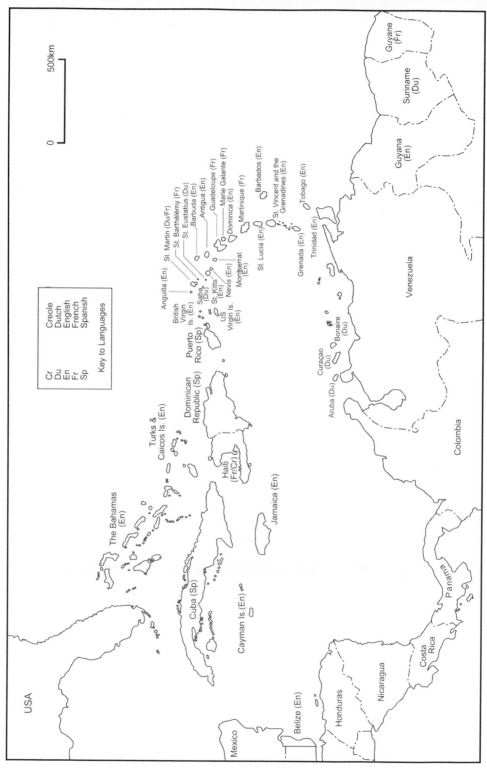

Map 1.4 A map to show the linguistic diversity of the Pan-Caribbean

Key to Languages

Cr	Creole
Du	Dutch
En	English
Fr	French
Sp	Spanish

USA

Mexico

Belize (En)

Honduras

Nicaragua

Costa Rica

Panama

Colombia

Venezuela

The Bahamas (En)

Cuba (Sp)

Cayman Is. (En)

Jamaica (En)

Haiti (Fr/Cr)

Dominican Republic (Sp)

Turks & Caicos Is. (En)

Puerto Rico (Sp)

British Virgin Is. (En)

US Virgin Is. (En)

Anguilla (En)

St. Martin (Du/Fr)

St. Barthélemy (Fr)

St. Eustatius (Du)

Barbuda (En)

Antigua (En)

Guadeloupe (Fr)

Marie Galante (Fr)

Dominica (En)

Martinique (Fr)

Barbados (En)

St. Vincent and the Grenadines (En)

Tobago (En)

St. Lucia (En)

Grenada (En)

Trinidad (En)

Saba (Du)

St. Kitts (En)

Nevis (En)

Montserrat (En)

Aruba (Du)

Curaçao (Du)

Bonaire (Du)

Guyana (En)

Suriname (Du)

Guyane (Fr)

500km

0

West African languages. In the Dutch Antilles of Aruba[5], Bonaire and Curaçao, Papiamentu (Papiamento) is widely spoken and is generally accepted as a linguistic meeting of Portuguese and West African languages. Even where islands are listed as speaking English the diversity of dialects and accents of each country are audible and expert listeners can invariably place speakers to their 'home' islands. Islands such as St. Lucia and Dominica, which had periods of French colonialism, are officially described as English speaking but the everyday language spoken there, especially in the rural areas, is in fact a Creole that has more affinity to French than English.

Representing the Pan-Caribbean

The Caribbean struggles to resist external representations which reduce it to sun, sand, surf and sex (see Chapter Five). The Caribbean is sold, marketed and stereotyped as a paradise for play, an idyll of adventure and a construct of consumption (see Sheller 2003). While parts of the Caribbean are indeed extremely beautiful and there *are* stunning beaches lapped by gorgeous turquoise seas, this is not all that constitutes the Caribbean. It is essential not to perpetuate persistent and uni-dimensional stereotypes of the Pan-Caribbean, but it is also important to remember why the places are so loved, enjoyed and admired by people who reside there and people who are privileged enough to visit. The three images selected for this chapter show some of the natural beauty of the Caribbean landscape and vernacular architecture, but at the same time, along with other images used in the text, serve as a reminder of the complex differences within the region. It is important to recall that, for many, behind the beauty lies persistent poverty (see Chapters Three and Five). Plate 1.1 is a photograph taken in

Plate 1.1 *An ox and cart being used to collect sugar cane and wood in rural Cuba.*
© David Howard

contemporary Cuba and shows an ox and cart being used to collect sugar cane and wood. Sugar represents a great deal in the Caribbean context. It was the subject of an economic and agricultural system which exploited slave labour, it was the reason for complex labour migrations and it remains an important cash crop. In the Cuban case it was the main commodity of economic exchange with the USSR in an attempt to beat the post-revolutionary US embargo (see Chapters Two, Three, Six and Seven).

The second image (plate 1.2) is a view of English Harbour and Falmouth, Antigua. At first glance it is the 'typical' representation of the region: sea, sun, sand, but it also represents more than this. Historically, the coves and bays would have been essential havens for ships in the wars between different European powers waged for territorial dominance in Caribbean waters. It shows the importance of tourism for the island state of Antigua and Barbuda, but makes us think of the environmental problems tourism brings. Nevertheless, the image can serve to show some of the natural beauty of the Caribbean landscape and hence remind us of the need for tourist development that is sustainable (see Chapters Two, Three, Five, and Eight).

Plate 1.3 shows a part of the Caribbean that is not often represented, the Dutch Caribbean. The careful decoration and design of this house front shows both a pride of place and a sense of hybridity as the designs are both Caribbean and Dutch.

The chapters which constitute this book provide an intellectually pleasing circularity and continuity. In Chapter Two, Cleve McD. Scott presents an historical analysis and Lennox Honychurch, in the final chapter, analyses cultural formations in the Caribbean beginning with the pre-colonial historical context. Circularity is a pervasive discourse in Caribbean writing, especially in relation to movements of people (Pessar 1997; Puri

Plate 1.2 *English Harbour and Falmouth, Antigua*

© David Howard

Plate 1.3 *House design and decoration in Sint Maarten, Netherlands Antilles*
© Tracey Skelton

2003) and in the telling and retelling of stories through literature, song, dance and theatre. Tracey Skelton, in Chapter Three, critiques the notion of development, which threads on through to Jessica Byron's critical commentary on globalisation and its impact on the region (Chapter Four) and Beverley Mullings' insightful take on tourism (Chapter Five). The complex circles of movements and identities of Caribbean people are described and analysed by Laurence Brown and David Howard in Chapters Six and Seven respectively.

This book can be read as a whole and as such provides a nuanced and complex insight into a region which is at once highly different and similar. The holistic reader will come across what appears to be snippets of repetition. For example, there is history in Chapter Six and stories of migration in Chapter Eight, tourism appears in Chapter Three as well as in greater detail in Chapter Five. This overlap is intentional. It can be thought of as a parallel to the Caribbean Sea which laps at the edges of each of the countries in the Pan-Caribbean. However, each chapter can be read independently as the contextual elements so necessary for understanding each subject remain present in each. This is similar to the way in which living in or visiting one Caribbean country can provide a distinctive experience but also an insight into the Pan-Caribbean. Living in, or visiting, one Caribbean country often stimulates a desire to live in, and see, others, especially in the Eastern Caribbean where neighbouring islands are visible on the horizon. We hope that reading one chapter of this book will stimulate you to read the others. We also trust that this book will serve as an intellectual map through one of the most fascinating parts of the world, through the Pan-Caribbean.

Notes

[1] One of the apparent omissions to our definition of the Caribbean is the island of Bermuda, which isn't mentioned explicitly in any of the chapters, but which is sometimes defined as Caribbean. It remains a British Overseas Territory but it is located in the North Atlantic rather than the Caribbean Sea. It has some commonalties of history and has been a site of Caribbean migration over time.

[2] In many caribbean texts, on web sites and maps there are two ways of spelling Surinam/Suriname. Throughout this text we use the spelling Suriname. I have been unable to find out why there are these differences in spelling.

[3] In the June and July of 2003, the reality and far-reaching aspects of the US embargo became apparent to other committee members of the UK-based Society for Caribbean Studies (www.scsonline.freeserve.co.uk) and myself. Each year we award a travel bursary in the name of Caribbean scholar and former member of the society, Bridget Jones, to a Caribbean-based artist, arts practitioner or arts researcher. For the conference of 2003 a Cuban academic, artist and activist, Felix Kindelan Delis, was the successful recipient of the award. As part of the bursary we needed to send him money via his bank account to pay for travel documents and visas. None of the usual companies would transfer the money because of the US embargo. This demonstrates two things. Firstly how the US embargo serves to stifle Cuba, Cubans and all aspects of Cuban life. Secondly how powerful the US is forcing even apparently non-US companies to obey its economic embargo. As I write this introduction we were still not sure whether Felix would make it to the UK and to our conference.

[4] The 12 non-independent territories are: Anguilla, British Virgin Islands, Cayman Islands, Montserrat, Turks and Caicos Islands; Martinique, Guadeloupe and Guyane; Aruba and the Dutch Antilles; Puerto Rico and the US Virgin Islands.

[5] Strictly speaking Aruba is no longer one of the Dutch Antilles but it is not fully independent either, it has autonomous federation status but remains an integral part of the Kingdom of the Netherlands (Alonso and Hicks 2002).

References

Alonso, I. T. (ed.) 2002: *Caribbean Economies in the Twenty-first Century*. Gainesville: University Press of Florida.

Alonso, I. T. and Hicks, D. R. 2002: 'The economic structure of the French- and Dutch-speaking Caribbean islands'. In Alonso, I. T. (ed.) 2002: *Caribbean Economies in the Twenty-first Century*. Gainesville: University Press of Florida. pp. 86–96.

Association of Caribbean States: http://www.acs-aec.org/members.htm (accessed 2nd July 2003).

Aud-Buscher, G. and Ormerod Noakes, B. (eds.) 2003: *The Francophone Caribbean Today: Literature, Language and Culture*. Kingston, Jamaica: UWI Press.

Burton, R.D.E. and Reno, F. (eds.) 1995: *French and West Indian: Martinique, Guadeloupe, and French Guiana Today*. London: Macmillan.

CARICOM: http://www.caricom.org (accessed 2nd July 2003).

Ferguson, J. 1999: *The Story of the Caribbean People*. Kingston, Jamaica: Ian Randle Publishers.

Gamaliel Ramos, A. and Israel Rivera, A. (eds.) 2001: *Islands at the Crossroads: Politics in the Non-Independent Caribbean*. Kingston, Jamaica: Ian Randle Publishers.

Gilmore, J. 2000: *Faces of the Caribbean*. London: Latin American Bureau.

Holger, H. and Reno, F. (eds.) 2003: *Modern Political Culture in the Caribbean*. Kingston, Jamaica: UWI Press.

James, C. and Perivolaris, J. (eds.) 2000: *The Cultures of the Hispanic Caribbean*. London: Macmillan.

McAfee, K. 1991: *Storm Signals: Structural Adjustment and Development Alternatives in the Caribbean.* London: Zed Press.

Massey, D. 1995: 'Imagining the world'. In Allen, J. and Massey, D. (eds.) *Geographical Worlds.* Oxford: Oxford and Open University Presses. pp. 6–51.

Oostindie, G. 1996: *Ethnicity in the Caribbean.* London: Macmillan.

Pattullo, P. 1996: *Last Resorts: The Cost of Tourism in the Caribbean* London: Cassell and Latin American Bureau.

Payne, A. and Sutton, P. 2001: *Charting Caribbean Development.* London: Macmillan.

Pessar, P. R. (ed.) 1997: *Caribbean Circuits: New Directions in the Study of Caribbean Migration.* New York: Center for Migration Studies.

Puri, S. (ed.) 2003: *Marginal Migrations: The Circulation of Cultures within the Caribbean.* Oxford: Macmillan.

Sheller, M. 2003: *Consuming the Caribbean.* London: Routledge.

Skelton, T. 1989: *Women, Men and Power: Gender Relations in Montserrat.* Unpublished Ph.D. thesis, University of Newcastle upon Tyne.

2

Unity in diversity?: A history of the Pan-Caribbean region from 1492 to the 1970s

Cleve McD. Scott

Introduction

The Caribbean, simply put, is problematic. It is a space that is difficult to define.[1] In the view of Ralph R. Premdas, 'the Caribbean as an unified region that confers a sense of common citizenship and community may be conceived as a figment of the imagination' (Premdas 1999: p. 4). Yet, no one can deny that, as Rex Nettleford (2001) has suggested, it is 'a distinguishable and distinctive entity … The typical Caribbean person … is part-African, part-European, part-Asian, part-Native-American but totally Caribbean' (Nettleford 2001). Consequently, the region is comprised of different peoples, cultures and languages; it is a diversified entity. While the geographical boundaries of the region have been highly debated, it is an incontestable fact that the region has several unifying perspectives; it has a history of colonialism, imperialism and exploitation.

This chapter provides a historical overview of the Pan-Caribbean, the territories in the Caribbean sea colonised by the various European powers, from colonisation to the 1960s, when the newly independent nations joined those older independent states of 'other languages'. Combined with these nation states were those territories which continued colonial relationships with France, the United Kingdom and the Netherlands. The analysis ends around the 1970s because this period highlights the continuities and disruptions, similarities and differences of the Pan-Caribbean region that largely remain to date.[2]

European colonisation

European colonisation of the Pan-Caribbean began when the Spanish, under the leadership of the Italian navigator, Christopher Columbus, first set foot on Caribbean soil in the Bahamas in October 1492. For much of the sixteenth century, the Spanish exploited the indigenous peoples of the region subjecting them to systems of forced labour. Overwork and diseases of European origin wreaked havoc on the Arawaks (one of the indigenous groups of people residing in the Caribbean), decimating their populations. Thereafter the Spanish overpowered the indigenous Caribs (Kalinago, Calipuna, Ciboney and Tiano peoples) and the Arawaks in various territories. By the

Plate 2.1 *Statue of Christopher Columbus and the first cathedral in the Americas, Dominican Republic*

© David Howard

mid-1500s the Spanish occupied much of the Greater Antilles, they settled in Cuba, Santo Domingo (now the Dominican Republic) and Puerto Rico (Plate 2.1) (see Chapter Eight for a fuller discussion about the original peoples of the Caribbean).

No sooner than it was reported that Spain was amassing hordes of gold and silver from its territories, albeit from Central and South America, other European nations launched an attack on the Spanish monopoly. This assault resulted in the French, Dutch, Danish and English establishing colonies in the Caribbean as well. So by the start of the 1600s, Spanish hegemony in the Caribbean was being undermined.

Slavery and the plantation system

Unable to find precious metals, the various European nations transformed these territories into agricultural production. Beginning with crops like tobacco, indigo and ginger, the colonies then moved into sugar cultivation at different times. This began the plantation system (see Chapter 7 for a discussion of the social consequences).

There were a few islands in the Windward Islands which managed to evade the plantation complex for much of the seventeenth and eighteenth century. Plantation agriculture did not arrive on islands such as St. Vincent until the late eighteenth century. St. Vincent had been declared a neutral territory under the Treaty of Aix-la-Chapelle in 1748, but at the end of the Seven Years War in 1763 it was one of the islands ceded to the British under the Treaty of Paris. One of the main reasons why the plantation system was late in coming was the stern resistance of the indigenous people called the Black Caribs or Kalinago. The Black Caribs showed utter disregard for British hegemony and this resistance was met with British military might (Waters 1964; Craton 1996). After years of conflict the British were finally able to overpower them in the Second Carib War, or Brigand's War, of 1796. In 1797, the British exiled close to 5,000 Black Caribs to a small island just off the coast of British Honduras called Roatan.[3] With the rebels out of the way the British were able to entrench the plantation system on St. Vincent.

The Dutch played a pivotal role in the movement towards sugar production in the region. Having been driven out of Brazil in 1640, the Dutch moved to the English and French colonies. In the islands they settled, the Dutch were able to foster the development of the sugar cane plantation complex because they possessed the capital, had the technological know-how and had access to enslaved Africans to provide labour.

The movement towards sugar cane cultivation constituted what many refer to as the 'Sugar Revolution'. It is described as a revolution because the change to sugar production affected every element of these colonies: economy, society, demography, law, politics and the landscape and the environment (Higman 2002). Sugar cane cultivation forced out the small farms that were prevalent during the tobacco era and the labour regime was also reconstituted. The indigenous people provided the labour force for the early economic activity, they were followed by indentured servants or bondsmen, white Europeans, some of whom had volunteered, many others who had been forced into servitude as a punishment. The move towards sugar production created a demand for a large, readily available, labour force and so the Europeans opted to enslave Africans, largely for economic and racist reasons. Enslaved Africans were supplied via the trans-Atlantic slave trade, a trade which linked Europe with Africa and the Americas.

African slavery is another factor which unifies the Pan-Caribbean region. African slavery, as an institution, has played a pivotal role in shaping the history of the Caribbean. The introduction of enslaved Africans changed the demographics in the Caribbean; not only did the predominant race in the region become African/black, but also a wide range of coloured persons or 'mulattos' were the result of black and white miscegenation. Many of these coloured persons were free, hence the constant reference to them in the historiography as the 'free coloureds' (Heuman 1997, p. 144). In the Hispanic Caribbean there were as many as 25 different categories of coloureds as the slightest difference in colour was considered important. Free coloureds in some slave societies achieved economic power. One such example is in St. Domingue where the 'gens du couleur' by 1790 owned close to 25 per cent of the slaves and about 25–50 per cent of the arable land (Heuman 1997, p. 147). In Barbados, where free coloureds 'were represented in a wide range of [occupational] activities in Bridgetown [the capital], several of them, including many women, went on to hold large properties in the city' (Welch and Goodridge 2000, p. 10).

The slave regimes of the different European colonies, though varied at times in the way they were managed and organised, were all harsh. The institution of slavery was maintained through the use of fear and violence. Although in law the enslaved were considered as property, many slave owners recognised the humanity of the enslaved, with the result that the enslaved were able to create their own world. N.A.T. Hall (2000), for example, has shown how the enslaved in the Dutch Virgin Islands 'made' a 'world' which contained attendance at church, market day activities, dancing at parties, cultivation of provision grounds and Christmas and New Year's celebrations. At such events the enslaved wore finery, which a 1786 sumptuary law had forbidden.

Enslaved blacks did all sorts of skilled and unskilled jobs. They were masons, carpenters and mechanics, and in some British colonies they even performed military duties on a few occasions. One such 'black corps' was the over 500-strong St. Vincent Rangers. It was raised in 1795 to strengthen the assault on the Black Caribs and contained enslaved blacks loyal to the plantocracy. The unit was incorporated into the second West India Regiment in October 1795 (Chartrand 1998).

The majority of enslaved blacks did manual labour in the fields, and the majority of field slaves were women. Men and women were equal under the whip in that they were treated as harshly, especially when it came to punishment. Women were also central to the existence of the slavery system as the slave status was tied to the womb, that is to say that a child of an enslaved woman was born into slavery.

Resistance and revolt

To control the enslaved, slave laws were enacted by the various colonising powers to add to the physical and psychological forms of control (other agencies of control included the militias and the navies). Despite the systems of control slave resistance was endemic, Hilary Beckles has suggested that 'the many slave revolts and plots . . . between 1638 and 1838 could be conceived of as the "200 Years' War" – one protracted struggle launched by Africans and their Afro-West Indian progeny against slave owners' (Beckles 1991, p. 363). The enslaved protested against slavery both violently and non-violently. Non-violent protest, or day-to-day acts of resistance, included actions such as sabotage, malingering and pretending to be stupid or ill. Women resisted slavery in unique ways that included infanticide, abortion and prolonging the lactation period to delay their next conception.

Armed resistance was the highest form of slave resistance. Among the heroes and heroines of the various armed slave revolts are Cuffy in Guyana, Nanny of Jamaica, Bussa in Barbados and Morales in Cuba. However, because of the militia and other mechanisms in place to put down revolts, armed resistance were largely unsuccessful. In fact, the only successful slave revolt in the Caribbean was the Haitian revolution of 1792–1804. In this case 'the Black Jacobins' with 'a self liberation ethos' were able to overthrow colonial slavery and in its stead establish the first black republic in the western hemisphere (Beckles 1991).

Another form of resistance was to run away from the plantation, this is referred to as marronage. Marronage was prevalent in the more mountainous territories such as Jamaica, which saw the emergence of several maroon settlements, and Suriname, whose maroons were called the Bush Negroes. In the less mountainous territories, such as Barbados, enslaved blacks resorted to maritime marronage, for example, enslaved blacks from Barbados often fled via sloops to neighbouring St. Vincent and the Grenadines (Beckles 1986). Slave resistance was therefore another 'aesthetic-political theme' that unites the region (Cudjoe 1980, p. 269).

Disintegration of the slavery system

After nearly 400 years of chattel slavery in the Pan-Caribbean region, which brought about 10 million enslaved Africans to the Americas, internal and external forces, including economics, abolitionists in Europe, politics and slave resistance or more precisely the 'self-liberation ethos' of the enslaved, colluded to precipitate the disintegration of the slave system and brought emancipation. Besides freeing themselves, the Haitians ended slavery in neighbouring Santo Domingo (now the Dominican Republic) in 1822 when they seized this Spanish colony.

Emancipation occurred throughout the Pan-Caribbean region at different times in the nineteenth century. Britain was the first to end slavery in its colonies, the Act to terminate slavery was passed in the British Parliament in 1833 and took effect in the colonies from 1 August 1834. This law was to take immediate effect in the Crown colonies (colonies without elected assemblies) while the colonies with representative government were to pass the measure in their assemblies (Knight 1997, p. 336).

Emancipation in the British territories was to be followed by a transitional period to full freedom called apprenticeship. However, some colonies like Antigua, opted not to implement it. Those who introduced apprenticeship saw the British government abandoning it in 1838, two years before it was due to expire, because of problems such as the corruption of the magistration responsible for overseeing the scheme and labour disputes.

The non-British territories lagged behind the British in their movement towards emancipation. With a revolutionary atmosphere prevailing in Europe, the French decided to end slavery in its territories in 1848. It was Victor Schoelcher (1804–1893), the French abolitionist writer, in his capacity as Secretary of State for colonies in the Provisional French Government, who had the privilege of declaring complete freedom in the French colonies. Following a slave revolt in the Danish colony of St. Croix in 1848, the Danes abolished slavery in their colonies as well. On 1 July 1863, some 15 years later, the Dutch ended slavery in their territories. This was following the passage of a law to this effect in Holland on 2 August 1862. The last Pan-Caribbean territories to outlaw slavery were Cuba and Puerto Rico. Slavery in Puerto Rico was ended on 22 March 1873, while in Cuba, complete emancipation was effected on 7 October 1886 (Knight 1997). Slavery and the plantation system, then, are intersecting historical phenomena that unify the Pan-Caribbean region.

Post-slavery society

The formerly enslaved population experienced tremendous difficulties in their efforts to create a new life, a life as free persons in post-slavery society. The immediate post-slavery society in the British Caribbean in particular was marked by an intense battle between the plantocracy and the formerly enslaved over rights as citizens. The plantocracy continued to exercise their hegemony in their interest, especially on issues of land and labour. For Nigel Bolland, 'the interrelated struggles for the control of labour and land constituted the central political issue' in post-slavery societies in the British Caribbean (2001, p. 3). Land has been 'both an economic and a symbolic resource' throughout the region's colonial history (Besson and Momsen 1987, p. 1), Hymie Rubenstein, an ethnologist, has testified to this historical importance of land. He observed:

> land is desired in its own right beyond its productive or commercial potential and it is the ambition of nearly every landless villager to own a piece of land. To own land symbolizes individual economic well-being and confers prestige and respectability on the owner. Equally important, land is something permanent and immovable, thereby conferring stability in a social system in which unpredictability and impermanence are constant elements. Finally land represents a legacy that may be passed on to one's heirs, thus ensuring that one will be remembered by one's descendants (1975, p. 165).

Although these comments were made in direct relation to the people of St. Vincent and the Grenadines, they are equally applicable to the rest of the Caribbean.

W. A. Green (1976) has advanced the land to population ratio to explain the movement of the newly freed blacks away from the plantations in the British Caribbean territories in the immediate post-slavery period. According to Green, blacks' aspirations were to obtain land and to cultivate, but such aspirations were limited by the availability of land itself. Islands such as Barbados, Antigua and St. Kitts were practically covered by the sugar plantations and, as such, black labourers in these islands had little alternative but to work on the plantations or leave the islands. Woodville Marshall (1993), on the other hand, has insisted that the flight from the plantations was precipitated by a labour relations problem, that is, by the failure of the plantation owners and management to provide sufficient incentives to encourage blacks to remain on the plantations. Interestingly, in some places women stopped working in the fields because of Victorian values of femininity (Shepherd 1999).

Having refused to work or to be continuously engaged in estate labour, the blacks in many territories established peasantries. This labour relations problem therefore created an artificial labour shortage in some colonies. Rather than encourage the blacks to remain on the estates, planters resorted to immigration to garner an adequate and continuous labour force. It is widely accepted that the planters in the Caribbean resorted to extra-regional immigration because they 'had been used to working with unfree labour' and emancipation had produced 'a free labour market' which they did not want to deal with. This position, however, has been challenged by recent research that suggest that 'in order to produce competitively, the plantations ... required a special type of labour' and that labour happened to be indentured labour (Emmer 2000, p. 156). Indentured labour gave the sugar plantations a new lease of life by providing the continuous and easily accessible labour they needed to function as they had during slavery.

While Hugh Tinker (1974) has labelled Asian indentureship 'a new system of slavery', Pieter C. Emmer has suggested that East Indian indentured labourers were better off in the region than at home. According to Emmer, while the formerly enslaved were disappointed with the reality that they experienced after emancipation, the East Indians 'seemed grateful to have migrated to the post-emancipation Caribbean' (Emmer 2000, p. 156). The majority of formerly enslaved did not profit from the opportunities presented by plantation agriculture and small-scale cultivation. In comparison, the East Indian indentured labourers reaped significant benefits. As a result the East Indians used land, organised their settlements and structured their families to create economic growth in a way in which the formerly enslaved did not. The reason for this difference in position, according to Emmer, was that the East Indians had learnt at home how the market economy functioned while the formerly enslaved had not, since during slavery the plantations were responsible for supplying food, shelter and health care to the enslaved whether they were 'productive' or 'non-productive' (Emmer 2000).

The French, Danish and Dutch territories, like the British, also resorted to immigration to meet their post-emancipation labour needs. The British allowed these European nations to import workers from India, one of its colonies and workers were also obtained from Africa and China. Cuba, on the other hand, was not so lucky, for the British refused to allow it to recruit East Indian labour, consequently Cuban planters got their post-slavery labour force from Spain and the Canary Islands (Emmer 2000).

The Asian indentured workers, 'the new arrivants', added to the cultural mix already existing in the region. Even though some of them became Christians, the majority remained Muslims and Hindus, religions they brought from India (Knight and Palmer 1989). They added to the economy as well by bringing rice, and planting cocoa and ground provisions. They also widened the ethnicity of and helped to further reconfigure Caribbean societies. The children of mixed African and Indian parentage were referred to somewhat pejoratively as 'douglah' (Allsopp 1996, pp. 200–201).

Post-slavery protests and political reform in the British Caribbean

The disintegration of the slave system inevitably presented a challenge to white hegemony for how could one expect the same practitioners of discrimination and exploitation to engineer an egalitarian society in the immediate aftermath of slavery? The result of this anomaly was that the new black citizens were denied their civil rights just as they had been under slavery. Blacks therefore continued to suffer exploitation and oppression. In such circumstances, many were forced to protest against their deplorable state, post-emancipation labour protests were frequent in the nineteenth century. In 1844 there was the 'Guerre Negre', an uprising against a census in Dominica. In British Guiana, in 1856, there were 'the Angel Gabriel' Riots when blacks attacked Portuguese emigrants. In St. Vincent, in 1862, there were the 'Vox Populi' riots and disturbances which erupted after workers on several estates downed tools and lit fires. In January 1876, there were the 'Belmanna Riots' in Tobago, a small island just off

Trinidad, when the labourers protested against the oppressive work regime and lit fires. Finally, in April 1876 there were the 'Confederation Riots' in Barbados when blacks raided potato fields after they were misinformed that confederation would lead to a return to slavery. Women were active in several of these violent protests, especially the Belmanna Riots and Confederation Riots (Craton 1997; Shepherd 1999).

Perhaps the most significant of these protests was the 1865 'Morant Bay Rebellion' in Jamaica. Poor people in Jamaica had been experiencing worsening conditions since the 1850s and they had been complaining to the governor about these conditions to no avail. The plight of the poor was later taken up by an English Baptist minister, Dr. Edward B. Underhill, who complained to London that the Jamaican government was to blame for the state of affairs. Underhill's assessment was discussed widely in the Jamaican press and the Colonial Office's response to Underhill's correspondence, known as the 'Queen's Advice', was distributed widely in Jamaica. This response, framed by Henry Taylor, a senior official at the Office, placed the blame for the dire straits the labouring population was in at their own feet, the 'Queen's Advice' called on the poor to exercise 'industry and prudence'. The result of such antagonism was that the people were further angered. Things came to ahead on 7 October 1865 when a huge crowd gathered at the courthouse in Morant Bay where a trial was in progress, assaulted the police and prevented them from executing their duty. Days later, violent unrest swept through Morant Bay.

The effect of the Morant Bay Rebellion, though the protest was isolated geographically, was that it helped to convince British colonial officials in London that a government selected by London would secure the interest of the black majority better than one elected by the largely white electorate. To put it another way, the rebellion showed London that it could not depend on a white minority government to govern in the interest of a black majority. London dealt with this dilemma by introducing Crown Colony government, a system of governance that effectively boosted the power of the governor and terminated elections for the legislatures. Such posturing was influenced by the Imperial policy of trusteeship, a paternalistic policy which maintained that the Crown must govern in the interest of colonial subjects until they were capable of using the vote prudently (Fergus 1985). Crown Colony government therefore unseated Representative Government in the British Caribbean during the period 1865 to 1877. By 1877, as many as twelve of the fourteen legislatures had changed their representative constitutions for Crown Colony rule (Millette 1970).

Haiti and civil war

The independence struggles in Haiti from the late eighteenth century had produced a nation with an infrastructure in need of repair. Other hinderances to the nation-building process continued into the nineteenth century and included the racial conflict between blacks and mulattoes. This conflict was manifest also in the discourse over land ownership, its use and labour (Beckles 1993).

Haiti experienced many years of civil war up until the 1840s. Hilary Beckles (1993) has described the blacks and mulattoes in Haiti during the early post-independence period as being 'divided to the vein'. Beckles' description of the scenario is quite unambiguous:

> the ideological forces of colourism were once again as clear as they were during the slavery period. Blacks and mulattoes represented two rival factions whose mutual distrust and dislike represented the principal destabalising political force within the new state. The two groups squared off to control their separate spaces, and the nation splintered after less than five years (1993, p. 501).

The leaders of the two factions involved in the civil war were Henri Christophe (1767–1820), president for life of the north, called Haiti, and Alexandre Petion (1770–1818), who was elected president of the Republic of Haiti (the southern part) by the senate located in Port-au-Prince. This war continued until 1818 when Petion died, and Jean-Pierre Boyer became president of Haiti. It was Boyer who was able to reunite the nation in 1820 after Christophe, who had declared himself to be King Henry I in 1811, committed suicide (Beckles 1993).

In the 1840s the state gradually reasserted control and this process was accompanied by the emergence of a liberal reform movement. This movement was responsible for the removal, in 1843, of the autocratic president, the mulatto Jean-Pierre Boyer (1776–1850), who had been in power since 1818. The liberal reform movement was, however, short-lived. The peasants in the southern part of Haiti could wait no longer to benefit from the expected democracy and so rebelled. This rebellion was met with governmental repression which entailed the use of the military. 'The result was the crushing of the nascent radical democratic polity and the maintenance of a military autocracy' (Peabody 2002). Mimi Sheller (2000) has found that the struggles for political agency by the peasants in Haiti and the Jamaican working class bear similarities to one another. Sheller has also suggested that the post-emancipation experiences of these two territories were similar to those of Cuba. Post-slavery protests therefore permeated the Pan-Caribbean region.

Francophone Caribbean

Unlike the British Caribbean, where blacks were denied the franchise during the apprenticeship period, blacks in French colonies became free persons and French citizens at the moment of Emancipation. Therefore, during the Second Republic (1848–51) blacks exercised the franchise. Napoleon III curtailed these rights of citizenship during his reign and it was not until the emergence of the Third Republic in the 1870s that these rights were restored (Burton 1995). It is Bridget Brereton's view that the coloured persons were the 'chief beneficiaries' of the emergence of the Third Republic in the French Antilles because they were able to ascend to political power, obtained higher education and controlled the administrative bureacracy (1994).

End of Spanish colonisation

The Spanish empire in the Caribbean came to an end in the nineteenth century. There were early indications that such a change would come after a new group obtained control of these colonies while France occupied Spain during the Napoleonic War of 1792 to 1815. Locally born persons or creoles, as against those born in Spain or peninsulars, took control of Spain's colonies, namely Cuba, Puerto Rico and Santo Domingo, during this period. Eventually, independence movements emerged all over Spanish America and so, in 1844, Spain gave Santo Domingo its political independence. On independence Santo Domingo was renamed the Dominican Republic. Meanwhile, Cuba experienced a decade-long war for independence starting in 1868. Finally, in 1897, Spain succumbed to the independence movements and granted Puerto Rico a charter for greater autonomy.

The Spanish empire in the Caribbean was effectively brought to the end by the Spanish–American war of 1898. The conflict was triggered by the alleged bombing of a US warship. At the end of the war, Spain signed a treaty with the USA in which it agreed to surrender control of Cuba and Puerto Rico. Consequently, Cuba obtained its independence in 1902 while Puerto Rico was annexed to the USA. In 1952 the United States Congress agreed to constitute Puerto Rico as a commonwealth.

Emigration from the Caribbean

The Caribbean and migration have always been synonymous. In fact, it is quite accurate to say that 'the Caribbean's diversity, its outstanding characteristic, is a diversity founded on migrations' (Sunshine 1988: p. 70). There have been significant population movements into and out of the region since 1492. However, Caribbean people, especially those from the British colonies, left their homeland in search of work from the mid-nineteenth century. The first movement from British colonies was inter-colonial with workers going to territories like Trinidad and British Guiana where higher wages were being paid. This migratory movement was relatively small scale.

Large scale emigration began in the late nineteenth century and expanded exponentially in the twentieth century. Workers from the British Caribbean went to Panama to work on the construction of the canal under the French between 1881 and 1888, and and from 1905 to 1913 under the Americans (Richardson 1992). Until the 1930s, when restrictions were placed on immigration, workers headed to South and Central America, including countries like Colombia, Nicaragua, Honduras, Guatemala and Costa Rica. These movements consisted mainly of Jamaicans and Barbadians and they worked largely on banana and sugar plantations (Proudfoot 1970). Cuba was the main migrant destination in the early 1920s. During the course of the Second World War there was emigration to Venezuela, Curacao and Aruba. In light of the extensive male emigration from the Eastern Caribbean, estates were forced to employ women as their main source of labour (Shepherd 1999). There was also a wave of emigration to the USA from around 1900, but this stopped in 1924 after the USA introduced The Immigration Act of 1924. This Act 'established immigration quotas according to the national origins system, and as of July 1, 1924, required all aliens arriving at the United States to present a visa'.

Migrant workers, especially those to the Panama Canal from 1905 to 1913 remitted significant sums of money to their homelands. 'Panama money' was used to buy food, clothing and land among other things (Richardson 1992.) However, Caribbean emigrants were not always better-off away from home. Howard Johnson (1998), for example, has shown that a group of Barbadian workers who went to the Putumayo district of the Amazon between 1904 and 1911 to harvest rubber experienced 'a continuation of the coercion which they had experienced in their homeland' (p. 185).

Of all the out migration one of the largest was to Britain between 1948 and 1973. During this period about 550,000 people from the British Caribbean migrated to Britain (Chamberlain 1997). The arrival of the *Empire Windrush* at Tilbury Docks on 21 June 1948 is considered the defining moment in post-Second World War migrations to Britain. About two of every three persons on this ship had done military service in Britain during the Second World War (Spencer 1997: p. 18; Wambu 1998). The arrival of the migrants on the *Windrush* was followed by frantic efforts by British officials to prevent continued immigration from the Anglophone Caribbean to Britain (Spencer 1997).

Other European colonial powers faced a similar dilemma in the post-war period. France, for example, received so many immigrants that Pierre Messmer, prime minister of France from 1972 to 1974, summed up the situation quite nicely when he said: 'This is a trap set by history. We in France and Europe have been accustomed to colonising the world. Now the foreigners are coming here to us' (Freeman 1987, p. 186). (For a full discussion of the complexities of Caribbean migration see Chapter Six.)

The Caribbean and the First World War

The Great War or the First World War broke out in August 1914 when Britain declared war on Germany and its allies. This war, which it was said would be over by Christmas, lasted until 1918. As Anthony Phillips has brilliantly put it, 'the First World War was peculiarly stupid, futile and disastrous: stupid in its origins, futile in its main campaigns and disastrous in its peace terms' (1998, p. 344).

The war allowed British and French West Indians to demonstrate their love and loyalty to the imperial powers (Fraser 1982; Burton 1995). The British colonies in particular showed this 'deep sense of patriotism and their feelings of loyalty to their King and to the cause' in tangible ways through donations (Scott 2002, p. 231). An excellent example of the pledges of loyalty was a telegram, which James Walvin has referred to, from the Barbados Assembly to the British Government with the reassuring words: 'Do not worry England, Barbados is behind you' though Anthony Phillips has argued that Walvin erred when he accepted this 'apocryphal' as 'fact' (see endnote 1, Phillips 1998, p. 418; Walvin 1984, p. 77).

Black people from the region were enlisted in the British and French armies. After some reluctance, the British enlisted black and coloured West Indians into the British West India Regiment (BWIR) with white commissioned officers and the story of these soldiers has been examined in detail by Glenford Howe (2002). Among the issues Howe surveyed were the problems which confronted West Indian soldiers on a daily basis, the workings of British War Office in relation to the BWIR, the largely non-combatant work done by the

West Indian soldiers and the problems of demobilisation and its aftermath. Discontent among demobilised soldiers of the BWIR was high in several British territories. However, it was only in British Honduras (Belize) that this discontent matured into riots (Bolland 1995). These men had experienced white racism in Europe and were convinced that the mother country did not want to see non-whites in a leadership position.

Black consciousness between the two World Wars

Garveyism

From around 1918 to 1925, the black consciousness movement gained considerable ground in the region. The main agency in this regard was the Universal Negro Improvement Association and African Communities League (UNIA). The UNIA was formed in Jamaica in 1914 by Marcus Mosiah Garvey (1887–1940), a black Jamaican, with the objective of boosting racial pride among Blacks. Garvey emigrated to the USA in 1916 and the following year he established Garveyism in Harlem (Hill and Bair 1987). Thereafter, the movement spread to Africa, Europe, North and South America and the Caribbean (Stein 1986). It may be hailed as the first authentic Pan-Caribbean organisation. There were many branches of the UNIA in Cuba especially in the districts where West Indian migrants worked. The spread of the Garvey movement may be attributed to the radicalism that emerged during the First World War, blacks' desire for black leadership, and their attraction to the ideas of self-reliance and black racial pride espoused by Garvey (Martin 1983) (see Chapter Seven for a discussion of Garveyism and resistance).

Garvey was imprisoned in the USA from 1925 to 1927 for mail fraud. On release from prison in 1927 he was expelled from the country and lived in Jamaica for a few years before moving to England. He died in England in 1940 a few days after having had the unfortunate experience of seeing his obituary in a London newspaper. After 1927 the UNIA experienced serious problems and went into decline. That the movement was never as strong as it had been was irrelevant, for Garvey's impact had been felt the world over and he has left a legacy which persists to this day.

Negritude

In the 1930s a movement that sought to glorify African culture and reject European culture emerged. 'Negritude,' as this philosophy was called, started as a literary movement and is credited to a large degree to L.G. Damas' *Pigments* (1937) and Aimé Césaire's *Cahier d'un retour au pays natal (Return to my Native Land,* 1939). Cesaire, a black writer from Martinique, is credited for having generated 'the neologistic term, Négritude' to stress the centrality of this ideology of adhering to Africanness. Négritude's overall position was that Africans were not culturally inferior (Ormerod 1998).

There have been Caribbean challenges to Négritude. One of its major critics is Edouard Glissant, perhaps one of the most influential Martinican novelists and poets since Césaire to have written about colonialism in the Caribbean. Recent literary critics have located Glissant within the circle of post-colonial theorists, like Frantz Fanon, Gayatri Spivak and Homi Bhabha (Britton 1999). Glissant has suggested that Caribbean cultural reality should focus less on the distant geographical and cultural African connection and more on the multi-ethnic constituents of Caribbean culture. Glissant's writings therefore promote the cultural concept of Antillanité or 'Caribbeanness' and not 'Africanness'.

Labour rebellions, riots, unrests and disturbances in the 1930s

There were several labour disturbances in the British Caribbean in the 1930s. Most historians agree that the series of troubles began in St. Kitts in January 1935, followed by the St. Vincent and the Grenadines unrests of October 1935. Nigel Bolland's contention that 'this period started in Belize, Trinidad and Guyana in 1934' is not so widely accepted (1995, p. 42).

Writing around 1939, Sir Arthur Lewis, a St. Lucian economist who was later to earn a Nobel Prize for economics, identified three contributory factors to the series of riots and disturbances in the 1930s. The first factor he pointed out was the deplorable economic condition of the region. According to Lewis, the price paid for major exports had declined, wages were slashed, taxes had increased and unemployment was rising. The second factor for Lewis was the rush of unemployed rural workers to the towns, in addition to the large number of returning migrant workers from Cuba and Santo Domingo who added to the unemployment situation. Thirdly, Lewis saw the Italian conquest of Abyssinia as an event which incited the people. He argued that West Indian people believed that Britain had betrayed Abyssinia because it was a black nation and this assumption made them lose faith in 'white government'. Thus, they became convinced that they should 'take their fate in their own hands' (Lewis 1939, pp. 11–12). Lewis therefore hypothesised that 'had there existed constitutional machinery for the redress of grievances, there might well have been no upheavals' (Lewis 1939, pp. 11–12).

Initially, British colonial authorities hesitated to acknowledge the real causes of the labour rebellions. In St. Vincent and the Grenadines, for instance, they insisted that the returning migrants from Cuba and Santo Domingo, countries where communist ideology was gaining ground, were responsible for the labour unrests. Hundreds of labourers emigrated to Cuba and Santo Domingo to work on sugar plantations for higher wages in the 1920s, these men were fingered as the ringleaders by the authorities. The authorities had stereotyped these returned migrants as communist sympathisers although in fact, of the 45 men sentenced to prison in St. Vincent for rioting on 21 October 1935, no less than 30 (or about 67 per cent) of them had lived in either Cuba or Santo Domingo. While the communist movement in Cuba expanded in the early 1920s, it was not until 1925 that the Cuban Communist Party was founded and it was banned two years later. The Dominican Republic, on the other hand, did not have a communist party in the 1920s, although communist sympathisers certainly existed there (Scott 2002; Suchlicki 1989; Simons 1996; Thomas 1998).

The labour rebellions and unrest influenced Britain's decision to alter its colonial labour policy in the region. Thereafter Britain introduced progressive labour legislation and constitutional reform in the Caribbean colonies. This cordial atmosphere also saw working class people joining forces with the middle class to establish labour and political organisations with the objective of drawing attention to their problems (Nurse 1992). In several territories labour organisations were formed called workingmen's associations. These were also partly political parties and partly mutual aid fraternities.

In all of this women were certainly active although they were disenfranchised until the late 1930s. They were present at political meetings, were canvassers and offered meaningful assistance in many other ways (Shepherd 1999). Elma Francios (1897–1944), a national heroine of Trinidad and Tobago, is an example of an outstanding Caribbean woman during this period. The St. Vincent-born Fancois, who emigrated to Trinidad in 1919, was one of the founders of the socialist-oriented Negro Welfare Cultural and Social Association (NWCSA). Formed in 1934, the NWCSA mobilised Port-of-Spain's unemployed through public meetings and protest action. For example, this organisation drew close to 1,500 persons to Woodford Square, Port-of-Spain on 30 October 1935 to condemn the St. Vincent government for its handling of the October 1935 unrest. The rally issued a petition demanding the 'unconditional release [of the] arrested demonstrators' and the arrest of the workers' 'murderers' (Scott 2002, p. 422; Reddock 1988; Brereton 1981).

The Caribbean and the Second World War

The Second World War lasted from 1939 to 1945 and was triggered to a significant degree by the issue of German unification. The actual declaration of war on Germany by England and France was over the issue of Polish independence. The conflict soon spread because Germany was resolved to create a huge empire in Central and Eastern Europe. German forces, in an astonishing, swift operation in May 1940, invaded and occupied France, the Netherlands and Belgium and forced them to surrender. The seizure of France and the Netherlands by the Axis powers put in doubt the future of the Caribbean colonies of these nations. The Dutch Monarchy had fled to England, then to Canada to escape capture by the Axis powers, yet the Dutch Caribbean colonies remained loyal to the Dutch empire and supported the Allies.

As had been the case in the First World War, the colonies rallied to the support of the Imperial powers. Besides the 'reaffirmation' of 'loyalty', British Caribbean colonies offered men, women, money and supplies to the mother country. In the case of Barbados or 'Little England', the colony contributed about 2,000 men and 85 women to the war effort, many of these persons served in the British Army and the Royal Air Force. This figure, however, excludes those who joined the Auxiliary Territorial Services as well as those who worked on the naval bases around the region. British Caribbean women were relatively visible during this conflict. In 1943 alone close to 30 women from the British Caribbean travelled to England to join the British Air Transport Auxiliary (ATA) (Shepherd 1999).

By the end of the war, Britain had become somewhat dependant on the USA having struggled to defend its empire, including the British Caribbean. Evidence of Britain's reliance on the USA for assistance was visible from as early as 1940 when the USA offered Britain warships in exchange for permission to construct naval bases on several British Caribbean colonies (Bolland 2001). While the USA had a 'strategic interest' in the British, French and Dutch Caribbean before the Second World War, it was during this conflict that its interest in the region expanded for geo-political reasons in face of German U-boat activity (Baptiste 1988).

For the British Caribbean the post-war period brought some improvements in the form of colonial development and welfare. The series of labour rebellions/revolts/ unrests/riots and disturbances in the British Caribbean in the 1930s had forced British colonial authorities to dispatch an enquiry into the causes of these troubles in 1939. The investigating body, a royal commission known as the Moyne Commission, in its report, published after the war, noted that there was an urgent need for development aid and government welfare (Bolland 2001). The Colonial Development and Welfare Act was therefore London's response to the suggestions outlined in the Moyne Commission's report.

The USA in the Caribbean after the First World War

As early as the mid-1800s, Denmark had offered to sell the USA its Caribbean colonies for $7.5 million. In an effort to expedite the sale, the Danes had gone as far as to draw up a treaty to transfer the territories, but the USA refused the offer in 1867 (Knight 1989a). In 1916 Denmark bowed to immense external pressures exerted on it and once more decided to sell its Caribbean colonies to the USA and the sale was finalised a year later, in the midst of the First World War. Under the terms of the sale the USA agreed to pay $25 million for St. Thomas, St. Croix, St. John and about another fifty tiny islands. The rationale the USA gave then for the purchase was that these islands were crucial strategic military locales, positions that could prevent Germany from establishing military bases in the region. It was widely held that if Germany captured Denmark, the Germans would use St. Thomas as a launch pad for naval attacks on ships transiting the Panama Canal (Phillips 1991).

Once in control of these islands, the USA congress had the right to decide on their constitutional status. The congress therefore put them under the Navy's charge in 1917. In 1931 USA authorities transferred the responsibility for the islands to the Department of the Interior following mounting complaints about Navy rule from the islanders and from persons in the USA. The first non-military governor was therefore appointed in 1931. One noticeable feature of both the Navy's and the Department of the Interior's rule was the retaining of the Danish colonial government it found in operation in 1917 until 1936.

The people of the Virgin Islands were made American citizens in 1927. Further constitutional advancement was introduced on 22 June 1936 when US president, Franklin D. Roosevelt, signed into law the Organic Act of 1936 to give the Virgin

Islanders virtually identical civil rights as Americans. This law also granted a greater level of local self-government while maintaining the far-reaching powers of the Federal government (Knight 1989a).

In the years following 1917 Americans made significant financial investments in the Caribbean region, mainly in Cuba, the Dominican Republic, Puerto Rico, Trinidad, Jamaica and Guyana. Around the 1950s, for instance, the renamed The United States Virgin Islands were being promoted by American investors as a premier vacation islands. (For more detailed discussion of the development of tourism see Chapter Five.)

The Cuban Revolution

Cuba had been governed by repressive and undemocratic regimes for much of the early twentieth century. Knight believes that:

> The enduring pattern of graft corruption, maladministration, fiscal irresponsibility, and social insensitivity to minority groups may have been a legacy of the colonial period and the repressive slave system abolished only in 1886 (Knight 1989b, p. 173).

This period of instability in Cuban politics and society began around 1902 and ended in 1959.

The undemocratic and repressive regimes presided over a country that was wealthy and served as a playground for Americans. Unfortunately, the vast majority of the Cuban populace did not benefit from this wealth and this made them amenable to anti-establishment protest. Coupled with economic discontent and American imperialism was the decadent political system and bureacracy. These factors helped precipitate the removal of Fulgêncio Batista in 1959. A former chief of the army, Batista was elected president in 1940 and served until 1944. In 1952 he returned to power after staging a coup d'etat. He then suspended the Cuban constitution and proceeded with what Franklin Knight has called 'outright repression' (Knight 1989a, p. 172).

In 1951, Fidel Castro, a law graduate, led a small guerrilla group in an unsuccessful attempt to overthrow the dictator Batista by first seizing the Moncada army barracks. Castro, who became the leader of a grouping called 'The 26 July Movement' after the foiled attack, was then exiled to Mexico. Unwilling to give up, Castro returned on a small sea craft, the *Granma*, in December 1956 to once again attempt to overthrow the government of Baptista. Unfortunately for him this mission failed as well, some of the guerrillas were killed and the others sought refuge in the hills called the Sierra Maestra. While Castro and his troops were in these hills, there were other developments that helped to weaken Baptista's stranglehold on Cuba. These developments included sabotage and unease among the military, and at the same time, the USA, which had supported Batista, withdrew its support. Batista responded to his misfortune by fleeing Cuba for the Dominican Republic. With Batista having beaten a hasty retreat, the revolutionary forces pressed on and the Cuban military surrendered. This was how Fidel Castro managed to become president in January 1959 (Ferguson 1999).

Cuba and the Cold War

From the point Fidel Castro assumed power the USA and Cuba had a strained relationship. The USA had economic interests in Cuba, but this capitalist exploitation was at ideological odds with the revolution. Added to this, Batista sympathisers in the USA joined with the US government to work to remove Castro's revolutionary government. The result of this bad blood was that Cuba moved further away from the USA and closer to its rival, the then USSR/Soviet Union. Sometime before Castro led the the revolutionary forces to victory he had formed an alliance with the communist party of Cuba.

From the end of the Second World War the world was entrenched in a Cold War, a war without armed battles between the belligerents involved. The two main countries in this war were the USA and the USSR. These countries had different ideologies. The USA was capitalist and democratic and the USSR communist and non-democratic. This conflict was reflected in the mistrust, the espionage, propagandising and the deception each nation practised.

Cuba's alignment with the USSR brought the world exceedingly close to war when a scenario developed that became known as the Cuban missile crisis. Castro's appropriation of American investments in Cuba angered the USA and it decided to end this. To manage this they tried using CIA trained Cuban exiles to invade Cuba. The attempted landing at the Bay of Pigs in April 1961 was a fiasco. The Cubans were prepared for the invaders and crushed them, making the USA a laughing stock. A news report published in the *New York Times* of 21 February 1998 quoted a declassified 1962 Central Intelligence Agency (CIA) report as having blamed 'its own arrogance, ignorance and incompetence' for the disaster. The report is said to have described the CIA's failed mission as 'ludicrous or tragic or both'.

The Bay of Pigs fiasco was followed by appeals from Castro for help to fend off further US sponsored insurgency. The Soviet leader Nikita Sergeevich Khrushchev (1894–1971) came to the rescue and offered Cuba medium-range nuclear missiles. These missiles would serve a dual purpose. From Cuba they put the Soviet Union in close striking range to the USA something that they could not achieve from the USSR. This is what President Castro had to say on the issue in an interview with the US television network CNN:

> I immediately appreciated the strategic importance of the presence of those missiles in Cuba. By that time, the Americans had already transported similar missiles to Turkey. I thought: if we expected the Soviets to fight on our behalf, to run risks for us, and even involve themselves in a war for our sake, it would be immoral and cowardly on our part to refuse to accept the presence of those missiles here (CNN).

In July 1962, Soviet ships transporting nuclear missiles headed for Cuba. These missiles in Cuba would put the USA at a strategic disadvantage. The Russians could attack them without warning and this was an obvious worry. The decision by Cuba to allow the Soviets to locate missiles there in the heart of the Cold War angered the

USA and they threatened to take drastic action if the Soviets went ahead with the plan. After considering military and economic manoeuvres, the USA resorted to diplomatic negotiations with the Russians. The negotiation produced results and the Russians decided to withdraw the missiles in return for the USA's assurance that it would not invade Cuba and would also remove its missiles from Turkey.

Economic development after the Second World War

Up to the 1950s, British Caribbean countries were still underdeveloped with agriculture dominating their economies. At the same time bauxite mining in Guyana and Jamaica and oil production in Trinidad were beginning to break the agricultural dominance (Ramsaran 2001). A few non-British territories had began to turn away from agriculture as well. In 1916 an oil refinery was established on Curacao and in 1918 bauxite mining commenced in Suriname.

The solution for fast-tracking the industrial development of the British Caribbean in the 1950s was called 'industrialisation by invitation', a terminology first used by Trinidadian economist Lloyd Best. While this development strategy is frequently associated with Sir Arthur Lewis, who articulated the ideas in a 1950 essay, there were other advocates besides Lewis such as the People's National Party as well as the trade unions in Jaimaica in the late 1940s (Mandle 1996). Under this plan, multinational corporations (MNCs) were invited to establish branches in the region to assemble goods for foreign and domestic markets. In return for establishing such industries governments provided incentives such as infrastructure, including factory shells, tax holidays, subsidies and guarantees such as access to the domestic market. This was an idea which Lewis had modelled from the Puerto Rican 'Operation Bootstrap' (for an examination of Operation Bootstrap, see for example, Dietz 1993). Lewis argued that the region could be industrialised using the excess labour existing particularly in agriculture. Lewis' idea was to create a modern industrial sector with local or imported capital utilising the plentiful supply of cheap labour. However, Lewis never suggested industry as a replacement for agriculture (Ramsaran 2001).

By the 1950s, legislation had been passed to encourage industrialisation, and this strategy was intensified in the 1960s. In the 1950s and 1960s import substitution was adopted as the major strategy to development in the manufacturing sector (Ramsaran 2001). However, despite the expansion in mining (bauxite and oil) and tourism, the plan did not work well. Market forces were not favourable. The international demand for the products produced wavered and the prices charged were not always competitive. In addition, many companies uprooted themselves after the incentives had expired. This approach therefore led to continued dependency and the underdevelopment of the economies of the British Caribbean.

Caribbean governments were willing to try the tourist industry to break the high level of dependence and economic underdevelopment (Bryden 1973). As Jean S. Holder (1993) has indicated, from as early as the 1940s tourism was considered by

Caribbean governments as an important economic sector. This faith in tourism was shown in the formation of the Caribbean Tourism Association (CTA) in 1957. The membership of the CTA was drawn from Cuba, the Dominican Republic and all the British Colonies. The organisation's mandate was to promote the region's tourism product. (See Chapter Five.)

From the 1960s there was a debate in the Caribbean 'as to whether tourism should be accepted as a viable development strategy, partially integrated into the short-term development planning, or essentially rejected as a contributor to socioeconomic growth' (Gale and Goodrich 1993, p. 4). Take the case of Antigua, in 1964, this country conducted research into contributions made to the national economy by the hotel industry in the tourism sector to determine the 'financial viability of the industry' (O'Loughlin 1964, p. 1). In the 1960s the main tourism establishments were managed by white foreigners while black locals were given the low paid menial jobs. This fact may have contributed to the perception of tourism as an extension of the colonialism in the region. Tourism in the region expanded in the 1960s and the number of tourist arrivals increased. The growth was said to be similar to that experienced by international tourism (Bryden 1973).

In the immediate post-independence period the economic strategy was mainly one of import substitution and a significant amount of government intervention in key sectors of the economy. Nationalisation was pursued by some states in an effort to exercise greater control of the economy in the hope of achieving economic independence (Ramsaran 2001).

The religious mix from the nineteenth century

A wide variety of religions are practised in the Pan-Caribbean. For much of the period under review, Christianity was the main religion, practised through the Roman Catholic, Anglican and Methodist churches. The Catholic Church was more dominant in the French and Spanish territories as well as those territories that were once under the French, namely St. Lucia, Dominica, Grenada and Trinidad. There were also the various protestant missionaries. The East Indian indentureds widened the religious mix in the nineteenth century with the introduction of Hinduism and Islam, especially in Trinidad, Guyana and Suriname.

From the 1920s onwards other churches appeared in the region. In St. Vincent, for instance, there was the less popular Church of Scotland. In Barbados and Trinidad, there were branches of the Greek Orthodox Church (see Plate 2.2). The African Orthodox Church, affiliated with the UNIA, also opened branches in Chappara, Cuba. The African Methodist Episopal Church (AME), originating in the USA, was active in Barbados and Cuba during the 1920s and 1930s (Scott 2002; Dodson 1998).

It has been traditionally suggested that religions in the region are syncretic or a synthesis, that is the 'blending of diverse cultures into new', as well as resistive, that is the 'borrowing of elements of culture and transforming them as a means of resistance'

Plate 2.2 *Ruins of a Greek Orthodox Church, Barbados*
© Cleve McD. Scott

(Sunshine 1988, p. 22). 'Syncretism … was the basis for the generation of a new Caribbean culture', what some writers called creole – born in the Caribbean (Taylor 2001, p. 3). Recent scholarship, however, argues that 'symbiosis' is more applicable to Caribbean religions than is either syncretism or creolisation, in that such a description allows for the recognition of the difference that characterises them. According to Desmangles, 'symbiosis refers to the spatial juxtaposition of diverse religious traditions from two continents, which coexist without fusing with one another' (Desmangles 1992, p. 8). Symbiosis, Desmangles insists, helps to pull the creoleists and pluralists together. The focal point of pluralism is the social and cultural differences that exist in the region.

The theoretical debate aside, it is quite obvious that in the Caribbean there developed Christian-oriented but highly Africanised religions (Austin-Broos 1997). Among these religions are the Shaker religion, also called Penitents, and Spiritual Baptists in St. Vincent and Trinidad, Revivalism and Bedwardnism in Jamaica, Shango in Trinidad. Voodoo continued to exist in Haiti. Alongside these religious beliefs was the belief in Obeah, the magical powers of the spirit world.

Among the newer religions, or religious movements as some prefer to say, is Rastafari. Rastafari originated in Jamaica in the late 1930s. It has a religious and political philosophy that is anti-colonial and pan-African. Rastafari also speaks reverently of Ethiopia largely because of the many biblical references to this African state. Its adherents don dreadlocked hair as an outward identification of their belief in the teachings and philosophy of Rastafari (Chevannes 1994; Taylor 2001). From the late 1960s Rastafari began spreading both around the Caribbean and internationally. Much of the attention drawn to Rastafari stems from the popularity of the Jamaican Rastafarian reggae singer, Robert 'Bob' Nesta Marley (1945–1981), Marley's songs of peace and love have become favourites among worldwide audiences since the 1970s.

Nation states, 1962–1970s

The West Indies Federation

British colonial authorities had been encouraging confederation from the eighteenth century. In fact several administrative unions were formed, most notably the Leeward Islands Federation. Several other attempts in the late nineteenth and early twentieth centuries were strongly resisted, these included the Barbados/Windwards Union proposed in 1876 and the Windwards Union/Confederation of 1884/85.

The sole objective for promoting federation was the desire to reduce the cost of administering the colonies. At the same time the people rejected union for they perceived it to be a possibly more oppressive form of government. This perception resulted from the misinformation fed to them by the white merchant/planter elite who were opposed to any diminution in their political control.

The West Indies Federation was formed out of the then British colonies in the West Indies in 1958. It consisted of Antigua, Barbados, the Caymans and Turks and Caicos Islands, Jamaica, Trinidad and Tobago, Montserrat, St. Kitts-Nevis-Anguilla, Grenada, St. Vincent, St. Lucia and Dominica. The Bahamas and the British Virgin Islands were not members of the Federation. The seat of government was Port of Spain, Trinidad. The Federation's flag consisted of a blue field bearing four equally spaced horizontal wavy lines with a gold disk over the middle two lines in the centre of the flag. The flag signified the Caribbean Sea and the sunshine of the region.

Slated for independence in 1962, the Federation did not live beyond the problem-plagued teething years. Fearing that it would have to shoulder the burdens of the economically underdeveloped members, Jamaica, the most populous and prosperous member, decided to hold a referendum on whether it should remain with the Federation. The result was a very slim majority against federation, but it was a majority which Jamaica considered sufficient to leave the Federation in 1962. 'Totally disenchanted', by Jamaica's decision to secede, the premier of Trinidad and Tobago, Dr. Eric Williams, declared: 'One from ten leaves nought'. This declaration was the last post for the Federation. It was an example of Williams 'exhibiting the exquisite, painful Trini gift for sublimating tragedy into comedy' (*Trinidad Express*, 24 August 2001). Having stated the principle of all or none, Williams decided to seek political independence for Trinidad and Tobago alone (Anthony 2002). This decision sealed the fate of the Federation which was eventually dissolved in May 1962. Tim Hector (1997), an Antiguan politician and intellectual, said that 'the End [of the West Indies Federation] was in the Beginning'. Hector saw clashes of Parochialism and Federalism just months after the Federation had begun and blamed these same forces for the demise of the Federation.

The Caribbean Community and Common Market (CARICOM) was the result of the failed British West Indies Federation. In 1962 a Common Services Conference was called to take decisions on services, such as the University of the West Indies (UWI) and the Regional Shipping Services. This meeting took the decision to continue inter-state cooperation. The trade agreement, creating what became known as the Caribbean Free Trade Area (CARIFTA), was signed on 1 May 1968. In October 1972, CARIFTA was converted into CARICOM.

Political independence

The territories colonised by other European powers were the first to attain political independence. St. Domingue was the first territory to become independent, it fought for and obtained its independence in 1804 and changed its name to Haiti. Santo Domingo, a country that shared the landmass known as Hispaniola with Haiti, was next. It became independent in 1844. Like Haiti it changed its name at independence and became known as the Dominican Republic. Cuba was the next country to become independent. This island was declared independent in 1902 following the Spanish–American War.

Haiti and the Dominican Republic did not fare too well after independence. For just over 30 years (1930–1961), the Dominican Republic was ruled by General Rafael Trujillo (1891–1961) with an iron fist. It was the USA who assisted his rise to power. Once in power the brutal president stole government funds while he ignored the plight of Dominicans. He also repressed his political opponents. Trujillo's rule was brought to an end when he was assassinated in 1961.

In 1946, just after the end of the Second World War, France decided to make its Caribbean colonies, namely Martinique, Guadeloupe, St. Barthelemy and St. Martin (French part) into three *Départements d'Outre-Mer* or DOMs (overseas departments) of the French Republic. These are (1) Martinique, (2) Guadeloupe along with the other islands and (3) French Guiana on the mainland. DOM status really meant that these territories were an integral part of France. As such they were to enjoy the same status as the other *Départments* in metropolitan France. In addition to having representatives in the Senate and Chamber of Deputies in France, the two *Départments* were allowed to elect a local General Council. Thus, these persons were effectively given the full benefits of French citizenship.

Departmentalisation was part of France's reconstitution of its colonial possessions in the post-world-war decolonisation process. It is a widely held view that the decision by Martinique, Guadeloupe and French Guiana to remain as DOMs allowed them to achieve a far superior standard of living to other parts of the Caribbean, especially the British Caribbean (Burton 1995) (see Chapter Three for more details). The downside to this, however, was the problem of identity. French West Indians were said to possess a 'double identity', that of French and West Indian. On the question of identity, Richard Burton has asserted that, 'the vast majority of coloured French West Indians were more than prepared to sacrifice West Indian-ness for the sake of Frenchness' (1995, 2).

The Dutch had shown a willingness to grant political independence to its Caribbean colonies since the 1940s. It had staged conferences in 1948, 1952 and 1954 to develop a new constitution. The final conference in 1954 led to a statute advancing a greater degree of autonomy to these territories. This law integrated the Dutch territories in the region as an autonomous department of the 'Tripartite' Kingdom of the Netherlands. Thus, Aruba, Curaçao and Bonaire (also known as the ABC islands), Suriname, St. Eustatius (or Statia), St. Maarten and Saba were given a new constitution making them semi-independent. These territories were given a governor, who was appointed by the Crown, as well the Staten, an elected legislature. As part of the 'Tripartite' Kingdom, citizens of these territories were given the same rights as citizens of the Netherlands. In 1969 violent protests broke out in Suriname and Curaçao. Dutch officials responded to this challenge by dispatching troops to quell the trouble. From this turbulence came independence for Suriname in 1975 (Brereton 1994, p. 55).

From the 1960s political independence was 'returned' to various territories in the region. Following the break up of the ephemeral West Indies Federation, decolonisation in the British Caribbean quickened, albeit 'at London's pace and on its own terms' (Brereton 1994, p. 53). Jamaica and Trinidad and Tobago became the first British Caribbean territories to become independent in 1962. British Guiana (called Guyana afterwards) and Barbados followed in 1966. In 1967 an Act of the British Parliament conferred a status called Associated Statehood on several of the smaller British Caribbean territories. Associated Statehood was a status that meant that these states were voluntarily associated with Great Britain and as such had full control of their internal affairs. The associated states were Antigua, Dominica, Grenada, St. Kitts and Nevis, and St. Lucia. St. Vincent and the Grenadines did not become an associated state until 1969.

From the 1970s onwards the associated states were moved to independence. Islands which gained independence in the 1970s and 1980s were: the Bahamas in 1973, Grenada in 1974, Dominica in 1978, St. Lucia, and St. Vincent and the Grenadines in 1979, Antigua in 1980, Belize in 1981 and St. Kitts and Nevis in 1983.

Not all British Caribbean territories were decolonised. The territories kept as colonies were: The British Virgin Islands, Anguilla, Monserrat, Turks and Caicos and the Cayman Islands. These territories seemed willing to continue the colonial relationship with Britain with some level of internal self-government. (See Chapter Three for a fuller discussion.)

Conclusion

Historical forces have shaped and fashioned the Pan-Caribbean territories into what they are today. The Pan-Caribbean is characterised by homogeneity as well as diversity, which stems from its colonial past. Catherine Sunshine sums it up brilliantly: 'The overwhelming cultural characteristic of the Caribbean, taken as the sum of its parts, is diversity. In race, in culture, in language and religion, it is one of the most heterogenous areas in the world' (1988, p. 19).

From around the 1990s, globalisation became a buzzword. The history of the Pan-Caribbean region shows that the region was perhaps the first true global village. Mary Chamberlain has pointed to the global nature of the Caribbean civilisation: 'Caribbean culture itself is global, a melange of European, and native Indian, African and Asian. Elements of each, old and new, have forged, and continue to forge, a unique syncretic cultural form which continues to adapt, incorporate and transform the local with the global' (Chamberlain 1998, p. 4). This is quite evident in the festivals in particular, such as Carnival, Phagwah and Divali, Eid-ul-Fitr, Hosein and the La Rose La Marguerite. The diversity of the region is also reflected in the Creole languages existing in the region. In the Dutch Antillean islands of Bonaire, Curacao and Aruba, for example, there is a Creole called Papiamento. (See Chapters Seven and Eight for more discussion.) This language was created from the interaction of African, English, Portuguese, Spanish missionaries, Dutch merchants, South American traders and Indians. Surely, there is unity in diversity in the Pan-Caribbean region.

Notes

[1] For a brief discussion of definitions of the Caribbean see the Introduction and also Blake 2000.
[2] Thanks to Tracey Skelton for her input into this conceptualisation.
[3] British Honduras is today called Belize and the descendants of the Black Caribs living there are called Garifuna. The deportation of the Black Caribs has created a Garifuna nation in Belize.

References

Allsopp, R. 1996: *Dictionary of Caribbean English Usage*. Oxford: Oxford University Press.

American Civil Liberties Union. 1939: *Civil Liberties in American Colonies*. New York: American Civil Liberties Union. [Online], Available:http://www.boondocksnet.com/ai/ailtexts/civillib.html [2002, May 29].

Anthony, M. 2002: *From Oxford Scholar to Father of a Nation: Dr Eric Williams*. [Online], Available: http://www.raceandhistory.com/historicalviews/williams.htm [2002, Dec. 9].

Austin-Broos, D. J. 1997: *Jamaica Genesis: Religion and the Politics of Moral Order*. Kingston, Jamaica: Ian Randle Publishers.

Baptiste, F. A. 1988: *War, Cooperation, and Conflict: The European Possessions in the Caribbean, 1939–1945*. Westport, Conn.: Greenwood Press.

Beckles, H. McD. 1986: 'From land to sea: runaway Barbados slaves and servants, 1630–1700'. In Heuman, G. (ed.). *Out of the House of Bondage: Runaways, Resistance and Marronage in Africa and the New World*. London: Frank Cass. pp. 79–94.

Beckles, H. McD. 1991: 'Caribbean anti-slavery: the self-liberation ethos of enslaved blacks'. In Beckles, H. McD. and Shepherd, V. A. (eds.) *Caribbean Slave Society and Economy*. Kingston, Jamaica: Ian Randle Publishers.

Beckles, H. McD. 1993: 'Divided to the vein: the problem of race, colour and class conflict in Hatian nation building, 1804–1820'. In Beckles, H. McD. and Shepherd, V. A. (eds.) *Caribbean Freedom: Economy and Society from Emancipation to the Present*. Kingston: Ian Randle Publishers. pp. 170–80.

Besson, J. and Momsen, J. (eds.) 1987: *Land and Development in the Caribbean*. London and Basingstoke: Macmillan.

Blake, B. 2000: 'The Caribbean — geography, culture, history, identity: Assets for economic integration and development'. In: Hall, K. and Benn, D. (eds.) *Contending with Destiny: The Caribbean in the 21st Century*. Kingston: Ian Randle Publishers. pp. 45–52.

Bolland, O. N. 1995: *On the March: Labour Rebellions in the British Caribbean, 1934–39*. Kingston, Jamaica: Ian Randle Publishers.

Bolland, O. N. 2001: *The Politics of Labour in the British Caribbean: The Social Origins of Authoritarianism and Democracy in the Labour Movement*. Kingston, Jamaica: Ian Randle Publishers.

Brereton, B. 1981: *A History of Modern Trinidad, 1783–1962*. London: Heinemann.

Brereton, B. 1994: 'Independence and the Persistence of European Colonisation in the Caribbean'. In Cobley, A. (ed.) *Crossroads of Empire: The Europe-Caribbean Connection, 1492–1992*. Cave Hill, Bridgetown, Barbados: Dept. of History, University of the West Indies. pp. 53–63.

Britton, C. M. 1999: *Edouard Glissant and Postcolonial Theory: Strategies of Language and Resistance*. Charlottesville: University Press of Virginia.

Bryden, J. M. 1973: *Tourism and Development: A Case study of the Commonwealth Caribbean*. Cambridge: Cambridge University Press.

Burton, R. D. E. 1995: 'Introduction: the French West Indies à l'heure de l'Europe: an overview'. In Burton, R. D.E. and Reno, F. (eds.) *French West Indian: Martinique, Guadeloupe and French Guiana Today*. London: Macmillan. pp. 1–19.

Chamberlain, M. 1997: *Narratives of Exile and Return*. London: Macmillan.

Chamberlain, M. (ed.) 1998: *Caribbean Migration: Globalised Identities*. London: Routledge.

Chartrand, R. 1998: 'Black corps in the British West Indies, 1793–1815'. In *Journal of the Society for Army Historical Research* 76, pp. 248–254.

Chevannes. B. 1994: *Rastafari: Roots and Indeology*. Syracuse: Syracuse University Press.

CNN Cold War Episode Script, episode 10, *Cuba 1959–1968*. [Online], Available: http://www3.cnn.com/SPECIALS/cold.war/episodes/10/script.html [2002, Dec. 18].

Craton, M. 1996: 'The Black Caribs of St. Vincent: a reevaluation'. In Paquette, R. L. and Engerman, S. L. (eds.) *The Lesser Antilles in the Age of European Expansion*. Gainsville, Florida: University of Florida Press.

Craton, M. 1997: 'Continuity not change: late slavery and post-emancipation resistance in the British West Indies'. *Empire, Enslavement and Freedom in the Caribbean*. Kingston, Jamaica: Ian Randle Publishers. pp. 324–347.

Cudjoe, S. R. 1980: *Resistance and Caribbean Literature*. Ohio: Ohio University Press.

Desmangles, L. G. 1992: *The Faces of the Gods: Vodou and Roman Catholicism in Haiti*. Chapel Hill, NC.: The University of North Carolina Press.

Dietz, J.L. 1993: 'Operation Bootstrap and economic change in Puerto Rico'. In Beckles, H. McD. and Shepherd, V. A. (eds.) *Caribbean Freedom: Economy and Society from Emancipation to the Present*. Kingston: Ian Randle Publishers. pp. 421–435.

Dodson, J. E. 1998: 'Encounters in the African Atlantic World: the African Methodist Episcopal Church in Cuba'. In Brock, L. and Castañeda F. D. (eds.) *Between Race and Empire: African-Americans and Cubans before the Cuban Revolution*. Philadelphia: Temple University Press. pp. 85–103.

Emmer, P. C. 2000: 'A spirit of independence' or lack of education for the market? Freedmen and Asian indentured labourers in the post-emancipation Caribbean, 1834–1917'. *Slavery and Abolition* 21.2, pp. 150–169.

Fergus, C. K. 1985: 'British imperial trusteeship: the dynamics of reconstruction of British West Indian society, with special reference to Trinidad, 1783–1838'. Ph.D. Thesis, UWI, St. Augustine.

Ferguson, J. 1999: *The Story of the Caribbean People.* Kingston: Ian Randle Publishers.

Fraser, P. 1982: 'Some effects of the First World War on the British West Indies'. *Collected Seminar Papers No. 29, Caribbean Societies, Vol. 1.* London: ICS.

Freeman, G. P. 1987: 'Caribbean migration to Britain and France: From assimilation to selection'. In Levine, B. B. (ed.) *The Caribbean Exodus.* West Port, Connecticut: Praeger.

Gale, D. J. and Goodrich, J. N. (eds.) 1993: *Tourism Marketing and Management in the Caribbean.* London: Routledge.

Green, W. A. 1976: *British slave emancipation: The Sugar Colonies and the Great Experiment, 1830–1865.* Oxford: Clarendon Press.

Hall, N. A. T. 2000: ' "Slaves" use of their "free" time in the Danish Virgin Islands in the later eighteenth and early nineteenth century'. In Beckles, H. McD. and Shepherd, V. A. (eds.) *Caribbean Slavery in the Atlantic World: A Student Reader.* Princeton, NJ: Markus Wiener. pp. 722–731.

Hector, L. T. 1997: 'The West Indies Federation – the end was in the beginning'. *Fan The Flame,* July 25.

Heuman, G. 1997: 'The social structure of the slave societies in the Caribbean'. In Knight, F. W. (ed.) *General History of the Caribbean vol 3: The Slave Societies of the Caribbean.* London: UNESCO/Macmillan. pp. 138–168.

Higman, B. W. 2002: 'The making of the sugar revolution'. In *In the Shadow of the Plantation.* Kingston, Jamaica: Ian Randle Publishers. pp. 40–71.

Hill, R. and Bair, B. (eds.) 1987: *Marcus Garvey Life and Lessons: A Centenial Companion to the Marcus Garvey and Universal Negro Improvement Association Papers.* California: University of California Press.

Holder, J. S. 1993: 'The Caribbean Tourism Organization in historical Perspective'. In Gale, D. J. and Goodrich, J. N. (eds.) *Tourism Marketing and Management in the Caribbean.* London: Routledge. pp. 20–27.

Howard, R. A. and Howard, E. S. (eds.) 1983: *Alexander Anderson's Geography and History of St. Vincent, West Indies.* Cambridge, Mass: Harvard.

Howe, G. D. 2002: *Race War and Nationalism: A Social History of West Indians in the First World War.* Kingston, Jamaica: Ian Randle Publishers.

James, C. and John, P. (eds.) 2000. *The Cultures of the Hispanic Caribbean.* Gainesville: University Press of Florida.

Johnson, H. 1998: 'Barbadian migrants in the Putumayo district Amazon, 1904–1911'. In Chamberlain, M. (ed.) *Caribbean Migration: Globalised Identities.* London: Routledge. pp. 177–187.

Knight, F. W. 1989a: 'The Caribbean: a regional overview'. In Knight, F. W. and Palmer, C. A. (eds.) *The Modern Caribbean.* Chapel Hill: North Carolina Press. pp. 1–19.

Knight, F. W. 1989b: 'Cuba: politics, economy, and society, 1898–1985'. In Knight, F. W. and Palmer, C. A. (eds.) *The Modern Caribbean.* Chapel Hill: North Carolina Press. pp. 165–184.

Knight, F. W. 1997: 'The disintegration of the Caribbean slave systems, 1772–1886'. Knight, F. W. (ed.) *General History of the Caribbean vol 3: The Slave Societies of the Caribbean.* London: UNESCO/Macmillan. pp. 322–345.

Knight. F. W. and Palmer. C. A. (eds.) 1989: *The Modern Caribbean.* Chapel Hill: North Carolina Press.

Lewis, W. A. 1939: *Labour in the West Indies: The Birth of a Workers' Movement.* London: V. Gollancz.

Mandle, J. R. 1996: *Persistent Underdevelopment: Change and Economic Modernization in the West Indies.* Amsterdam: Gordon and Breach Publishers.

Marshall, W. 1993: ' "We be wise to many more things": black hopes and expectations of emancipation'. In Beckles, H. McD. and Shepherd, V. A. (eds.) *Caribbean Freedom: Economy and Society from Emancipation to the Present.* Kingston: Ian Randle Publishers. pp. 170–80.

Martin, T. 1983: *The Pan-African Connection: From Slavery to Garvey and Beyond.* Massachusetts: The Majority Press.

Millette, J. 1970: *The Genesis of Crown Colony Government: Trinidad, 1783–1810.* Curepe, Trinidad: Moko.

Nettleford, R. 2001: *Texture and Diversity: the Cultural Life of the Caribbean.* [Online], Available: http://www.princeclausfund.nl/source_eng/archive/Nettleford.doc [Accessed 2002, May 29].

Nurse, L. A. 1992: *Trade Unionism and Industrial Relations in the Commonwealth Caribbean: History, Contemporary Practice and Prospect.* Westport, Conn.: Greenwood Press.

O'Loughlin, C. 1964: *Financial and Economic Survey of the Hotel Industry in Antigua.* Eastern Caribbean: Institute of Social and Economic Research.

Ormerod, B. 1998: 'The Martinican concept of "creoleness": A multiracial redefinition of culture'. *MotsPluriels* [Online], Available: http://www.arts.uwa.edu.au/MotsPluriels/MP798bo.html. [accessed 2002, Jul. 20].

Peabody, S. 2002: *Peasant Political Culture in Post-Emancipation Haiti and Jamaica.* H-NET book review. H-Caribbean@h-net.msu.edu.

Phillips, A. D. V. 1998: ' "Go Ahead, England; Barbados is Behind You": Barbadian responses to the outbreak of the First World War in 1914'. In Moore, B. L. and Wilmot, S. R. *Before and After 1865: Education, Politics and Regionalism in the Caribbean.* Kingston: Ian Randle Publishers. pp. 343–50.

Phillips, Di. E. 1991: 'The U.S. "Special Relationship" with the Virgin Islands: definition and prospects for independence'. In Lisowski, J. (ed.) *Caribbean Perspectives: The Social Structure of a region.* New Brunswick: Transaction Books. pp. 1–17.

Premdas, R. R. 1999: 'The Caribbean: ethnic and cultural diversity and a typology of identities'. In Premdas, R. R. (ed.) *Identities, Ethnicity and Culture in the Caribbean.* pp. 3–12.

Proudfoot, M. J. 1970: *Population Movements in the Caribbean.* New York: NUP.

Ramsaran, R. 2001: 'Patterns of growth and social development in the Anglophone Caribbean'. *Iberoamericana. Nordic Journal of Latin American and Caribbean Studies* 31(2). pp. 37–64.

Reddock, R. 1988. *Elma Francois: The NWCSA and the Worker's Struggle for Change in the Caribbean.* London: New Beacon.

Richardson, B. C. 1992: *The Caribbean in the Wider World, 1492–1992: A Regional Geography.* Cambridge: Cambridge University Press.

Rubenstein, H. 1975: 'The utilization of arable land in an Eastern Caribbean valley'. *Canadian Journal of Sociology* 1 (2): pp. 157–67.

Scott, C. McD. 2002: 'The Politics of Crown Colony Government: Land, Labour and Politics In a Colonial State, St. Vincent and The Grenadines, 1883 to 1937'. Ph.D. Thesis, UWI, Cave Hill, Barbados.

Sheller, M. 2000: *Democracy after Slavery: Black Publics and Peasant Radicalism in Haiti and Jamaica.* Gainesville: University Press of Florida.

Shepherd, V. A. (ed.) 1999: *Women in Caribbean History.* Kingston: Ian Randle Publishers.

Simons, G. 1996: *Cuba: From Conquistador to Castro.* Basingstoke: Macmillan.

Spencer, I. R. G. 1997: *British Immigration Policy since 1939.* NY: Routledge.

Stein, J. 1986: *The World of Marcus Garvey: Race and Class in a Modern Society.* Baton Rouge: Louisiana State University Press.

Suchlicki, J. 1989: *Cuba: From Columbus to Castro.* Washington: Pergamon-Brassey's.

Sunshine, C. A. 1988: *The Caribbean: Survival, Struggle and Sovereignty.* Washington, D.C.: Ecumenical Program on Central America and the Caribbean.

Taylor, P. (ed.) 2001: *Nation Dance: Religion, Identity, and Cultural Difference in the Caribbean.* Bloomington: Indiana University Press.

Thomas, H. 1998: *Cuba, or, the Pursuit of Freedom.* New York: Da Capo.

Tinker, H. 1974: *A New System of Slavery: The Export of Indian Labour Overseas, 1830–1920.* Oxford: Oxford University Press.

Trinidad Express. 2001: '20 most memorable statements in T&T politics'. Aug. 24.

Walvin, J. 1984: *Passage to Britain.* Harmondsworth: Penguin.

Wambu, O. 1998: *Black British Literature since Windrush.* [Online], Available: http://www.bbc.co.uk/history/society_culture/multicultural/windrush/literature01.shtml [accessed 2002, Oct. 31].

Waters, I. 1964: *The Unfortunate Valentine Morris.* Chepstow, Wales: Cheapstow Society.

Welch, P. L.V. and Goodridge, R. A. 2000: *Red and Black Over White: Free Coloured Women in Pre-Emancipation Barbados.* Bridgetown, Barbados: Carib Research.

3

Issues of development in the Pan-Caribbean: overcoming crises and rising to challenges?

Tracey Skelton

Introduction

Development is arguably in a period of crisis. As a process, a practice and a project it is not doing what it was intended to do (Crush 1995; McAfee 1991; Rist 1997; Skelton 1996a; Visvanathan *et al* 1997). In the Caribbean this 'failure of development' is apparent in widely divergent ways, but there have also been some development success stories.

Contemporary commentaries on Caribbean development have revolved around the *crises* of the 1990s and have more recently turned their attention to the *challenges* the region needs to focus upon in the twenty-first century (Alonso 2002a and b; Bartilow 1997; Gafar, 2002; González Vilaseca 1997; Hall 2001; Jessen and Rodríguez 1999; Payne and Sutton 2001; Ramsaran 2002; Stark 2001; Thomas 1988). However, while much of this literature provides an insight into the economic development issues within the Pan-Caribbean region there is a lack of analysis relating to social and cultural contexts of development (Skelton 1996b; 2003). In addition, the literature cited above tends to present a range of challenges as something which the Caribbean, the region and individual states, has to meet. The challenges are almost accepted as the inevitable consequence of globalisation. There is relatively little critical theorisation about the inequalities created by the global economic system, the OECD-dominated economic model of neo-liberalism and the structural adjustment programmes (SAPs) imposed by the World Bank and the International Monetary Fund (IMF). The shift away from dependency analysis (Girvan 1991; Payne and Sutton 2001) has not been replaced by further critical theorisation, with a few interesting exceptions which will be discussed below.

'Development'[1] as a process is problematic within the Pan-Caribbean context and yet it is essential to our understanding of the region and the ways in which countries connect and compete with each other. Inevitably, globalisation is the contextual backdrop to contemporary development issues, and Jessica Byron expertly deals this with in the following chapter. Here, this chapter provides an insight (however partial) into some of the key development factors at play in the Pan-Caribbean. It provides data to enable us to view the diversity and semblance within and across the region. The focus is then on four case studies to examine the discourses around development as they apply to particular groupings of 'states' or individual states. This selection provides a genuine take on aspects of the Pan-Caribbeanness of the 'development project' as it focuses on the independent Commonwealth Caribbean (the English-speaking independent nations), Cuba (a Spanish-speaking socialist state), Haiti (a Creole- and French-speaking independent nation) and the remaining 'dependent' or 'colonial' territories of the region. The latter group is very hard to collate statistical data for because the majority are not listed in the UNDP's figures nor those of the World Bank because they are legally part of their metropolitan/colonial power (Britain, France, The Netherlands and the USA). Nevertheless, a brief overview is an important step towards making some of their development issues more visible. In conclusion, the chapter will critique the potential for a future of effective and sustainable development.

What is the 'development' situation within the Pan-Caribbean?

While the Pan-Caribbean is not the poorest region in the world (as will be shown below in selections from UNDP and World Bank data) it does, along with Latin America, have the greatest levels of inequality (Carlson 1999; Economic Commission for Latin American and the Caribbean (ECLAC) 1997 and 2002). In addition, there is enormous diversity within the region itself. The Caymen Islands had a Gross Domestic Product (GDP) per capita of $24,500 (US)[2] in 1997 (Alonso and Hicks 2002b), whereas Haiti's GDP per capita was just $1,800 (US) in 2001 (Alonso and Hicks 2002a). The Cayman Islands are one of world's richest 'states'[3], Haiti is one of the poorest countries in the world and yet geographically the two are very close to each other. This diversity can make it difficult to write about development within the Pan-Caribbean region without resorting to vague generalisations, which becomes more likely when one considers that data from the UN, the World Bank, and ECLAC tend to combine the Caribbean with Latin America. Finding the specifics of the Caribbean within such an analysis can be complicated and very time-consuming. Nevertheless, some detail is provided below in an overview of some of the key features relating to, and how, development matters in the Caribbean.

What is now very clear is that the 1990s was a decade of remarkable and rapid change in the Caribbean. Stark states that the Caribbean was involved in 'neo-liberal economic restructuring and state reforms but also the strengthening of civil society and shifts in understanding and expectations of citizens and political leaders in relation to national development' (2001, p. 1). The goal remained economic growth but more complex discussions created the space for questions about social equity, democratic participation, unemployment, the role and possibility of sustainable development and how social services were to be provided and delivered (Carlson, 1999; Stark: 2001). This growing discourse within the region has in part framed the following overview of some of the key issues relating to 'development'.

Debt in the Caribbean

One of the terrible ironies of the development project of the 1960s and 1970s is that money loaned for development through modernisation in those early decades suddenly became very expensive money. This was due to the oil crises of the 1970s and the pushing up of interest rates by the majority of the OECD countries. Caribbean countries, attempting to follow the industrialisation path to a 'developed' condition, were, and are, trapped in a state of indebtedness which has exacerbated a whole range of economic, social and cultural problems. The Debt Crisis continues to cripple most countries and territories in the Caribbean as they struggle to repay the money borrowed decades before. In order to reschedule debts and borrow more money the region has been forced to adopt structural adjustment programmes (SAPs) established by the IMF and the World Bank. Region-wide figures are hard to gather, but in 1998 the Dominican Republic owed a little under $4 billion and Antigua (with a population of 65,000 people) owed $327 million (Ferguson 1999, p. 329). McAfee and Bartilow report that between 1980 and 1988 total debt in the Caribbean grew by 125 per cent (1991, p. 14; 1997, p. xii, respectively). The region's debt continues to escalate even though in many cases countries are selling more but receiving less in payment. Much of what they do earn in foreign exchange is turned around and paid out in debt repayment. Currently the Caribbean is paying out considerably more in repayments than it receives in fresh loans. The total foreign debt of the Caribbean countries is not as large as its neighbouring region of Latin America but as a percentage of the region's combined gross national product (GNP) it constituted 70 per cent in the 1980s (McAfee, 1991) and has probably increased during subsequent years. The Pan-Caribbean debt is largely owed to the IMF which affords less flexibility in terms of rescheduling or even the cancelling of some debts when compared to private banks or national governments that have loaned money to individual countries.

Although debt is debilitating for the future prospects of Caribbean countries, and can be directly witnessed in the cuts in education and health, the declining infrastructure and stagnation of wages, the World Bank list of economies for April 2003 records several Caribbean countries in rather surprising ways (see Table 3.1).

For example, Antigua and Barbuda is classified as 'upper middle income and less indebted'. The range of income for an upper middle economy' is $2,976–$9,205. In 2001 the GDP (now called GNI by the World Bank) per capita for Antigua and Barbuda was $8,200 (Alonso and Hicks 2002b, p. 79). St Lucia is classified in exactly the same way, 'upper middle income and less indebted' yet the actual the figure for GNP per capita for this country is $4,500 (Alonso and Hicks 2002b: 80). This indicates that generalised categories can mask considerable inequalities in terms of income and indebtedness. Economic based data often tell us little of the reality of indebtedness experiences as they are lived on the ground by ordinary Caribbeans. (For a full discussion of economic issues, trade relationships and global economic impacts see Chapter Four.)

Economy	Income Group[1]	Indebtedness[2]
Antigua and Barbuda	upper middle income	less indebted
The Bahamas	high income (non OECD)	debt not classified
Barbados	upper middle income	less indebted
Belize	lower middle income	severely indebted
Cuba	lower middle income	severely indebted
Dominica	upper middle income	moderately indebted
Dominican Republic	lower middle income	less indebted
Grenada	upper middle income	moderately indebted
Guyana	lower middle income	severely indebted
Haiti	low income	moderately indebted
Jamaica	lower middle income	moderately indebted
Netherlands Antilles	high income (non OECD)	debt not classified
Puerto Rico	upper middle income	debt not classified
St. Kitts and Nevis	upper middle income	moderately indebted
St. Lucia	upper middle income	less indebted
St. Vincent and the Grenadines	lower middle income	moderately indebted
Suriname	lower middle income	less indebted
Trinidad and Tobago	upper middle income	less indebted
Virgin Islands (US)	high income (non OECD)	debt not classified

TABLE 3.1 *Table to show income group and level of indebtedness allocated to Caribbean countries by the World Bank*

Source: World Development Indicators data base, World Bank located at http://www.worldbank.org/data/onlinedatabases/onlinedatabases.html (accessed 25th June 2003)

[1] Income groups are calculated from 2001 gross national income (GNI) per capita, calculated using the World Bank Atlas method. *Low income* = $745 or less; *lower middle* = $746–2,975; *upper middle income* = $2,976–9,205; *high income* = $9,206 or more.
[2] *Severely indebted* means present value of debt service to GNI exceeds 80 per cent or present value of debt service to exports exceeds 220 per cent. *Moderately indebted* means that either of the two key ratios exceeds 60 per cent but does not reach the critical levels. All other classified low-income and middle-income economies are listed as *less indebted*.

Social features of development

One of the key features of the social situation in the Caribbean throughout the 1990s, and which will continue through into this century, is the decline in birth rates and the demographic shift towards an ageing population in some countries. The exception is Haiti which has a birth rate of 31.68 per 1,000 people, whereas the region's average in 2001 was 18 births per each 1,000 residents (Alonso 2002c, pp. 30–31)[4]. In Haiti the life expectancy in 2002 was just 49.55 (CIA 2002). Table 3.2 shows the key demographic profiles and HDI (see below) rating for the Caribbean countries in 2002. This gives an indication of population size and all the significant demographic indicators that are often utilised in evaluations of socially related development[5].

Other general trends in social development reported by ECLAC in 2002 were reported as: a relative decline in poverty but rising inequality in several countries, progress towards gender equality with more women in paid employment and improved structural changes in social policy (2002, p. 45) (for more on gender as a social construction and issues of development see Chapter Seven).

A very useful analysis of social development is the Human Development Report produced by the United Nations Development Programme (UNDP) (see Box 3.1). The Human Development Index is designed to measure average achievements in human development and demonstrate this through one set of figures. The HDI includes three measures of human development: life expectancy, educational attainment and per capita income measured in real terms, and listed as 'purchasing power parity' (PPP)[6].

■ Box 3.1 What is 'human development'?

'The basic purpose of development is to enlarge people's choices. In principle, these choices can be infinite and can change over time. People often value achievements that do not show up at all, or not immediately, in income or growth figures: greater access to knowledge, better nutrition and health services, more secure livelihoods, security against crime and physical violence, satisfying leisure hours, political and cultural freedoms and sense of participation in community activities. The objective of development is to create an enabling environment for people to enjoy long, healthy and creative lives.' Mahbub ul Haq (n.d.)

Human development is about much more than the rise or fall of national incomes. It is about creating an environment in which people can develop their full potential and lead productive, creative lives in accord with their needs and interests. People are the real wealth of nations. Development is thus about expanding the choices people have to lead lives that they value. And it is thus about much more than economic growth, which is only a means – if a very important one – of enlarging people's choices.

Source: UNDP web site page http://hdr.undp.org/hd/default.cfm accessed June 26th 2003

Fifteen Caribbean countries are included in the Human Development Report for 2002 and five of them are listed in the *high human development* category: Barbados, The Bahamas, St. Kitts and Nevis, Trinidad and Tobago and Antigua and Barbuda (listed in ranked order). Cuba, Belize, Dominica, St. Lucia, Suriname, Grenada, Jamaica, St. Vincent and the Grenadines, The Dominican Republic and Guyana are all ranked as *medium human development*. Haiti is the only Caribbean country assessed in the *low human development* category (see Table 3.2). To try and put this into some perspective, 173 countries in the world are included in the HDI, 53 of them are ranked in the high category, 84 in the medium listing and 36 in the low ranking category. The variation within these categories is significant and this, like many statistical data, masks inequalities within countries. In relative terms, for people's everyday lives, minimal access to basic facilities and problems of insecurity and vulnerability to economic and other changes

TABLE 3.2 Key demographic profiles and HDI ranking for Caribbean countries in 2002

Country	population 1000s	population growth %	fertility rate per woman	birth rate per 1000	death rate per 1000 pop.	infant mortality 1000/live births	life exp. in years	HDI rank
Anguilla	12,446	2.44	1.77	14.94	5.54	23.68	76.5	not ranked
Antigua and Barbuda	67,448	0.69	2.29	18.84	5.75	21.61	71.02	52
Aruba	70,441	0.59	1.8	17.54	7.47	7.98	78.2	not ranked
The Bahamas	300,529	0.86	2.28	18.69	7.49	17.08	69.87	41
Barbados	276,607	0.46	1.64	13.32	8.38	11.71	73.49	31
Belize	262,999	2.65	3.96	31.08	4.6	24.31	71.46	58
British Virgin Islands	21,272	2.16	1.72	15.09	4.42	19.55	75.85	not ranked
Cayman Islands	36,273	2.03	2.03	13.45	5.24	9.89	79.18	not ranked
Cuba	11,224,321	0.35	1.6	12.08	7.35	7.27	76.6	55
Dominica	70,158	-0.81	2.01	17.3	7.11	15.94	73.86	61
Dominican Republic	8,721,594	1.61	2.94	24.4	4.68	33.41	73.68	94
French Guiana	182,333	2.57	3.13	21.66	4.78	13.22	76.49	not ranked
Grenada	89,211	0.02	2.5	23.05	7.63	14.63	64.52	83
Guadeloupe	435,739	1.04	1.92	16.53	6.03	9.3	77.35	not ranked
Guyana	698,209	0.23	2.09	17.89	9.33	38.37	65.59	103
Haiti	7,063,722	1.42	4.3	31.42	14.88	93.35	49.55	146
Jamaica	2,680,029	0.56	2.05	17.74	5.45	13.71	75.64	86
Martinique	422,277	0.89	1.79	15.37	6.4	7.62	78.56	not ranked
Montserrat	8,437	8.43	1.81	17.54	7.47	7.98	78.2	not ranked
Netherlands Antilles	214,258	0.93	2.06	16.16	6.4	11.06	75.15	not ranked
Puerto Rico	3,957,988	0.51	1.9	15.04	7.82	9.3	75.96	not ranked
St. Kitts and Nevis	38,736	0.01	2.39	18.61	9.04	15.83	71.29	44
St. Lucia	160,145	no data	2.34	21.37	5.3	14.8	72.82	66
St. Vincent and The Grenadines	116,394	0.37	2.01	17.54	6.12	16.5	72.82	91
Suriname	436,494	0.55	2.44	19.97	5.67	23.48	71.9	74
Trinidad and Tobago	1,163,724	-0.52	1.8	13.66	8.81	24.2	68.59	50
Turks and Caicos Islands	18,738	3.28	3.18	24.18	4.38	17.46	73.76	not ranked
US Virgin Islands	123,498	1.04	2.24	15.85	5.85	9.21	78.43	not ranked

The figures for Montserrat are rather strange due to the dynamic fluctuations in migration to and from the island because of the volcanic crisis. There is also a substantial inward migrating population from Dominica, Guyana and Dominican Republic as people seek work in the reconstruction of the island.

Source: CIA Worldfact Book 2002 at http://www.cia.gov/publications/factbook/geos and Human Development Index Trends at http://hdr.undp.org/reports/global/2002/en/indicator/ (both accessed 23rd June 2003).

can be profound. Poor people might live in a country ranked 50th in the world for the HDI (Trinidad and Tobago) but their sense and experience of development may not be ranked as 'high' by any stretch of the imagination. Furthermore, comparison with the 1998 Human Development Index provided in Alonso (2002c, p. 34) demonstrates that the apparent 'development success' placements for 2002 are in fact slippages down the world ranking for 8 of the 13 countries listed here and by Alonso. Four countries (with the exception of St. Lucia) have moved up a couple of ranks and Trinidad and Tobago has remained in the same place. Several Caribbean countries have therefore experienced a decline in HDI rather than an increase.

Poverty

It is clear from its HDI ranking that Haiti is a country where poverty is common and probably highly visible (for more detail on Haiti see below). However, levels of poverty, in a development context can be hard to measure, evaluate and witness. Nevertheless there are distinctive issues related to poverty that are important to address in the context of the Pan-Caribbean. Most of the Pan-Caribbean countries export primary goods. Currently world commodity prices are low, so although more is produced and sold less and less income is earned. For the Caribbean a process of poverty reduction must include their more open and equitable access to markets in the world's richer countries and there has to be debt relief and debt forgiveness. As Gafar (2002, p. 235) clearly states: 'Debt payments contribute to poverty, since scarce foreign exchange is diverted from improving health, education and the physical infrastructure'. (See Plate 3.1 for a visible representation of poverty.)

Plate 3.1 *Visible evidence of poverty and almost non-existent infrastructure in a low-income neighbourhood, Dominican Republic.*

© David Howard

The 1997 ECLAC (Economic Commission for Latin America and the Caribbean) report *The Equity Gap* argues that for all households in the Caribbean and Latin America the incidence of poverty declined from 41 per cent to 39 per cent from 1990–95 but that this was not sufficient to off-set the increases of the 1980s. In absolute terms, it argues, there are more people living in poverty than ever before. Where there has been a reduction in poverty in the Caribbean it has been due to a range of factors: economic growth, reduction in inflation, the continuing effort, despite SAPs, to increase social expenditure and with several processes of restructuring in state sectors, and more efficient systems of allocation. Success in poverty reduction appears most likely where there are high growth rates over a period of years, a reduction in unemployment and an increase in employment chances for those in the poorest households. What the report stresses, however, is that economic growth alone does not secure better income distribution. Even where there has been good economic growth it has not necessarily led to a reduction in relative poverty and inequity has worsened.

The crushing burden of poverty is most acutely felt at the household level and women bear the brunt of the responsibility of devising coping strategies in order to try and protect their children and households from the most damaging effects of all that poverty drags with it. In the Caribbean, women are evident in society as survivors, copers and strugglers (Box 3.2) (see Mohammed and Shepherd, 1999 for a wide range of essays which consider issues relating to women and gender and development in the Caribbean).

■ Box 3.2 Caribbean women's resistance and resilience: roles women can, and do, play in development

'The women's movement in the Caribbean … recognizes that many of the most important activities that sustain life and make life worth living do not come with a high school or university degree and are not saleable in the labor market. Until development strategists and popular organisations also recognize and take into account the essential role of these activities, many of which are carried out by women, development that is sustainable and socially and psychologically healthy will not be possible. As one starting point, the channeling of development resources directly to women could result in the liberation of women's creativity and productive power.'

(Kathy McAfee 1991, p. 201)

'The women's movement in the [Netherlands] Antillean islands, and its feminist components, have influenced the direction and pace of the advance made by Antillean women. The residual effects of the history of slavery, and continued migration in and out of the region, however, is still evident in the complexity of social and gender relations which exist today. A careful and systematic analysis needs to be carried out in the Netherlands-Antilles as much of this history remains hidden in our archives and our memory … The greatest victory in the future would be

■ Box 3.2 Continued

genuine respect for women as individuals and as a social group, on all levels, irrespective of social class or racial grouping. Perhaps at that point, one can start to build a society free of oppressive disequilibria.'

(Sonia Magdalena Cuales 1998, p. 98)

'Haitian women have struggled to make their voice heard. An analysis of their social conditions shows that whatever their class, their tremendous contribution to their country and to the economy has never been thoroughly assessed. This social and economic 'invisibility' has been reproduced in the field of culture. As writers and artists, they are seen as deviant and marginalised. However, these women have challenged quietly yet decisively male stereotypes concerning them … They have tried to redefine themselves, subverting the dominant male discourse that sought to silence them. The new narrative strategies they crafted have enriched the body of Haitian literature. Most of these writers were at the same time involved in social activism and feminist struggles. They paid a dear price during the Duvalier's dictatorship. Today, despite the volatile political climate and the harsh conditions of life in Haiti, women are trying to create a protected space from which will emerge new prospects for their country.'

(Marie-José N'Zengou-Tayo 1998, p. 138)

Poverty is also experienced harshly by children of the region. Children and young people are often a neglected part of development discourse. Apart from data about birth rates, infant mortality rates and age structures, they barely feature in development discussion. This is problematic given each child and young person is the future for any country. Two important texts published by Save the Children provide some degree of insight into the lives of children and their role in environmental change in the Caribbean (Green 1998; McIvor 1999). When cut backs are made in education it is children who suffer. They might be prevented from attending school altogether because of imposed costs, or for those that can still attend, the standard of resources, the quality of teaching and the learning environment may steadily decline. Loss of access to education can be brought about because of natural disaster, not just economic restructuring. At the time of the Montserratian volcanic eruption, in 1995, and during the ensuing crisis, one of the most serious concerns for parents was that while schools were being used as shelters for evacuees from the villages in the path of the pyroclastic flows there was no formal education for their children. For many who relocated off the island gaining adequate education provision for their children was a central reason for their choice.

When children experience a reduction in opportunities, experiences and investment in them as individuals, whether by their families because of poverty or by the state because

Plate 3.2 *A Montserratian child enjoying a mango before the volcanic crisis. This part of the island is now destroyed.*

© Tracey Skelton

of balance of payments deficits, the structural basis of all manner of social, cultural and economic inequalities is already established. Poor children are likely to die younger, get sick more often and find it harder to recover from even basic infections because of poor nutrition (Green 1998). Their lack of education means they will earn less as adults, girls are more likely to have their first child at a younger age and to have more children. With inadequate education children and young people are at risk from exploitation in the workplace and run higher risks of catching socially transmitted diseases such as HIV. Poor people realise this, hence their commitment to their children's education, but inadequate and inappropriate development processes alongside poverty can make this impossible. The Caribbean's future lies with its children and young people. There has to be an improved (or in some cases carefully maintained) commitment to the provision of accessible and relevant education as a way forward for the region.

Sustainable development and environmental issues

The first Earth Summit in Rio de Janerio in 1992 built upon the Brundtland Commission's report of 1987 *Our Common Future*. What was becoming apparent was that mismanaged economic growth, which was part of development, was causing environmental degradation on a massive scale (Lloyd Evans *et al* 1998). Southern countries were (and are) very critical of the Northern nations' remedies against global environmental problems which appeared to be thwarting attempts by the South to industrialise (McIvor 1999). Out of Rio came an emphasis on sustainable development which as a concept demanded that the environment be considered as an integral part of development programmes, and not just there for exploitation. The principles of protection and conservation of the environment for future generations and for possible development became powerful and emotive aspects of development discourse, especially post-Rio. The idea of 'stewardship' of resources by one generation for the next began to be expanded away from the issue of the environment to all sorts of aspects of development. What is becoming increasingly clear is that sustainable development will never be achieved if development/economic institutions and nations adhere to economic growth being the highest goal of development (Lloyd Evans *et al* 1998).

For the Caribbean environmental degradation locally and globally, especially in the form of global warming, is especially worrying as the majority of people live in the urban areas and almost all of these are in the coastal zones (Thomas-Hope 2002) (see Plate 3.3). The environment, poverty and debt are closely linked. Poor farmers, for example, may be forced into environmentally damaging practices (Pemberton *et al* 2002). Agriculture remains very important throughout large parts of the Caribbean and is still a significant earner of foreign exchange. Traditionally local farmers have had good conservation knowledge, but with increased pressures to produce for a cash crop system and earn foreign exchange, the environments are severely at risk through excessive use of pesticides and herbicides (McAfee 1991; Barker and McGregor 1995).

> The present environmental crisis can be attributed to increasing poverty, economic restructuring, inappropriate industrial policy, rapid urbanization and social deprivation associated with informal activity.　　　　　　　　　　　　　　　(Lloyd Evans *et al* 1998, p. 12)

I would also argue that poverty is due to environmental degradation as farmers and householders struggle to produce crops and raise livestock on impoverished ground.

Plate 3.3 *The coastal capital of St. George's, Grenada*

© Tracey Skelton

Much of the Caribbean consists of island states and sustainable approaches are essential to their survival – there is no other landmass to move on to once some part is destroyed. For the mainland countries safeguarding their natural resources is slowly becoming incorporated into development strategies. However, when faced with a northern logging company promising hard foreign currency payments for the rights to log a section of the interior and the IMF demanding certain levels of debt repayment, the environment and, in the case of Guyana, the indigenous Amerindian populations are all too often the losers in the 'development' game (Colchester 1997).

Pan-Caribbean examples of development: case studies from across the region

This section of the chapter selects two groups of territories and two specific countries for closer examination within the context of development. The selections are based upon an attempt to present a Pan-Caribbean perspective on the complex aspects of development process, practice and projects. It will, by perforce, have to be relatively brief. Nevertheless each will provide an introduction which hopefully will stimulate further interest on the part of the reader.

The first case study selected is the largest single group within the Caribbean in terms of the number of territories. It is the independent English-speaking Commonwealth Caribbean (while the British Overseas Territories of Anguilla, British Virgin Islands, Cayman Islands, Montserrat and the Turks and Caicos Islands are part of the Commonwealth they are considered in the fourth case study). The second case study under scrutiny is Cuba because of its anomalous position politically, economically and in terms of development. It is also an example of the Hispanic-Caribbean. Haiti is the third case study and is chosen because of its unenviable position as the poorest country of the region and is the one Creole/French-speaking island in the Caribbean that is not a *Départment d'Outre-mer* (DOM) of the French metropole. The final case study focuses on a collection of places that make the Caribbean such a distinctive region in terms of political status. These 'countries' are the remnants of a colonising era in Pan-Caribbean history in which European powers, and later the USA, fought for domination over particular spaces. This case study considers the French Départments, the Netherlands Antilles, the British Overseas Territories, and the US Virgin Islands and the Commonwealth of Puerto Rico.

The Independent Commonwealth Caribbean

This section charts aspects the economic development that have had held sway in the constituency since the 1950s and 1960s. For this section we are concentrating on the 11 nations of Antigua and Barbuda, The Bahamas, Barbados, Belize, Dominica, Grenada, Guyana, St. Lucia, St. Kitts and Nevis, St. Vincent and the Grenadines, Trinidad and Tobago. This sub-region is English-speaking and so has a strong connection through communication with the USA. It also includes some of 'wealthier' nations of the Caribbean; it incorporates all five of the countries which lie in the 'high human development' category of the 2002 HDI (see above). A fuller analysis can be found in Anthony Payne and Paul Sutton's excellent book *Charting Caribbean Development* (2001) which considers the whole of the Commonwealth Caribbean[7].

Payne and Sutton identify four phases in the context of development for this part of the Pan-Caribbean (2001, pp. 1–2). The first era dates from the end of the Second World War and political independence, which for most was in the 1960s and early 1970s. The central development theory and practice utilised was linked to modernisation and industrialisation as countries attempted to shift from agriculture-based economies and for some to develop further their mineral extraction processes, although this was complex because so much of it was owned externally. The plan was to shift towards manufacturing – following the pathway based on the European and US processes of development. Foreign companies were invited in but the level of actual production was minimal, just 'finishing off' products which brought little added value. In attempt to capitalise on their natural resources there was a strong push towards tourism but this brought its own problems (see Chapter Five for Beverley Mullings' lucid examination of this process). Neo-liberalism promotes free trade and the Caribbean Free Trade Association (CARIFTA) was established in 1968 as an attempt to harmonise tariffs and also to promote trade within the Commonwealth Caribbean.

By the early 1970s it was clear that the region was experiencing growth without development and countries were competing against each other to provide the same products. The sub-region was more divided than ever, but a second era began. At one of the Commonwealth Caribbean's other institutions, The University of the West Indies, academics were formulating their own critical commentary on development as it was then being practiced. They placed the fact that the sub-region's economy was dependent on the advanced industrialised nations as central to their analysis. They reflected on the ways the contemporary development processes were repetitions of the plantation system which locked the Caribbean into an iniquitous relationship with the metropoles. The problem with the dependency critique was that while it had genuine critical insight into modernisation it couldn't stimulate such a thorough analysis of the ways forward. This lack of an effective alternative was compounded by the oil crises of the 1970s and the onset of the conditions of debt. There were alternative paths trodden in some countries, Guyana adopted 'co-operative socialism', Jamaica 'democratic socialism', Grenada had a populist revolution towards socialism (Payne and Sutton 2001, p. 9). However, none was a successful alternative for a range of reasons, one of which was linked to the presence of a powerful 'anti-socialist' state, the USA, which brought its will to bear on smaller countries.

Still, in the 1970s, and effectively overlapping with some of the processes described above, was what Payne and Sutton have named 'the neo-liberal revolution' (2001, p. 11). The 1970s were a time of crisis and failure that meant as the region entered the 1980s there still was no possible alternative either as theory or possible economic or political practice. The USA under Ronald Reagan was determined to re-assert its hegemony and part of this plan in relation to economics was the push towards market-based economies.

The Caribbean Basin Initiative was announced in 1982 and was supposed to offer preferential access of selected Caribbean goods, although not the ones the Caribbean was best able to produce, to the US market. The reality was far less generous than was promised and the Initiative focused much more on military assistance to anti-communist/socialist regimes (Bernal 2001; Boodhoo 2002). The second part of the push were SAPs imposed by the IMF, World Bank and US Agency for International Development (USAID) (Payne and Sutton 2001). The social costs were profound: unemployment, inflation, a sharp decline in living standards that stimulated riots in Jamaica and industrial action in Guyana. There were some small perceptible benefits from a trickle-down process in Barbados and some Eastern Caribbean states (Payne and Sutton 2001, p. 14).

This shove (and I use that term deliberately) towards neo-liberalism during the 1980s came from outside the region and left the Caribbean both open and vulnerable to what Payne and Sutton describe as the fourth phase; globalisation and regionalism. Without the leverage of the possible turn towards socialism afforded to the Commonwealth Caribbean by the Cold War the Caribbean became a marginalised region in US foreign politics. The Commonwealth region was now suitably 'west-like' in its politics and economics as far as the US was concerned; the Commonwealth was anxious about becoming 'off-shore platforms for the US economy' (Payne and Sutton 2001, p. 16) and being forced into total dependency. Leaders of the region established the West Indian Commission to report to CARICOM on the questions of future development and the context of globalisation. The report, *Time for Action* (1992) demonstrated that the Commonwealth Caribbean was oriented towards both the USA and the European Union (EU) and would have to make a decision about which was its best future. It also recommended that CARICOM should expand to include more countries and also consolidate its integration. It was a precursor to the establishment of the Association of Caribbean States in 1994 which is a genuinely Pan-Caribbean/Caribbean-Americas organisation. The report received high praise but little of it was put in to action. US hegemony in the region was reinforced by the Enterprise of the Americas Initiative (EAI) in 1990 which in practice has narrowed the options for Commonwealth Caribbean states even further.

The 1990s, as we have seen above, demonstrated some degree of economic growth, and in several countries this has been translated into some improvements in social development. However, the gains have not yet matched the losses of the 1980s. What of the future? The sub-region is struggling to find an economic place in a globalised world; it has to look towards a place in the proposed Free Trade Area of the Americas (FTAA) but threatens to be dwarfed in the wider region. What the region could once offer to external investment – raw materials and cheap labour – is no longer what is required. TNCs are seeking professional and technical labour and well developed telecommunication resources, expertise and infrastructure, which only Barbados is currently able to potentially supply (Alonso and Hicks 2002b; Watson 1997). (The final section of this chapter considers future possibilities for the wider Caribbean region.)

Cuba

Cuba is the largest country in the island-Caribbean and is just 145km south of Florida, which has been a significant feature of its geopolitical history (see Chapter Two by Cleve McD. Scott). Cuba has for a long time been an exception in the Caribbean in relation to social development achievements. The revolutionary government took over the means of production and developed state programmes which focused on employment and social services. Its policies were, and are, informed by commitments to egalitarian redistribution and social welfare (Dilla Alonso 2000; Ferguson 1999). In less than 30 years Cuban development in relation to education and health was dramatic.

> In 1953, 57 per cent of the population lived in urban areas, illiteracy affected slightly less than 25 per cent of the population, and only 11 per cent of the people had a middle-school education or higher. By 1981 these figures had changed significantly: approximately 69 per cent of the population lived in urban areas, illiteracy had been virtually wiped out, and 41 per cent of the population had six or more years of education. By 1989, the last year the statistical yearbook was published, the population was reported at 10.5 million, 73 per cent of whom lived in urban areas ... more than 140,000 were receiving high-school instruction. More than half of the 33,199 graduates from Cuban universities in that year were women.
> (Dilla Alonso 2000, pp. 33–34)

> For the last 37 years the Cuban National Health System has itself been a social project to assure the equity, accessibility, and universality that all citizens require. The health indicators of the Cuban people have outstripped those of underdeveloped countries. Cuban indicators have been in the forefront because the country's organization in the health field gives special importance to disease prevention and the promotion of health, and to participate in the entire community and all sectors.
> (Dr. Dotres Martinez 1997)

The investment and commitment to education and health provision for all is evident when we consider a range of demographic and social indicators (also see Box 3.3). In 2001 Cuba's population was about 11.2 million and growth was estimated at 0.37 per cent. Its infant mortality rate is one of the lowest in the Caribbean at just 7.39 deaths per 1000 live births and its life expectancy was the highest at 76.41 years. It also has the second highest (after the Dutch Antilles) literacy rates as 95.7 per cent of the population over 15 can read and write (Alonso and Hicks 2002a, p. 42). Its combined primary, secondary and tertiary gross enrolment ratio was 76 per cent in 1999, which placed it third in the Caribbean countries listed by the UNDP after Suriname (82 per cent) and Barbados (77 per cent). It is ranked at 55 in the HDI, second to Mexico in the *medium human development* ranking (UNDP 2002).

The World Bank ranks the Cuban economy as 49th in a total of 208 countries and defines it as *lower middle income* but *severely indebted* (World Bank 2003). It is difficult to estimate economic factors because the US embargo on Cuba means there is effectively no exchange rate for the peso. Its purchasing power parity GDP per capita was $1,700 in 2001, which places it marginally above Haiti. Hence income is very low in the country but health care and education is free along with other welfare provision. It

■ Box 3.3 Cuba's revolutionary commitment to education, health and innovative technology

'Throughout the 1970s and 1980s health, education and housing remained priorities for the government, which achieved impressive results in reducing illiteracy and poverty-related illness. Cuba's reputation as an active supporter of third-world liberation struggles was also enhanced as the island opened up its medical facilities to victims of conflicts in Africa and Central America. In 1979, some 30,000 Cubans volunteered to assist the revolutionary programme in Nicaragua with its literacy programme.'

(James Ferguson 1999, p. 306)

'Cuba's health care system has been unrivaled since the 1959 revolution … The national health system includes a network of institutions that provide coverage to 100% of the population. In every community, there is a family doctor and nurse who live and work there. In 1992, there were over 18, 500 family doctors on the island. Between 1959 and 1989, Cuba's electrification program brought the electrified population up to 95%. Still, there are over 300 family doctors living and working in remote rural areas without electricity from either the national grid or the many micro-hydro systems around the country … The fall of the Soviet Union added to the already difficult circumstances caused by the economic blockade imposed by the United States, which has been in place for over 30 years. Cuba desperately needed to cut back on its oil consumption. Despite these hardships, Cuba has forged ahead with the plan to bring adequate health care to every Cuban citizen … CUBASOLAR is a non-governmental organization promoting the use of renewable energy and energy consciousness. [The village of El Mulato's] health clinic became the first in Cuba to be electrified with photovoltaics [which uses solar energy].'

(Laurie Stone 1998)

'Concentrated, hard or conventional energy (this is oil, coal and nuclear reactors) is a weapon. Since a long time ago, the principle causes of wars in the world have been energy. Who controls the energy, controls the world. It was also used against the Cuban Revolution, when one of the first measures that was taken against Cuban was to cut us off from the oil delivery. Conventional energy responds to the interests of the rich, of the powerful, makes the poor each day poorer, more indebted, more enslaved. Renewable, soft or nonconventional energy (this is solar), is a weapon against capitalism and is against imperialism, yet it is for everyone. The sun shines for the Chinese, the Blacks, the Indians and the Whites; for women, men, elderly and children; for the poor and it is so generous it also shines for the rich. The sun can't be blockaded, it can't be dominated, it can't be destroyed. Solar energy is the weapon of the people. It is the only thing that can produce the true economic and social development that humanity needs'.

(Luis Berriz, President of CUBASOLAR – quoted by Stone 1998) is these commitments to social and welfare development delivery which rank the island relatively high on the HDI (6th out of the 16 Caribbean countries ranked) but it is the GDP (PPP) per capita which pulls it down.

Faced with the US embargo the Cuban government and the Cuban people have had to be highly adaptive and inventive (see Box 3.3 about the use of solar energy). In order to maintain most of the social welfare provision and to try and earn much needed foreign exchange Cuba has tried to develop niche products and areas of expertise. One such area is biotechnology and biomedical research and Cuba has a growing export market in medical-pharmaceuticals. It has also invested in the rural sectors and agriculture to reduce its food import bill. In 1988 its food and beverages import bill was $730 million; in 1998 this had reduced to $665 million (Alonso and Hicks 2002a). However, the Cuban people still receive subsidised basic foodstuffs through ration systems.

In the 1980s and early 1990s the Cuban economy faced almost total collapse with the end of the Soviet Union which was its main trading partner and source of aid. The government was forced to abandon total state control of the economy and it has moved slowly, and often with difficulty, to a more open system, it has effectively gone through 'economic restructuring' (Dilla Alonso 2000, p. 35). Tulchin argues that:

> Cuba is far better prepared to attract and utilize foreign investment than any of its island neighbours. Its economy is one of the largest and most diverse of the Caribbean basin, and its infrastructure, the education and skill level of its people, and its medical and high technology industries are among the most developed in the Latin America' (1997, pp. xii–xiii).

Some commentators argue that the careful and measured state reform could be a version of a people-centred capitalist-socialist (or socialist-capitalist) combined economy (Carranza Valdés 1997; Tulchin 1997) However, there is also concern that the economic changes and the relaxation of the state might establish the space for entrepreneurial and individualistic people to then become the basis for a re-establishment of capitalism in the country (Dilla Alonso 2000, p. 38). There has, of course, always been dissent within Cuba against what for many is experienced as heavy-handed state control and restriction. For Bryan (1997) there is also the concern in the wider Caribbean of the potential threat Cuba's superior economic qualities and large internal market might pose if it became fully integrated into the regional economy.

What role Cuba continues to play (it has already been remarkably generous to its Caribbean neighbours through an extensive programme of educational scholarships, including training for medicine and vetinary science) and has yet to play in the Caribbean, is something that is very difficult to speculate about. What should be determined, however, is that it is a negotiation between *Cuba* and the *Caribbean* without continued US interference. If Cuba is to maintain its excellent development achievements it must safeguard itself against the harsh vagaries of capitalism.

Haiti

As Cleve McD. Scott has explained in Chapter Two, Haiti has the proud historical distinction of becoming the first black republic in the western hemisphere in 1804.

However, through complex and brutal political events it is now distinguished as the poorest nation in the Caribbean. There is not the time here to examine all the political events of the island, but some political context is important in relation to prospects for development (see Nicholls 1996 and Sheller 2000 for historical and political analysis).

The political dictatorships of 'Papa Doc', François, and 'Baby Doc', Jean-Claude, Duvalier established a pattern of intense extremes of wealth and abject poverty. The exploitation and terrorisation of the Haitian people over two generations of Duvaliers was the total antithesis of any human-centred form of development. Even now, democracy in the island is fragile and any sustainable development plans seem very difficult to achieve.

In the past external power was directed at trying to achieve some process of political change. In 1981 France's president, Mitterand, ended French aid to the island in protest at human right abuses[8]. The Catholic Church, not known for its support of dissent (consider its attitude towards liberation theology in central and south America), became more critical of Baby Doc's regime. In 1983 there was active papal support for Catholic priests to become more involved in struggles against the dictatorship. Indeed this dissent brought to the fore Jean-Bertrand Aristide, a radical priest who was to become the first democratically elected president in 1991 after the fall of dictatorship (see Plate 3.4 representing the campaign for Aristide's election). Although there had been a civilian president before him, Ertha Pascal-Trouillot, the first Haitian woman head of state, who tried to establish some sort of power base of social order until the elections were held in December 1990 (Ferguson 1998, pp. 312–314). However, yet another military coup forced Aristide into exile and the USA to intervene in September 1994. They conducted a 'peaceful' invasion for 'Operation Uphold Democracy', the Haitian military gave up and dissipated and Aristide returned to power in October of the same year. Ferguson reports that it was 'the first time that the USA

Plate 3.4 *Mural of Aristide, Port-au-Prince, Haiti*

© David Howard

had intervened in a Caribbean country to oust a military regime and install and radical civilian rather than vice versa' (1998, p. 315). This reinstatement of Aristide however came after major international sanctions were imposed on Haiti from 1991–94[9]. This was a devastating blow for economic development and reinforced the desperate levels of poverty experienced by the majority of Haitian people.

In terms of social indicators of development Haiti stands out in the Caribbean region, indeed in the whole western hemisphere. The 2001 population was about 7 million people and the annual growth rate is 1.4 per cent; between 65 and 70 per cent of people live in rural areas. Children aged 0–14 constitute a huge 40 per cent of the total population and hence population growth will continue at relatively high rates for some time to come. This 'youthful' population is despite an infant mortality rate of 95.2 deaths per 1,000 live births and the island had a life expectancy of just 49.4 years in 2001, although this is recorded as 52.6 years in the Human Development Report for Haiti 2002. So while this is still a very low expectancy rate there appears to be some prospect of improvement. Haiti has the lowest literacy rate in the region with just less than 50 per cent of the population being able to read and write. There is compulsory education for children aged 6–12 but there are not enough teachers or schools to educate all of the children within this age group (Alonso and Hicks 2002a). Hence an increase in the levels of adult literacy seems unlikely for some time to come which means very high numbers of illiterate and low-skilled people, which does not bode well in the current development context where skilled personnel are what is required. In 2002 Haiti's HDI ranks it at 146 out of a total of 173. All of the countries below Haiti in the ranking are all in Africa (UNDP 2002).

The island fares very badly in terms of social development but also in relation to economic growth. The GDP (PPP) per capita is just $1,467. However, in ten years (1990–2000) the GDP in Haiti currency, the gourde, increased from G12.5 billion to G77.6 billion. Nevertheless, the island experienced negative growth from 1988 to 1994 because of economic sanctions, intense political upheaval and labour unrest. In 1992 the growth rate was ⁻14.8 per cent but in 1994 was ⁻8.3 per cent. The growth rate just tipped over into positive from 1995–2000 at slightly over 1 per cent (Alonso and Hicks 2002b). However, as part of Haitian people's adaptability and resilience there is a substantial informal economy which involves complex smuggling operations, and while these can mean the difference between collapse and survival for households and communities this type of activity is not formally recorded. The state still owns the majority of infrastructure provisions which places it on the wrong side of neo-liberal programmes, so the island struggles to get funding from the World Bank and IMF. Haiti's agricultural sector, despite acute problems of land degradation (Lundahl 2001), remains a very important part of the economy and employs two-thirds of Haitian workers. It is largely small-scale subsistence farming but it supplies 70 per cent of all food consumed in Haiti and coffee, cacao, sisal and mangoes are very important earners of foreign exchange (Alonso and Hicks 2002b).

Mats Lundahl (2001) asks whether sustained growth in Haiti is a genuine possibility. He outlines in stark terms the environmental crisis that faces the majority of the island's population, in particular the acute and ongoing deforestation. The forest resource will survive only a few decades if tree felling for fuel continues at present rates. He argues that the economic sanctions of 1991–94 resulted in further erosion as export crops such as coffee trees (which act to protect against soil erosion) were uprooted to make way for food crops. Coffee could no longer reach export markets and more food was needed as less and less could be imported (2001, pp. 163–4). Haitian farmers are getting poorer and poorer, however, this could be changed with a concerted effort of ending soil erosion. Save The Children have a range of projects in Haiti trying to work with children and young people towards successful reforestation projects and changing approaches to the land to prevent erosion. In one scheme the children involved in tree-planting recoup the revenues from selling fruit and timber to help pay their school fees. This project has a 90 per cent survival rate for the trees, whereas other projects have had only 10 to 15 per cent success rates (McIvor 1999, p. 12). Children can see that their energy and time investment brings them positive rewards. When this happens in development it is the most successful and sustainable form. Poor people are willing to try new methods, adapt to new approaches and invest in alternative systems when there is a direct benefit for themselves and their communities.

Lundahl discusses and critiques a range of economic possibilities for Haiti including agricultural reform, manufacturing through assembly industries and the promotion and investment in Haitian handicrafts and tourism. He identifies two key inputs that are required for future economic growth: education and infrastructure. However, he is pessimistic about the possibilities for sustained economic growth, describing it as a 'remote possibility' (2001, p. 185). What is missing from Lundahl's presentation, however, is any recognition of the tremendous resilience and determination to survive shared by Haitians. To have lived through all that they have experienced and to still be there means they have an extraordinary tenacity.

There is an important question to be raised here as a conclusion to this brief discussion about Haiti. If one of Haiti's key social development problems is the lack of educational provision then we have to ask; if the state is forced to sell off its main assets where can funding for education possibly come from? How will people benefit from a privatised water system, for example? Haitian people do not need economic competition in relation to their water supply; they need teachers and classrooms for their children. If another acute problem currently is the large pool of 'unskilled' labour then support must be given to the current agricultural system as this has the capacity to feed large proportions of Haiti and also provide significant sources of income for so-called unskilled labour. In which case, is industrialisation the best pathway for Haiti given its current state? Why not provide the infrastructure and technical support to restore and conserve the land, develop better agricultural extension practices and establish better communications and infrastructure systems to transport agricultural produce to markets. We could argue that first, the international community lashed out at the ordinary Haitian people through imposed economic sanctions (even if they might have been for sound political reasons), and then later has another swipe at them in the form of enforced neo-liberalism. Development has to be holistic, focused on the current resources, community-based, gender inclusive and framed within the contemporary Haitian context. External, top-down, growth-obsessed 'development' strategies are unlikely to deliver any effective form of development gains for the ordinary people of Haiti.

The non-independent Caribbean

This final section of the Pan-Caribbean is dedicated to some of the development issues which face the non-independent territories of the Caribbean: the British Overseas Territories, the French *Departéments-d'Outre-Mer* (DOMs), the Netherlands Antilles, and the US Commonwealth of Puerto Rico and US Virgin Islands[10]. Development data for these territories are extremely difficult to find (with the exception of Puerto Rico) because they are invariably subsumed within data for their colonial power. None of them appear on the UN's Human Development Indicators although the Cayman Islands, the Netherlands Antilles and Puerto Rico appear on the World Bank list of economies for 2003, listed 36, 136 and 154 out of 208 respectively.

What all of these territories have in common is their continued colonial status, although is has to be acknowledged that in several cases this is as a result of democratic choice, through elections or referenda, on the part of the Caribbean territories. For their part the UK and Netherlands would quite happily say a political and economic goodbye to their territories but the residents on 'their' islands, in the majority, wish to remain aligned with their metropolitan power. The form of colonialism is not the same as in the past. Internal political decision-making is largely autonomous and citizenship has been conferred on all residents in the territories since May 2002 (when the UK finally came into line with the other territorial powers on the subject of legal and political citizenship). In reality, the standard of living, provision of education, health care and infrastructure combined with economic growth in the territories is among some of the best in the whole Caribbean region. In times of crisis, such as after hurricane catastrophes and during the current volcanic crisis in Montserrat,[11] the level of economic and redevelopment support from the colonial powers is much higher than that experienced by independent islands who seek help from other financial sources such as USAID or the UN. However, these places remain in a state of dependency and are viewed by institutions such as the UN and a range of pro-independence groups as an anachronism in the twenty-first century. They are likely to always be a source of political frustration and complexity.

The British Overseas territories include the Cayman Islands, which are one of the richest economies in the world and Montserrat, which since 1995 and the onset of the volcanic eruption has seen its standard of living and development status decline dramatically and is in receipt of substantial bilateral aid from the UK. Anguilla, in 1999 had a GDP (PPP) per capita income of $8,2000, earned largely from high-class tourism, off-shore banking and fishing. The British Virgin Islands (including Tortola, Virgin Gorda and Anegada) have almost double the GDP (PPP) per capita of Anguilla at $16,000 and they enjoy relatively low inflation and unemployment rates. Similarly to Anguilla, their income is mostly through tourism and off-shore banking. The Cayman Islands enjoy one of the highest per capita incomes in the world at $24,000. Seventy per cent of their GDP comes from tourism and off-shore banking is important. The Turks and Caicos Islands, like Anguilla, depend on tourism, fishing and off-shore banking. Their GDP per capita was $7,300 in 1999 (Alonso and Hicks 2002b).

The French DOMs (Guadeloupe, Martinique and French Guiana[12]) are very rarely accounted for separately from France as they have been part of France in all respects since 1946 and all residents became French citizens entitled to all the same rights and benefits as mainland French people. In 1974 Guadeloupe and Martinique were granted more control over their internal affairs but they remain dependent on aid and subsidies from France. The territories also benefit substantially from European Union funding as they were designated as a disadvantaged region of Europe and received substantial development funding. France was a contributing power in the founding of the Association of Caribbean States and so Guadeloupe and Martinique were able to become members (currently they would not be able to join CARICOM). Guadeloupe is the name of one island in cartographic terms but politically it is constituted of Basse-Terre, Grande-Terre, Marie-Galante, La Désirade, Îles des Saintes, Saint Barthelemy and part of St. Martin. Guadeloupe's infant mortality rate is 9.53 deaths per 1,000 live births, life expectancy is 77.16 years and 90 per cent of the population over the age of 15 is literate. Its GDP (PPP) per capita is $9,000 which it earns from services (largely related to tourism), industry and agriculture. France is obviously its main trading partner and source of aid. Martinique has a lower infant mortality rate of 7.8 deaths per 1000 live births, a higher life expectancy at 78.14 years and 93 per cent of its population can read and write. Its GDP (PPP) per capita was $11,675 in 1995[13]. The Martinican economy is based on tourism, industry and agriculture (Alonso and Hicks 2002c).

The Netherlands Antilles numbered six (Aruba, Bonaire, Curaçao, part of Sint Maarten, Saba and Sint Eustatius) until 1986 when Aruba separated from the Antilles and planned for full independence from the Netherlands, but this was abandoned in 1994 (see Plate 3.5). Hence it remains attached to the Netherlands and receives considerable financial support from its European metropole. The Antilles of Five has a population of 212,226 with a low growth rate of 0.97 per cent. The infant mortality rate is 11.4 deaths per 1000 live births, life expectancy is 74.94 years and literacy rates for those over 14 is an impressive 98 per cent. The GDP (PPP) per capita is $11,400 which compares well with French- and English-speaking neighbouring islands. As with the other small islands tourism and off-shore banking are the mainstays of the economy along with petroleum refining and transshipment. Its economy is based mostly on services and industry, agriculture plays a negligible role. Aid is received from both the Dutch government and the EU. The islands face different obstacles to development; the 'northern' three islands are prone to hurricane damage whereas Bonaire and

Plate 3.5 *Dutch-style architecture in Sint Maarten, Netherlands Antilles*
© Tracey Skelton

Curçao have problems with high unemployment levels. The islands went into structural adjustment programnmes with the IMF and the Dutch government in the mid-1990s and while there is evidence of economic re-growth and a reduction in deficits it is hard to evaluate the social development costs (Alonso and Hicks 2000c).

It is often forgotten that the USA has a colonial presence in the Caribbean. It owns the dependent territory of the US Virgin Islands and the Commonwealth of Puerto Rico (see Chapter Two for more details of the historical political events). The US Virgin Islands (Saint Croix, Saint Thomas and Saint John) have a population of 122,211 which grows at about 1.06 per cent annually. Their GDP per capita was $15,000 in 2000 and 70 per cent of its GDP is earned from tourism which also provides the bulk of its employment. Oil refining is another important source of revenue and St. Croix has one of the largest oil refineries in the world (Alonso and Hicks 2002b).

Puerto Rico is Spanish-speaking and hence has a complex political relationship with the USA. However, despite its different language and culture to the USA and its affinity with Latin America, Puerto Rico consistently votes to remain a commonwealth. Puerto Ricans argue that they only have to look at the economic, political and development 'disaster' of neighbouring Dominican Republic to understand why independence is not a positive perspective (Ferguson 1998). Nevertheless the island has distinct development problems of its own. It was one of the first islands to attempt industrialisation by invitation through the US-devised 'Operation Bootstrap' introduced in the 1940s which provided tax exemptions, good infrastructure and cheap labour. As Colón-Warren and Alegría-Ortega (1998) demonstrate, much of this industrialisation relied on women as a cheap and docile source of labour. They show the ways in which this led to some positive outcomes for women but that they also faced displacement and women-headed households in particular were pushed deeper into poverty from the 1960s onwards.

In the 1970s the emphasis changed from labour-intensive industrialisation to capital-intensive, again a US stimulated strategy. Puerto Ricans enjoy a relatively high standard of living compared with other parts of the Caribbean but in 1998 an estimated 60 per cent of Puerto Ricans live in poverty as defined by the US government. Welfare support is very important for many Puerto Ricans, especially food stamps, which creates a context of dependency. There are serious concerns about the lack of agriculture which means the island has a huge food import bill, drug related crime is growing in the cities and industrialisation is taking its toll on the environment (Ferguson 1998, p. 318). The island's population structure is ageing and it has one of the largest older populations in the Caribbean. Its infant mortality rate is 9.51 deaths per 1,000 live births (interestingly Cuba's is lower at 7.39) and life expectancy is 75.76 years. Eighty-nine per cent of its population over 15 can read and write. Its GDP (PPP) per capita was $10,000 in 2000 (Alonso and Hicks 2002a). Hence it would range relatively high in HDI terms but not as high as other dependent territories in the region. In 1994 a new model for economic development was proposed by the Puerto Rican government to emphasise the island's well-trained, bilingual workforce and its very advanced telecommunications and infrastructure. This, it is hoped, will bring new forms of economic investment into the island to help further economic growth. However, this is being combined with wholesale privatisation plans in which the government is selling off telecommunications, shipping, health care, water distribution, hotels etc. This has been heavily resisted by trade unions, as there is serious concern about the impacts of this on social welfare and development (Alonso and Hicks 2002a). The island might be able to demonstrate very impressive rates of economic growth in the future but whether this will reduce features such as 60 per cent of its population living in poverty remains to be seen.

What are the possible futures for Pan-Caribbean development?

This chapter has already alluded to some of possible futures for effective, sustainable and egalitarian development in the Caribbean region. What is clear is that economic growth alone cannot achieve development for the majority of the people unless there is a strong commitment to social provision. What is also clear is that decades of attempts at 'first world' style development models have not delivered as much social and welfare improvement as people have expected. In many cases people's standards of living have deteriorated rather than improved. What is required as one of the challenges facing the Pan-Caribbean in the twenty-first century is a different perspective to development which can genuinely bring about a better quality of life for more people in the region. It is likely that the best form of development is one which is initiated *in* the Caribbean, *by* the Caribbean *for* the Caribbean.

One of the issues which is claimed to be a disadvantage in relation to economic development (and in some people's thinking to social development) is the small size of the islands. However, Gray (2002) states that this assumption can be erroneous and that small 'states' can have particular advantages. He states that it can be important to be 'insignificant in the international community' (1998, p. 98) and that in a small place a little can go a long way. It might be possible to get a better consensus in a small state and mobilise people towards a collective development effort. This is an interesting critique of the notion that smallness is always a development disadvantage. If effective development (as has been proved in many contexts throughout the world) is one where the people who wish to benefit from development are involved in its construction and implementation, then small size can be a distinct advantage (see Plate 3.6 in which Montserratians are encouraged to participate in a 'grow your own food' campaign to improve nutritional health and reduce the heavy burden of food imports).

The other key factor in future successful development is the importance of a commitment to sustainability. Caribbean development futures have to include the environment if it is to have any hope of passing down the resources for well being to the future generations. The custom of family land (Skelton 1996a and b) demonstrates that there is already a social and cultural practice of sustainability. This tradition should be included in future development planning. It is Caribbean people themselves who need to critically determine the way sustainable development can be achieved (Lloyd Evans *et al* 1998).

Plate 3.6 *Grow your own food development campaign in Montserrat as part of the post-volcanic eruption recovery programme*

© Tracey Skelton

At the conclusion to their introductory chapter Payne and Sutton ask 'whither Caribbean development?' (2001, p. 20). They discuss an approach which is described as 'anti-development' in its thinking (2001, p. 23). This theoretical and conceptual approach places emphasis on the ways in which ordinary Caribbean people have worked at transforming their life worlds for the better through their own agency. This invariably involves new social movements and non-governmental organisations. Other authors have called for such approaches as long ago as 1991, namely Norman Girvan and Kathy McAfee. In wider development theoretical contexts such an approach is called 'post-development'. It recognises that the development policy, practice and programmes we have worked with since the 1950s, when 'development' as an industry and master plan began in earnest, have not worked for the vast majority of poor people. Poverty has not been alleviated let alone eliminated and wealth inequalities have increased exponentially. Ordinary Caribbean people live with the consequences of rich nations' economic and development planning but despite this they continually strive to escape poverty and to create a better life world for their children. It is time that Caribbean development strategies emerge *from*, and work *with* and *for*, the people of the Pan-Caribbean and not against them.

Note

[1] The term 'development' is written in this way to show that I am problematising the notion. It is often taken for granted that development means success, progress, a positive way forward. However, as we shall see in the remainder of this chapter that is not always, nor indeed often, the case. In some situations what goes under the guise of 'development' such as SAPs can actually be harmful to the quest for social development and equity within a community or country.

[2] All figures denoted as $ (dollars) are in US dollars.

[3] The Cayman Islands are in fact a newly named British Overseas Territory. Prior to the British Overseas Territories Act 2002 such territories were known as British Dependent Territories Overseas. The change in the constitution which forms part of this act reaffirms the colonial status of the Cayman Islands but allows all residents to apply for British Citizenship. Consequently the Cayman Islands do not officially constitute a state or nation, but all of their internal affairs are legislated for, and administered by, an elected parliament.

[4] The world birthrate is 21.4 per 1000 and for developing countries the average is 26 per 1000 (Alonso 2002c; CIA 2001)

[5] Although the CIA World Factbook is a publicly available source it is important to remember that many of the figures are estimates. In many cases Caribbean countries have not yet published their most recent census data.

[6] The UNDP chooses to use PPP US$ as part of its HDI calculation as explained below in response to frequently asked questions on their web site (http://hdr.undp.org/statistics/faq.cfm#16) 'To compare economic statistics across countries, the data must first be converted into a common currency. Unlike conventional exchange rates, PPP rates of exchange allow this conversion to take account of price differences between countries. GDP per capita (PPP US$) accounts for price differences between countries and therefore better reflects people's living standards. In theory, at the PPP (Purchasing Power Parity) rate, 1 PPP dollar has the same purchasing power in the domestic economy as 1 US dollar has in the US economy.'

[7] For a very thorough and wide-ranging analysis of Caribbean Community, CARICOM, which includes all of the English-speaking Caribbean countries and more recently the Dominican Republic, Haiti and Suriname see Kenneth Hall's comprehensive edited collection of 76 essays on the subject (2001).

[8] Although, just five years later, France accepted Baby Doc Duvalier and his family as exiles, even though his regime had been the one guilty of human rights abuses which stimulated French action against Haiti in 1981.

[9] Jean-Bertrand Aristide was elected president of Haiti again in 2000 (Alonso and Hicks 2002a).

[10] It is important to remember, not least because of its importance in geopolitical terms and its recent significance in the USA 'war' on terrorism, to remember a small section of Cuba that remains a US military installation, Guantanamo Bay. There are a range of web sites on this Naval Base, including the online edition of the Guantanamo Bay Gazette which proudly declares 'The source for local news and information from the only U.S. Naval Base on communist soil'. (http://www.gtmo.net/gazz. Accessed July 3rd 2003.)

[11] For more discussion on the volcanic crisis and the complexities of the colonial context for Montserrat see Skelton 2000 and 2003.

[12] I have been unable to find any comparative development data for French Guiana. It is a much neglected territory in Caribbean texts although please see Jones and Stephenson (1995) for a whole chapter dedicated to the country.

[13] To provide some comparison with neighbouring parts of the English-speaking Caribbean the equivalent GDP (PPP) per capita for Barbados was $14,500; for Jamaica $3,700; Trinidad and Tobago $9,500; Antigua and Barbuda $8,200 and Dominica $4,000. Hence, aside from Barbados, we can see the relative wealth of the French Caribbean DOMs.

References

Alonso, I. T. (ed.) 2002a: *Caribbean Economies in the Twenty-first Century*. Gainesville: University Press of Florida.

Alonso, I. T. 2002b: 'Prospects for the Caribbean in the twenty-first century: an introduction'. In Alonso, I. T. (ed.) *Caribbean Economies in the Twenty-first Century*. Gainesville: University Press of Florida. pp. 3–9.

Alonso, I. T. 2002c: 'Social conditions in the Caribbean'. In Alonso, I. T. (ed.) *Caribbean Economies in the Twenty-first Century*. Gainesville: University Press of Florida. pp. 28–40.

Alonso, I. T. and Hicks, D. R. 2002a: 'The economic structure of the northern Caribbean: Cuba, the Dominican Republic, Haiti and Puerto Rico'. In Alonso, I. T. (ed.) *Caribbean Economies in the Twenty-first Century*. Gainesville: University Press of Florida. pp. 41–65.

Alonso, I. T. and Hicks, D. R. 2002b: 'The economic structure of the English-speaking Caribbean islands'. In Alonso, I. T. (ed.) *Caribbean Economies in the Twenty-first Century*. Gainesville: University Press of Florida. pp. 66–85.

Alonso, I. T. and Hicks, D. R. 2002c: 'The economic structure of the French- and Dutch-speaking Caribbean islands'. In Alonso, I. T. (ed.) *Caribbean Economies in the Twenty-first Century*. Gainesville: University Press of Florida. pp. 86–96.

Barker, D. and McGregor, D. F. M. (eds.) 1995: *Environment and Development in the Caribbean: Geographical Perspectives*. Kingston, Jamaica: The Press, University of the West Indies.

Bartilow, H. A. 1997: *The Debt Dilemma: IMF Negotiations in Jamaica, Grenada and Guyana*. Basingstoke: Macmillan.

Bernal, R. 2001: 'The case for NAFTA parity for CBI countries'. In Hall, E. O. (ed.) *The Caribbean Community: Beyond Survival*. Kingston, Jamaica: Ian Randle Publishers. pp. 492–503.

Boodhoo, K. I. 2002: 'US-Caribbean relations in the Post-Cold War era: implications for globalisation and development'. In Ramsaran. R. (ed.) *Caribbean Survival and the Global Challenge*. Kingston, Jamaica: Ian Randle Publishers. pp. 149–162.

Bryan, A. T. 1997: 'Cuba's relations with the Caribbean: reversal of bad fortune?'. In Tulchin, J. S., Serbín, A. and Hernández, R. (eds.) *Cuba and the Caribbean: Regional Issues and Trends in the Post-Cold War Era*. Wilmington, DE: Scholarly Resources Inc. pp. 163–178.

Carlson, B. A. 1999: 'Social dimensions of economic development and productivity: inequality and social performance: an overview'. In Carlson, B. A. (ed.) *Social Dimensions of Economic Development and Productivity: Inequality and Social Performance* Santiago, Chile: United Nations. pp. 9–19.

Carranza Valdés, J. 1997: 'Economic changes in Cuba: problems and challenges'. In Tulchin, J. S., Serbín, A. and Hernández, R. (eds.) *Cuba and the Caribbean: Regional Issues and Trends in the Post-Cold War Era.* Wilmington, DE: Scholarly Resources Inc. pp. 191–206.

Colchester, M. 1997: *Guyana: Fragile Frontier: Miners, Loggers and Forest Peoples.* London: Latin American Bureau.

Colón-Warren, A. E. and Alegría-Ortega. 1998: 'Shattering the illusion of development: the changing status of women and challenges for the feminist movement in Puerto Rico'. *Feminist Review* 59 Summer, pp. 101–117.

Crush, J. (ed.) 1995: *Power of Development.* London: Routledge.

Cuales, S. M. 1998: 'In search of our memories: gender in the Netherlands Antilles'. *Feminist Review* 59 Summer, pp. 86–100.

Dilla Alonso, H. 2000: 'The Cuban experiment: economic reform, social restructuring and politics'. *Latin American Perspectives* 27 (1), pp. 33–44.

Dotres Martinez, C. 1997: Preface. In: *Master plan of investments in the health of Cuba.* Havana. Minister of Public Health, Republic of Cuba www.cubasolidarity.net/hoption accessed June 27th 2003.

Economic Commission for Latin America and the Caribbean, 1997: *The Equity Gap: Latin America, the Caribbean and the Social Summit.* Santiago, Chile: United Nations.

Economic Commission for Latin America and the Caribbean, 2002: *The Sustainability of Development in Latin America and the Caribbean: Challenges and Opportunities.* Santiago, Chile: United Nations, Economic Commission for Latin America and the Caribbean, United Nations Environmental Programme.

Ferguson, J. 1999: *The Story of the Caribbean People.* Kingston, Jamaica: Ian Randle Publishers.

Gafar, J. 2002: 'Poverty measures, dimensions and some strategies for its reduction in the Caribbean', *Caribbean Studies* 30 (1), pp. 205–243.

Girvan, M. 1991: 'Rethinking development: out loud'. In Wedderburn, J. (ed.), *Rethinking Development.* Kingston, Jamaica: Consortium Graduate School of Social Sciences, UWI. pp. 1–13.

González Vilaseca, M. 1997: 'Beyond NAFTA: current options for Caribbean nations'. In Tulchin, J. S., Serbín, A. and Hernández, R. (eds.) *Cuba and the Caribbean: Regional Issues and Trends in the Post-Cold War Era.* Wilmington, DE: Scholarly Resources Inc. pp. 109–121.

Gray, N. 2002: 'Small size and the transformation of the countries of the organization of the Eastern Caribbean states'. In Alonso, I. T. (ed.) *Caribbean Economies in the Twenty-first Century.* Gainesville: University Press of Florida. pp. 97–113.

Green, D. 1998: *Hidden Lives: Voices of Children in Latin America and the Caribbean.* London: Cassell in association with Latin American Bureau, Save the Children and Rädda Barnen.

Hall, K. O. (ed.) 2001: *The Caribbean Community: Beyond Survival.* Kingston, Jamaica: Ian Randle Publishers.

Hicks, D. R. 2002: 'Economic geography of the Caribbean'. In Alonso, I. T. (ed.) *Caribbean Economies in the Twenty-first Century.* Gainesville: University Press of Florida. pp. 13–27.

Jessen, A. and Rodríguez, E. 1999: *The Caribbean Community: Facing the Challenges of Regional and Global Integration.* Buenos Aires: Inter-American Development Bank and Institute for the Integration of Latin America and the Caribbean.

Jones, B. and Stephenson, E. 1995: 'Society, culture and politics in French Guiana'. In: Burton, R. D. E. and Reno, F. (eds.) *French and West Indian: Martinique, Guadeloupe, and French Guiana Today*. Basingstoke: Macmillan. pp. 56–74.

Lloyd Evans, S., McGregor, D. F. M. and Barker, D. 1998: 'Sustainable development and the Caribbean: geographic perspectives'. In McGregor, D. F. M., Barker, D. and Lloyd Evans, S. (eds.) *Resource Sustainability and Caribbean Development*. Kingston, Jamaica: The Press, University of the West Indies. pp. 3–25.

Lundahl, M. 2001: 'Sustained growth in Haiti: pipe-dream or realistic possibility?' In Danielson, A. and Dijkstra, A. G. (eds.) *Towards Sustainable Development in Central America and the Caribbean*. Basingstoke: Palgrave. pp. 161–191.

McAfee, K. 1991: *Storm Signals: Structural Adjustment and Development Alternatives in the Caribbean*. London: Zed Press.

McIvor, C. 1999: *The Earth in Our Hands: Children and Environmental Change in the Caribbean*. London: Save The Children.

Mohammed, P. and Shepherd, C. (eds.) 1999: *Gender in Caribbean Development*. Kingston, Jamaica: Canoe Press. (2nd edition).

N'Zengou-Tayo, M-J. 1998: ' "Fanm se poto mitan": Haitian woman, the pillar of society'. *Feminist Review* 59 Summer, pp. 118–142.

Nicholls, D. 1996: *From Desalines to Duvalier – Race, Colour and National Independence in Haiti*. Basingstoke: Macmillan. (Revised edition)

Payne, A. and Sutton, P. 2001: *Charting Caribbean Development*. London: Macmillan.

Pemberton, C. A., Wilson Garcia G. W. and Khan, A. 2002: 'Sustainable development of Caribbean agriculture'. In Goodbody, I. and Thomas-Hope, E. (eds.), *Natural Resource Management for Sustainable Development in the Caribbean*. Jamaica: Canoe Press. pp. 277–306.

Ramsaran. R. (ed.) 2002: *Caribbean Survival and the Global Challenge*. Kingston, Jamaica: Ian Randle Publishers.

Rist, G. 1997: *The History of Development: From Western Origins to Global Faith* London: Zed Press.

Sheller, M. 2000: *Democracy after Slavery: Black Politics and Peasant Radicalism in Haiti and Jamaica*. Gainesville: University Press of Florida.

Skelton, T. 1996a: 'Globalization, culture and land: the case of the Caribbean'. In Kofman, E. and Youngs, G. (eds.) *Globalization: Theory and Practice*. London, Cassell. 1st Edition. pp. 318–328.

Skelton, T. 1996b: ' "Cultures of land in the Caribbean": a contribution to the debate on development and culture'. *The European Journal of Development Research*. 8 (2), pp. 71–92.

Skelton, T. 2000: 'Political uncertainties and natural disasters: Montserratian identity and colonial status'. In *Interventions: International Journal of Postcolonial Studies* 2 (1): pp. 103–117.

Skelton, T. 2003: 'Globalizing forces and natural disaster: what can be the future for the small Caribbean island of Montserrat?' In Kofman, E. and Youngs, G. (eds.) *Globalization: Theory and Practice*. London: Continuum. Revised 2nd edition. pp. 65–78.

Stark, J. 2001: 'Introduction: the challenge of change in Latin America and the Caribbean: Development amid globalization in the 1990s'. In Stark, J. (ed.), *The Challenge of Change in Latin America and the Caribbean*. Miami: North-South Center Press. pp. 1–16.

Stone, L. 1998: 'Revolutionary health care PV-powered'. In *Home Power Magazine*. www.globalexchange.org/countries/Cuba/sustainable/Cubahealth accessed June 17th 2003.

The West Indian Commission 1992: *Time for Action: Report of the West Indian Commission*. Bridgetown, Barbados: CARICOM.

Thomas, C. 1988: *The Poor and the Powerless: Economic Policy in the Caribbean*. London: Latin America Bureau.

Thomas-Hope, E. 2002: 'Introduction: managing nature as resource'. In Goodbody, I. and Thomas-Hope, E. (eds.), *Natural Resource Management for Sustainable Development in the Caribbean*. Jamaica: Canoe Press. pp. 1–11.

Tulchin, J. S. 1997: Introduction. In Tulchin, J. S., Serbín, A. and Hernández, R. (eds.) *Cuba and the Caribbean: Regional Issues and Trends in the Post-Cold War Era*. Wilmington, DE: Scholarly Resources Inc. pp. xi–xxii.

Tulchin, J. S., Serbín, A. and Hernández, R. (eds.) 1997: *Cuba and the Caribbean: Regional Issues and Trends in the Post-Cold War Era*. Wilmington, DE: Scholarly Resources Inc.

UNDP. 2002: *Human Development Report 2002* (http://hdr.undp.org/reports/global/2002).

US Central Intelligence Agency (CIA) 2002. *The 2002 World Factbook*. Available from http://www.cia.gov/cia/publications/factbook/access date June 1, 2003.

Visvanathan, N., Duggan, L., Nisonoff, L. and Wierersma, N. (eds.) 1997: *The Women, Gender and Development Reader*. London: Zed Press.

Watson, H. A. 1997: 'The techno-paradigm shift, globalization, and western hemisphere integration trends and tendencies: mapping issues in the economic and social evolution of the Caribbean'. In Tulchin, J. S., Serbín, A. and Hernández, R. (eds.) *Cuba and the Caribbean: Regional Issues and Trends in the Post-Cold War Era*. Wilmington, DE: Scholarly Resources Inc. pp. 59–87.

World Bank. April 2003: *World Bank Development Indicators Database*. http://www.worldbank.org/data/databytopic/CLASS.XLS (accessed June 20th 2003).

4

The Caribbean in a globalised world: responses to a changing international political economy

Jessica Byron

Introduction

There is much controversy about the meaning and consequences of globalisation. There is a fairly widespread recognition, however, that the effects of globalisation are spread quite unevenly among and within states, and that there are many more victims than beneficiaries of the process. In the case of the Caribbean, globalisation has undoubtedly heightened the region's economic vulnerability to external trends with potentially dire consequences for some of its main export sectors. It has also 'reconfigured' the political and social networks of the Caribbean as the old links with metropolitan countries are transformed, and as new hemispheric relations multiply (Payne 1994). Finally, it has stimulated the formation of new multilateral structures and agreements as the region struggles to keep its footing in an international environment increasingly dominated by global and regional regimes.

This chapter begins with an overview of some key issues associated with globalisation. Then I identify significant effects on the Caribbean, such as the impact on preferential trade arrangements, developments in the offshore financial services sector and new directions in Caribbean regionalism. I discuss the greatly increased mobility of capital and labour across the Caribbean Basin as well as the region's institutional responses in the form of new multilateral initiatives and the restructuring of existing regional organisations.

The term 'Caribbean' in this context refers to the Greater Caribbean, a region that has struggled into being, stimulated both by external forces and by actors within the area, since the early 1980s. This area covers both the archipelagic Caribbean and the bordering mainland territories of Central America, the Guyanas and parts of Mexico, Colombia and Venezuela[1]. It is a geographical area characterised by tremendous cultural, political and economic heterogeneity in addition to the shared features of the Caribbean Sea, the proximity of the USA and the various legacies of European colonialism. It graphically demonstrates the contradictions that are being played out in the regional dynamics of global processes, as its state and non-state actors grope to forge common responses, where possible, to the threats and challenges posed by globalisation. Although external pressures have made co-operation a more urgent imperative, the actors have major difficulties in reconciling their divergent or competing interests.

The debate on globalisation

Globalisation refers to the tremendous interconnectedness of most parts of the globe that has taken place over the last thirty years or so. This is partly a technological phenomenon, wrought by advances in communications and computer technologies that have enabled commercial actors and individuals to transcend time and distance in their activities (Scholte 2000). However, in addition to the application of new technologies, globalisation has been facilitated by the concerted promotion of the Neoliberal ideology and economic policies by Western governments, the Bretton Woods institutions and the World Trade Organisation (Benn 2000). Thus, the worldwide spread of policies of liberalisation and deregulation has allowed global commercial actors to penetrate most of the world's national spaces and markets (Plate 4.1).

Jan Aart Scholte identifies the quintessential element of globalisation as the transcending of spatial boundaries, and he lists socio-economic activities which have been integral to the process, like global communications technology, transnational production and marketing, and deterritorialised monetary transactions and financial operations (Scholte 2000; Friedman 2000). These globalised commercial operations have also been the catalyst for the establishment of global management and regulatory bodies. The sheer scale of industrial production in the second half of the twentieth century has resulted in global ecological threats. Finally, the combination of globalised economic and media

Plate 4.1 *Imported Coca-Cola arrives in a low-income neighbourhood, Dominican Republic*
© David Howard

activity, global governance attempts and the heightened vulnerabilities and insecurities engendered by all these processes have caused the development of a kind of 'global consciousness' in people's conception of the space in which they exist (Scholte 2000).

Globalisation has generated major transformations in global economic processes and in the international division of labour. Gary Gereffi points out that in this new environment, 'development' for Southern countries depends on achieving a competitive export position and maintaining it by advancing to more highly skilled, value-added forms of production. He observes that:

> globalization is not inevitable, nor is it an unmixed blessing … (it) generates substantial social and cultural resistance because of its uneven and in some cases marginalizing consequences within as well as between countries and regions … For (most) regions of the world…problems remain as countries try to escape wage-depressing export strategies, low productivity and marginal forms of integration to the world economy (Gereffi in Mittelman 1997, p. 78).

Others are even more pessimistic about the marginalising impact on developing areas of the world. Samir Amin speaks of 'global polarization' and the ever-growing cohorts of reserve labour that are permanently excluded from global production processes. Hoogvelt envisages the world as concentric circles, rather than as countries or geographical regions. The smallest circle consists of transnational economic elites. The second circle, also small, comprises those who are employed on competitive and insecure terms. The largest circle consists of millions who are completely excluded from the global market economy, either as producers or as consumers (Amin 1997; Hoogvelt 1997).

Globalisation has triggered a new, critical examination of national and international modes of governance. On the one hand, it is clear that the role and functions of the state have been greatly affected, rendering meaningless traditional notions of sovereignty, and calling into question the traditional form of state. All states, and especially developing countries, have experienced reduced capabilities to control a wide range of economic, socio-political and environmental phenomena affecting their societies. The loss of control by the state has been highlighted by a surge of criminality that has accompanied domestic socio-economic decline and the globalisation of illicit industries, such as narco-trafficking, as well as legitimate industries. A paradoxical aspect of globalisation is that while the state's capacity to control economic activities or to provide security within its borders has been reduced, at the same time the state apparatus is expected to assume complex new regulatory functions to facilitate and monitor the operations of a liberalised world economy. This is leading to the emergence of new national and sub-national governance coalitions within countries. Likewise, regionalism has been revived as a strategic response to many of the challenges associated with globalisation (Gamble and Payne 1996; Grugel and Hout 1999; Hettne, Inotai and Sunkel 1999).

Finally, globalisation has stimulated practical and academic interest in appropriate forms of governance. Multilateralism has boomed as an approach to managing global processes. On the other hand, globalisation has also thrown into the spotlight the limited capabilities of the existing multilateral organisations, and the tremendous inequalities in the international system, which work to render it dysfunctional and unstable. Benn (2000) points out that, notwithstanding the pervasive free market rhetoric of globalisation, in the latest rounds of international negotiations on economic and environmental issues, there are many instances of the developed countries seeking to apply principles of liberalisation selectively so as to enhance their own areas of competitive advantage while prising open even more developing country markets for their multinationals. A number of critics argue that the institutions of globalisation must be redesigned to promote equity, representativeness and some measure of control over unbridled market forces to mitigate the social mal-effects (Held 1997; Sen 2000; Woods in Hurrell and Woods eds. 1999). As we shall see in the case of Caribbean countries, the mushrooming of global governance processes has also greatly increased the strain on the limited diplomatic resources of small, financially strapped countries who struggle to participate in many multilateral fora.

The normative debate on globalisation has waxed stronger since the Asian financial crisis of 1997–98. It has gained great impetus after the series of counter-globalisation protests at international conferences between 1999 and 2001; the terrorist attacks on the USA on September 11, 2001; and the latest economic crises in Argentina, Brazil and Uruguay 2001–02. Globalisation and neo-liberal policy prescriptions are now presented less stridently as a universal, inevitable and permanent state of affairs. This has given more space in which to contest the legitimacy of globalisation and to propose reforms to its modes of operation (Benn and Hall 2000a; Held and McGrew 2000; Scholte 2000; Sen 2000).

Globalisation and the Caribbean

All these perspectives on globalisation echo resoundingly in the Caribbean context. There are those who argue that the Caribbean is no stranger to globalisation. It was incorporated into the global capitalist economy and its societies thrown together turbulently via that process over four hundred years ago (Klak 1998; C.Y. Thomas in Benn and Hall 2000a). Proponents of that thesis express the hope that Caribbean societies possess the resilience and creativity to adapt to this latest phase in a long history of global pressures on their existence. Most writers also concede, nonetheless, that the contemporary era of globalisation is significantly different from earlier ones. It has dramatically speeded up the region's long evolution out of a neo-colonial political economy and it has changed relationships within the region, with the hemisphere and with the rest of the world. Caribbean experiences in a globalising world have demonstrated many of the risks faced by small societies attempting to restructure their economies and negotiate niches for themselves in a tremendously transformed international environment.

Debates on the pros and cons of small size have been a constant theme running through Caribbean economic development strategies and foreign policies since the 1960s. Globalisation has intensified this focus on small size and has introduced some new perspectives on the issue. The Commonwealth Report on Vulnerability and Small

States (1997), which had considerable input from Caribbean policymakers and technocrats, states:

> Small states have a susceptibility to risks and threats set at a relatively lower threshold than for larger states … their small size gives them less margin for coping than in larger states … Of most concern are economic threats linked to the globalisation of trade, investment, finance and production; environmental threats relating to the increased incidence and scale of natural disasters and the mounting damage of global warming; and threats to the fabric of society contained in the spread of transnational values. Expanding transnational activity has encouraged the growth of international crime which small states have found difficult to counter. (Commonwealth Secretariat 1997, p. xi)

The prognosis has therefore been one of heightened vulnerability for small states in a globalised environment. Globalisation, however, is regarded as an inevitable fact of life to which small states, like other actors, must adapt. This has led to an institutional focus on the measures that can be taken to reduce such vulnerability and to support their transition to greater economic liberalisation. The Commonwealth Secretariat Task Force/World Bank Report of 2000, for example, ends with a list of programmes and measures adopted by multilateral donor agencies to assist small states in gaining access to sources of investment capital, institutional capacity building, reducing the unit costs of essential infrastructure and public services, risk management, disaster mitigation and fuller participation in the institutions of the liberalised world economy.

Another debate on small size arose in the context of the Western Hemispheric negotiations towards the establishment of a Free Trade Area of the Americas which have been in train since 1995. While Commonwealth Caribbean countries in their international diplomacy had always consciously identified themselves as small states requiring special programmes of assistance, such an explicit definition had not necessarily underpinned the international strategies of the Central American grouping or other small states in the hemisphere, such as Uruguay. A hemispheric consensus finally emerged around the concept of a 'smaller economy', rather than a 'small state'. Moreover, countries were free to designate themselves as smaller economies or not, although their eligibility for any special measures derived from this status would then be determined on a case-by-case and sector-by-sector basis. Although some countries have not chosen to designate themselves collectively as smaller economies, much ground has been covered in exploring the characteristic weaknesses of such economies in the hemispheric context and in proposing special measures that might facilitate their full participation in a hemispheric free trade grouping. Constraints have been identified such as their undiversified economies, a high export concentration, dependence on trade taxes and the very small size of firms which inhibits research and development and investment. It has been recognised that such economies will have high transition and social adjustment costs in making their economies more competitive, and will not easily attract large inflows of foreign investment (Bernal 1998). Measures proposed to address these issues include more flexible timetables for complying with market liberalisation and with the technical requirements of the trading system, assistance with institutional capacity-building and with the costs of international economic negotiations and dispute settlement procedures, measures to improve investment inflows (Bernal 1998; Ceara Hatton 1998). Additionally, Bernal (2000) proposes 'strategic global repositioning' as a foreign policy response for small Caribbean states. Elements of this approach include export diversification, the forging of strategic corporate alliances by national firms, the rethinking and reinvention of regionalism and the formation of new alliances with Caribbean diasporas.

The outlook for adjustment for the smallest Caribbean states still looks bleak. Klak (1998) points out that new era export market niches, in such products as offshore financial services, data processing or cut flowers are very competitive and precariously maintained. He compares niche marketing to the 'historical and geographical crevices allotted to Afro-Caribbean people under colonialism ... both crevices then and niches now offer Caribbean people very narrow windows of opportunity for advancement within an international political economy dominated by outside powers' (Klak 1998, pp. 9, 10). He observes that although Caribbean states have become more integrated into the globalised economy and committed to neo-liberal policy agendas, they have simultaneously become more marginalised geopolitically in a post-Cold War global landscape that mainly features large market economies and regional blocs (1998, p. 12).

Significant effects on Caribbean countries include the progressive deterritorialisation of their societies in successive waves of labour migration (Basch, Glick-Schiller and Szanton-Blanc 1994; Klak 1998; Foy Olwig 1993), with obvious implications for the state. C.Y. Thomas reports the demise of the 'post-colonial developmental state' under the weight of globalisation and the US strategic agenda, and the emergence of neo-liberal, denationalised Caribbean states. Paradoxically, the very factors which would seem to underscore the need for a strong post-colonial state, acting in the public interest to reduce poverty, territorial challenges, regional disparities, increased transnational criminal activity and ethnic conflict, have also incapacitated it, leading to ever increasing problems of governance (Thomas, 1998). In sum, contemporary globalisation poses tremendous challenges of adjustment and survival, both domestically and in the international context, for Caribbean state units. For many Caribbean people and societies, it ushers in yet another era of a nomadic existence characterised by labour migration, transnationalisation and deterritorialisation, in which cultural practices and historical memories of place become essential elements of identity wherever they may be located in the global marketplace.

Twilight zone for preferential commodity arrangements: the cases of bananas and rum

Sugar cane and bananas were the Caribbean export staples of the colonial era. Special marketing arrangements based primarily on political relationships with former colonial metropoles were maintained thereafter for many Caribbean producers who only had direct interface with global market conditions at some point during the past decade.

The Caribbean banana industry best exemplifies the changes and the contradictions wrought by globalisation. The restructuring of the European banana market that has taken place since the establishment of the Single European Market in 1992, and the World Trade Organisation in 1995, has given rise to major conflicts of interest among the various producers in the Greater Caribbean, who produce and market their bananas under distinct conditions and in collaboration with distinct sets of partners[2].

■ Box 4.1 Europe, Latin America and the USA enter banana war: countries split over trade policy

Those who believe the old saw that money doesn't grow on trees ought to take a trip south. In half a dozen countries in Central and South America, it does. The locals call their cash crop 'green gold'. The rest of the world, it seems, is going bananas about bananas …

But a bitter fight over trade policy in Western Europe has put the banana boom on hold for Latin American producers. The debate pits Germany against Britain, France and Spain; big-time Latin American producers against small growers in Africa, the Caribbean and the Pacific; and giant American multinationals against a few of their European counterparts.

At stake in the banana war are hundreds of millions of dollars in profits, the principle of free trade and open markets in the unifying, wealthy economies of Western Europe and the economic health of dozens of poorer countries and islands straddling the Equator …

'The lowly banana has become a real symbol of free trade – the last bastion, a line in the sand', said a U.S. banana company executive.

(Excerpts from article by Lee Hockstader, *Washington Post*, July 1, 1992)

The negotiation of the fourth Lomé Convention on trade and development co-operation between the EU and the ACP states in 1988–89 marked the opening volleys of a long, bitter struggle over market shares and trade preferences. The then European Community was simultaneously engaged in dismantling all remaining internal barriers between its domestic markets in preparation for the Single European Market of 1992. This would inevitably disrupt British and French domestic market arrangements for their privileged suppliers. English-speaking Caribbean states, sometimes in alliance with the French DOMs, fought a rearguard action against the inexorable drift towards the liberalisation of the EU banana market. On the other side of the trenches were the Latin American dollar banana producers and the Multinational Corporations (MNCs) that controlled banana production in those states. Both groups were anticipating much larger market shares with the establishment of the Single Market and the expansion of the EU. There were also EU member states, like Germany, the Netherlands, Belgium and Denmark, who favoured more liberal market arrangements.

In June 1993, the first phase of the banana saga ended with the EU's adoption of Council Decision 404, which was intended to provide a transitional market arrangement for the next ten years. The new regime continued some measure of protection for EU (DOM) bananas, and for a specified volume of bananas from ACP traditional suppliers.

However, the 1993 European Banana Regime was dogged with controversy from the beginning. Some EU member states, particularly Germany, were deeply dissatisfied as it raised the price of bananas for their consumers and maintained artificial price controls in the banana market. The Latin American banana producers were also deeply opposed to the regime, feeling it was discriminatory and designed to restrict their overall market share in the Single Market. They brought two cases against the EU and the regime before the General Agreement on Tariffs and Trade (GATT) in 1993. The GATT rulings found that the EU's GATT obligations took primacy over Lomé trade preferences and that the EU had to apply to the GATT for a waiver before implementing any such agreements. The second panel also ruled that the new banana regime contravened GATT trade law (Sutton, 1997). Finally, new legal challenges were launched in the successor organisation to the GATT, the World Trade Organization (WTO), in February 1996 by the USA acting on behalf of US based banana multinationals[3], plus Guatemala, Honduras, Ecuador and Mexico. In 1997, the WTO ruled against major aspects of the regime, and in March 1999, the USA imposed trade sanctions to the value of US$520 million against a range of EU products (later reduced to US$191 million). The banana dispute between the EU and the USA was not settled until April 2001 when the two parties agreed on an EU Three-Phase Plan to introduce a market regime based only on tariffs by January 2006[4]. In July 2001, the US Trade Representative announced that the US would be lifting its trade sanctions against the EU in response to the EU's implementation of Phase One of their agreement (*Tradewatch* 4/7/2001).

The consequences of these events for Caribbean actors have been many and varied. Divisions deepened among all the banana producers. The rift between ACP and dollar banana producers not only deepened, the Latin American producers were ultimately divided among themselves. The alliance between the DOMs and the ACP producers proved short-lived, as the DOMs were, in the final analysis, within the EU and had access to compensatory financing to cushion the impact of a collapse of their banana industry. Cracks emerged within the ranks of ACP states in general, and also among the Caribbean ACP states over the amount of time, money and diplomatic effort that should be expended on defending an industry that appeared doomed. The banana war eventually became a battle between two of the world's largest economic actors, the EU and the US, with the other players being relegated to mere onlooker positions although they would suffer painful fallout from the outcome.

The experience of marginalisation was especially strong for the Caribbean ACP producers. Despite membership first of the GATT and then the WTO, they had to fight to be heard at the successive dispute panels, since they were third parties to all the disputes. Although their vital economic interests were at stake, they had very limited capacity to influence the outcome of the EU's internal decision-making processes, the deliberations within the GATT and WTO dispute settlement bodies or the conflict between the EU and the USA.

The era of the 1990s has generally been one of uncertainty and instability in the EU banana market. Some small Caribbean producers, with the assistance of the EU, embarked on a restructuring programme intended to improve their competitiveness. Nonetheless, their industry remained highly vulnerable to price fluctuations and the long-term global trend towards falling prices for bananas (Lewis, 2000). Not even the Fair Trade initiative in Europe provided the same degree of security as had the fading era of protected markets[5].

Another interesting case study on 'global repositioning' is provided by the Caribbean rum industry, possibly the only traditional sector considered to be genuinely competitive in a liberalising European market. Initially, the Single European Market promised the industry opportunities for expansion after many years of quota restrictions. However, the outlook changed drastically in March 1997 when the EU and the USA bilaterally agreed to open the EU rum market by 2003 to all rum producers worldwide[6]. As a result, the West Indies Rum and Spirits Producers Association (WIRSPA) lobbied strongly in 1998 and 1999 for a special transitional assistance programme within the EU–ACP framework to enable it to progress to the production of higher value branded rums between 2000 and 2006. It also sought more adjustment time by lobbying for the tariff quota regime to be extended beyond 2003 (see *Inside Europe*, 1999; Jessop 1999). As in the case of bananas, here again the major actors became the EU and the US, with Caribbean producers caught in the middle and playing a predominantly defensive role. As one private sector analyst expressed it:

> the Caribbean will be seen to have had the misfortune to be caught in early transatlantic battles on matters of principle relating to the role the US and the EU believe they should play in trade liberalisation and the process of globalisation. (CCE Newsletter, 27/10/2000).

Moreover, the rum issue again divided the Caribbean into ACP and non-ACP producers, with Puerto Rican and Cuban producers standing to possibly benefit significantly from the world market liberalisation that may ensue from the 1997 EU–US Agreement while WIRSPA faced a more sombre prospect.

Globalisation and the offshore financial services sector[7]

Analysts of Caribbean political economy like C.Y. Thomas have long pointed to the geopolitical advantages the region possessed in attracting offshore financial flows from the North American mainland, as well as the potential for humanmade advantages like lax financial regulation (Thomas 1988, p. 167). The development of the offshore financial services sector as an alternative and somewhat dubious path to growth began in earnest in the Caribbean in the late 1960s. Maingot (1994) points to a phenomenal increase in the flow of funds to tax havens located in the Western Hemisphere since the beginning of the 1970s, attributing this to US corporations' search to reduce their tax payments, to the increasing movement of funds generated by the international drugs trade and finally to capital flight funds. In the 1970s to mid-1980s, the principal offshore financial centres in the Caribbean Basin were Panama, the Bahamas, the Cayman Islands and the Netherlands Antilles. By the mid-1990s, the number had increased to include the British Virgin Islands, Anguilla and Montserrat, most of the Eastern Caribbean micro-states and Barbados. The range of services offered had also grown and the offshore financial services sector had become a significant source of revenue and employment for some Caribbean territories. Caribbean countries which specialised in tourism and financial services had higher growth rates than the rest and a growing number of policy-makers viewed the development of their own service exports as the way to secure a competitive niche in the post-industrial global economy.

However, in 1999–2000, the offshore financial industry became the target of a concerted drive for tougher regulation by the OECD countries, partly triggered by global financial instability in 1997–99, and their recognition of the vulnerability of the international financial system in a globalised era. This, together with the greatly increased incidence of money laundering, was the justification for pressing for tighter regulation of offshore financial jurisdictions. Governments of the EU were also reinforcing their efforts against tax evasion by business corporations and, after European Monetary Union, were grappling with the knotty issue of fiscal harmonisation among themselves.

The OECD issued reports in 1998 and 1999 on Harmful Tax Competition. Fifteen countries from the Caribbean region were listed as being among the locations for offshore financial services which could cause capital flight and damage to the tax regimes of OECD member states. They also indicated that they would apply sanctions against the countries concerned if they did not enact regulatory legislation by June 2001. In May 2000, the Financial Stability Forum, established by the Group of Seven countries (G-7), also published a list ranking offshore financial centres according to their supervisory and transparency measures. This listed twelve Caribbean territories as having various types of supervisory and regulatory weaknesses. The IMF was urged to assist such countries to adhere to international standards. However, Caribbean actors concerned maintained that such standards have not yet been clearly established and are largely being determined in OECD fora by OECD actors, who have not fully reached consensus among themselves, let alone with the wider international community, on such issues. This suggests quite a deficit in the global governance process in this area.

In June 2000, the Financial Action Task Force (FATF) published a list of 'non-co-operating countries or territories'. Five English-speaking Caribbean territories were named as having inadequate measures in place against money laundering. The FATF assessment differed significantly from that of its subsidiary body, the Caribbean Financial Action Task Force, a body in which Caribbean states are themselves represented, which stated that Caribbean jurisdictions were, in fact, tightening their money laundering regulatory and legislative framework, but that the FATF assessment was seeking to unilaterally introduce a range of new benchmarks.

In response to the pressure, most Caribbean territories quickened the pace of legislative and regulatory reform in their financial services sector. They also strengthened regional diplomatic co-ordination and sought to be proactive in their negotiations on financial services. In January 2001, in concert with Pacific countries with similar concerns, they met in Barbados with the international financial institutions, the Commonwealth Secretariat, regional organisations and OECD member state representatives to discuss taxation and competition issues. This was certainly a diplomatic advance for the Caribbean and Pacific offshore financial centres present, in that it gave them a seat at the table and a voice in future international consultations on regulating offshore financial flows. Tangible results have been their inclusion in the Joint Working Group that was set up to maintain transparent tax regimes and to co-operate against harmful tax practices, and the IMF's offer in May 2001 of a technical assistance package to the CARICOM states to tighten the regulation of their financial sectors. Another possible indicator of diplomatic success is the fact that the 2001 Annual Money Laundering Report of the Financial Action Task Force removed the Bahamas, the Cayman Islands and Panama from the list of so-called Non-Co-operating Countries. However, three Caribbean micro-states remained on the list, vulnerable to the threat of international sanctions being applied by OECD countries.

Moreover, the Caribbean effort to develop a coherent policy position on the governance of international financial activities seemed to shift focus somewhat in the changed international climate after the terrorist attacks in the USA on September 11 2001. This came in response to the USA's announcement of global hard-line measures against money laundering as part of the fight against terrorism. In the CARICOM Nassau Declaration on International Terrorism of October 12, 2001, many Caribbean governments pledged full co-operation with the international community on money laundering matters in general, and specifically in the tracing and freezing of assets that could belong to terrorists. All these developments have injected heightened uncertainty and consequent instability into the offshore banking sector throughout the region. It no longer seems as promising a growth area as it did ten years ago. Although a few Caribbean territories may manage to maintain a competitive edge in the global offshore financial sector, it might turn out to be a sunset industry for many others.

International trade negotiations: the emergence of new norms and structures

On the 1st January, 1995 the World Trade Organisation came into being. This new international institution wielded a stronger mandate to liberalise the world trading system and to regulate the activities of its member states than its predecessor, the General Agreement on Tariffs and Trade (GATT), did. The advent of the WTO had major implications for the content and scope of all future trade agreements. Since then,

Caribbean countries have been engaged in a series of multilateral trade negotiations, most of which have departed significantly from the earlier trend of non-reciprocal trade preferences for developing countries. Under the categories used by the WTO, only one Caribbean country, Haiti, currently qualifies as a Least Developed Country and is entitled to special assistance measures which may be agreed on for such countries. The Special and Differential Treatment measures for developing countries in general are voluntary on the part of the developed world and not legally enforceable[8].

Recent trade negotiations in the Greater Caribbean have tended to fragment the region even further. No negotiation has included all the countries in the region and in each major set of trade talks, participating countries have had widely divergent interests. The two most important trade negotiations have been the Cotonou Agreement (2000) and the ongoing negotiations toward a Free Trade Area of the Americas (FTAA). Additionally, the implementation of the North American Free Trade Area (NAFTA) in 1994 triggered a long, arduous process of lobbying for NAFTA Parity for beneficiaries of the Caribbean Basin Initiative[9].

The Lomé Conventions on preferential trade and development assistance, initiated in the 1970s between the EU and the Africa-Caribbean-Pacific countries (ACP Group), came to an end in 2000[10]. Preliminary consultations on a post-Lomé arrangement had started in 1996, and formal negotiations began in September 1998. The stark differences in perspective in these negotiations were vividly portrayed by the fact that the EU spoke of 'Post-Lomé talks', indicating their interest in mapping out a new trade regime, while the ACP referred for a long time to the 'Lomé V talks', underscoring their desire to maintain the status quo in the trade and aid relationship. In particular, they fought to defend the non-reciprocal trade preferences that they had enjoyed for over 90 per cent of their exports to the EU market, and to prevent the introduction of new political conditionalities into the development co-operation relationship.

Ultimately, an agreement was negotiated to span the next 20 years . It differed radically from the 25 year cycle of Lomé accords. The Cotonou Agreement has a strong political dimension. It requires political dialogue to take place on a wide range of issues. It has strong conditionalities of human rights, democracy and the rule of law, and co-operation will be suspended if these norms are violated. It also introduces a new criterion of good governance aimed at discouraging corruption. The development relationship now goes beyond the intergovernmental dimension to incorporate collaboration between the EU and both private sector and civil society groups in ACP countries. Finally, to a far greater extent than previously, the ACP countries are not treated as a discrete whole, but interact with the EU as regional groupings with distinct trade, developmental and political issues peculiar to each region.

The trade provisions also depart radically from earlier norms. There is a transitional period of eight years (2000–08), during which a Lomé-type preferential trade regime continues[11]. Such non-reciprocal preferences will be maintained thereafter for the LDCs in the ACP. For the non-LDC ACP countries, the effect of the transition period is itself diluted by the EU's 'Everything but Arms' proposal – the decision to extend to 48 Least Developed Countries, with effect from 2002, duty free access to the EU market for all their products except arms (ECLAC 2001). In September 2002, a new round of EU–ACP negotiations started, aimed at the eventual establishment of Regional Free Trade Agreements between the EU and the non-LDC countries in the ACP.

The EU's stated objective is to fully integrate the ACP countries into the global economy, i.e. to gradually shift the underlying rules and principles of the EU–ACP partnership so as to reconcile it with the WTO regime and with EU trade policies vis-à-vis the rest of the world. Thus, the WTO norms and frameworks are steadily erasing the contours of neo-colonial, special relationships embodied in agreements like the Lomé Conventions. For their part, the Caribbean ACP actors have had to engage in multiple levels of negotiations since 1996 to establish common positions and to maintain ACP solidarity at the same time as they struggle to gain maximum time for the transition from protected markets to open competition with all other producers.

Despite the considerable time and resources spent on EU–ACP trade arrangements, and the controversies generated thereby, the Caribbean ACP countries accounted for only 2 per cent of the EU's trade with Latin America and the Caribbean between 1999 and 2000. Mexico, which signed a Free Trade Agreement with the EU in 2000, accounted for 25 per cent and the Central American countries accounted for 4 per cent. The latter group is singular in the Americas in that it has maintained a trade surplus with the EU and, together with Mexico, has achieved a substantial diversification of exports to the EU away from traditional agricultural products to manufactures[12]. These facts, together with the overall trade liberalisation trends in the Western Hemisphere, influence the thinking of EU officials as they nudge Caribbean ACP states towards an eventual free trade agreement.

NAFTA came into being in January 1994. It created the world's largest free trade area with a population of 404 million and a combined GDP of over US$8 trillion (IDB 1999). It was also the first such free trade zone to merge a developing country with two highly industrialised countries. The NAFTA bloc is an enormous vortex of economic activity, representing approximately 8/9 of the GDP for the Americas as a whole. Its establishment heralded a major restructuring of trade arrangements in the Pan-Caribbean. It meant a decisive shift in Mexico's geostrategic interests towards its Northern partners. Likewise, NAFTA brought about an erosion of US trade preferences and some disinvestment for CBI countries like the Dominican Republic and Jamaica – a relocation of CBI industries from their shores to Mexico because it was now much more attractive to produce there. CBI countries have lobbied persistently since 1993 for increased market access that would put them on par with Mexico. This finally resulted, in May 2000, in the enactment by the US Congress of the Caribbean Basin Trade Partnership Act (CBTPA). It extends NAFTA-like trade preferences to several new products and has provided a boost for textile and apparel exports. The

CBTPA, however, is only for a limited time period and has imposed many new conditionalities on its beneficiaries, mostly designed to speed up the liberalisation of their economies. The preferences last until 2008 or until the FTAA is implemented, if that happens earlier (IDB 2000).

NAFTA, the quintessential neo-liberal trade agreement[13], became a highly influential model for subsequent trade agreements which have incorporated several of its features. Moreover, it occasioned a spurt of new alliance formations as Caribbean Basin countries, most of whom depend on the US market for at least 50 per cent of their export trade, sought to guard against the spectre of a Fortress North America. Mexico now has bilateral free trade agreements with Costa Rica and Nicaragua, and multilateral trade agreements with Venezuela and Colombia on the one hand, and El Salvador, Honduras and Guatemala on the other. Canada is negotiating a free trade accord with Costa Rica while the USA has begun the preliminary procedures to negotiate a free trade agreement with the five countries of the Central American Community (Miller 2002).

■ Box 4.2 Background on the free trade area of the Americas

Objectives: To progressively eliminate barriers to trade and investment in the Americas by 2005.

Membership: Open to all countries in the Americas with representative democratic forms of government. Cuba is not a party to the negotiations.

Structure of Negotiations:Ministers of Trade: grant final approval – meet every 18 months   Trade Negotiations Committee: Supervisory Body, meets at least twice a year.

Nine Negotiating Groups which meet regularly during each year: Market Access; Investment; Services; Government Procurement; Dispute Settlement; Agriculture; Intellectual Property Rights; Subsidies, Antidumping and Countervailing Duties; Competition Policy.

Special Committees: Smaller Economies; Civil Society, E-Commerce (now inactive), Institutional Issues.

Geographic Representation: The chairship of the entire negotiating process and of the various committees has been regularly rotated to ensure maximum participation by the parties. The venues for the talks have shifted, based on the same principle. Phase One: Miami, USA, March 1999–February 2001; Phase Two: Panama City, March 2001–February 2003; Phase Three: Puebla, Mexico, March 2003–December 2004.

Administrative and Technical Support: The FTAA Secretariat, which services the negotiations, is located at the rotating venue. Technical and analytical support is provided by a Tripartite Committee made up of the Interamerican Development Bank, the Organization of American States and the UN Economic Commission for Latin America and the Caribbean.

Sources: *Overview of the FTAA Process* www.ftaa-alca.org; *The FTAA Process: Overview*, SICE Foreign Trade Information System, www.oas.org

The sequel to NAFTA was the decision by 34 countries in the Western Hemisphere in December 1994 to begin negotiating a FTAA. The talks are scheduled to end by 2005. If successfully concluded, they will create the largest free trade area in the world with a population of 800 million and a GDP of US$9 trillion. It will be a highly asymmetrical FTA with four very large economies, namely the US, Canada, Mexico and Brazil and 21 very small economies, mostly located in the Caribbean region. Its operation will also be heavily influenced by the two major economic blocs, NAFTA in the North and the Market of the Southern Cone (MERCOSUR) in the South.

1995–98 was the preparatory phase of the talks, during which eleven working groups compiled and published information from all the countries and sub-regional trading groups on current trade patterns, institutions and regulations. The guiding principles, definitions, norms and structures for the negotiations were also agreed on. The main principles underpinning the negotiations are as follows:

- Decisions will be taken by consensus.
- Negotiations will be conducted transparently.
- The FTAA will be consistent with WTO rules and disciplines, improving on them where possible.
- The FTAA will be a single undertaking in which everything is agreed on simultaneously.
- The FTAA will co-exist with bilateral and sub-regional agreements; countries may negotiate and accept the obligations of the FTAA individually or as members of a sub-regional integration grouping.
- Special attention will be paid to the needs of the smaller economies.

(Overview of the FTAA Process www.ftaa-alca.org 10/29/2002)

A more intense phase began with the formal launch of the negotiations in Santiago de Chile in April 1998. Since then, there has been an average of 60 meetings of the Negotiating Groups per year. Two landmark meetings were the Fifth and Sixth Trade Ministerial Meetings, held in Toronto, November 1999 and Buenos Aires, April 2001, respectively. The former meeting agreed to implement a series of administrative measures intended to stimulate intra-hemispheric commerce and capitalise on the momentum of the FTAA negotiations even before the agreement is completed. Some measures relate to customs procedures while others relate to transparency and greater availability of information on trade, travel and investment regulations in the different countries of the FTAA zone. At the Buenos Aires meeting, the first draft of an eventual treaty was tabled and made publicly available, although there were still major areas to be agreed upon. This was intended to promote awareness about the trade talks among the populations of the hemisphere and to stimulate dialogue with hemispheric civil society. A more technical phase of the negotiations began with market access talks in 2002 which ended with the tabling of a second draft treaty at the Seventh Trade Ministerial Meeting in Ecuador at the end of October 2002. The final phase of the FTAA talks will run from April 2003 to the end of 2004. Puebla, Mexico will be the venue while Brazil and the USA will co-chair the talks.

The FTAA trade talks are a marathon multilateral process spanning a ten-year period. They mark a watershed, in several ways, for the international relations of the Western Hemisphere. They involve all but one of the independent states of the Americas and the negotiations have produced a number of innovations, including the establishment of a mechanism to consult with civil society groups in the Americas. What are the overall implications of this new configuration for the actors of the Caribbean Basin? Negotiating positions have varied markedly across the region. Actors' stances seem to be determined by their overall strategies vis-à-vis globalisation and by geography and geo-economics. While CARICOM has chosen to negotiate as a group and to lobby for special and differential treatment for smaller economies, the small Central American economies elected to negotiate individually. Mexico's stances toward the FTAA are determined primarily by its NAFTA membership, while Venezuela and Colombia operate within the Andean Group of countries. It is also evident that the sheer size and technical nature of the negotiations have stretched to the limit the capacity of the smallest Caribbean countries to participate, notwithstanding the collective negotiating strategy adopted by CARICOM and the technical assistance offered by the Inter-American Development Bank and the OAS.

The FTAA will doubtless generate more intra-hemispheric trade and investment in the long run. The major beneficiaries, at least initially, are likely to be the larger and more globally competitive economies and producers in the hemisphere. It is likely to make a lasting impact on the structures of trade in the Western Hemisphere, including the dismantling of the preference scheme extended to the CBI countries by the USA and ultimately influencing the trade provisions contained in a number of sub-regional agreements like CARICOM. A specific challenge is posed for many archipelagic Caribbean countries by the structure of their economies. They depend on tourism and financial services for a large share of national income and are likely to benefit less from the potential increase in trade in goods promised by the FTAA. They are, moreover, obliged to dismantle the systems of trade taxes on which they currently rely heavily for government revenue, and to redesign their taxation systems. The reshaping of institutions for the FTAA promises to extend well beyond the taxation regime to many areas of regulation and will require major public administration reforms (Lopez-Cordova 2001). Civil society groups in the Caribbean area have critiqued the FTAA process and have urged that the goals of poverty reduction and social development be added to modify its neo-liberal economic agenda. Their demands include provisions to assist and rehabilitate displaced workers, assistance for highly indebted countries, adequate long term protection for vulnerable sectors in very small economies and protection for agriculture geared towards domestic consumption (Caribbean Reference Group 2000).

Caribbean responses to external challenges
Earlier on, the impact of globalisation on certain economic sectors in the Caribbean was discussed. This final section examines other types of Caribbean responses to the changing international environment – intergovernmental initiatives, individual country

strategies and the increased transnational flows of trade, investment and people evident in the Pan-Caribbean region.

The first type of response has been that of regionalism, now recognised by many scholars as an integral part of globalisation (Grugel and Hout 1999; Hettne *et al* 1999). New regional groups have emerged, most significantly the Association of Caribbean States (ACS), and existing ones have been restructured, notably CARICOM and the Central American Integration System (SICA). The Association of Caribbean States, agreed to in July 1994 and established in 1995, is the first Pan-Caribbean regional body, in that it offers the possibility of membership or associate membership to every state and non-independent territory in the Greater Caribbean area. Its major sponsors were the CARICOM states, Mexico, Venezuela and Colombia. It reflected, on the one hand, the search of small Caribbean actors for a wider regional forum and new alliances in an uncertain international environment, and on the other hand, the interest of larger regional players in institutionalising their presence in the Caribbean. Despite initial recommendations by some of its sponsors that it should focus primarily on functional co-operation (Gill 1996), the ACS found itself confronting political and ideological issues from its inception[14], and was constrained in developing a trade agenda by the widely divergent trading interests and alliances of its member states. Nonetheless, it has been slowly developing a viable co-operation agenda in the areas of sustainable tourism, marine environmental conservation, natural disaster management, air and sea transport networks in the Caribbean and cultural co-operation (Byron 1998).

Both CARICOM and the CACM have tried to re-invent themselves in the decade of the 1990s, but with varying results. Following prolonged paralysis during a decade of civil wars and regional conflict, attempts were made to revive the Central American Community in the context of the Central American peace agreements in the late 1980s. It was felt that regional democratic structures and renewed economic integration arrangements would preserve peace and stability in the sub-region. The Protocol of Tegucigalpa (1991) established the Central American Integration System (SICA), which incorporates a plethora of subregional organs, among them the Central American Court of Justice and the Central American Parliament. Despite numerous summits and high-level political declarations and agreements during the 1990s, however, economic integration made little progress, and most Central American organs enjoy only partial membership and limited support from the countries in the sub-region. Regional integration and economic development goals received further setbacks from the region-wide devastation of Hurricane Mitch in 1998 and the earthquake in El Salvador in 2001. The fragility of regional integration in Central America was demonstrated by an upsurge in border disputes between 1999 and 2001 involving Nicaragua–Honduras over maritime boundaries in the Caribbean Sea, Belize–Guatemala over 50 per cent of Belizean territory and Guatemala's access to the Caribbean Sea, Costa Rica–Nicaragua over the San Juan River, and Guatemala–Honduras–El Salvador–Nicaragua over the Gulf of Fonseca on the Pacific Coast. No regional institution has been an effective instrument for dispute settlement, regional trade and mobility have stagnated and there have been various calls for the rationalisation of the cumbersome, under-funded subregional institutional network. Subregional integration has declined under the impact of hemispheric integration, as most Central American actors have shown greater interest in pursuing stronger economic links with the USA, their major trading partner, and with Mexico via bilateral or multilateral free trade agreements and the recently announced Plan Puebla-Panama which is intended to stimulate investment and sustainable economic development in the Southern Mexican and Isthmus region. They also participate in the hemispheric FTAA trade talks but voice national, rather than collective positions.

In the early 1990s, CARICOM embarked on a process of deeper integration in response to fears of globalisation and economic marginalisation. This took various forms, including the restructuring of the organs of the Community, moves to establish a Single Market and Economy (CSME) and the expansion of membership to include Suriname in 1995 and Haiti in 1997. Additionally, trade agreements were concluded with Venezuela in 1991, Colombia in 1994, Cuba in 2000 and the Dominican Republic also in 2000. Finally, faced with the prospect of having to participate simultaneously in several complex multilateral trade negotiations between 1998 and 2005, CARICOM formed a loose body called the Regional Negotiating Machinery, which negotiates on behalf of the group in the FTAA and co-ordinates regional positions in the Cotonou and WTO negotiating fora (EIPU 2000; Nicholls *et al* 2000.

■ Box 4.3 The Caribbean Regional Negotiating Machinery (RNM)

The RNM was created by CARICOM governments in 1997 to develop and put into action a negotiating strategy for several trade-related negotiations in which the region is involved. Its mandate comes from the Conference of CARICOM Heads of Government, but it has also worked closely with the governments of Cuba and the Dominican Republic on ACP–EU trade talks and the FTAA respectively. The RNM's initial focus was on trade talks in the WTO, the ACP–EU Cotonou and post-Cotonou negotiations and the FTAA negotiations. It has also been called on increasingly to manage other trade negotiations between CARICOM and individual countries or groups.

The RNM briefs and advises participating governments about the progress of the different negotiations, works with various regional and national interest groups to develop Caribbean positions on the issues being negotiated, co-ordinates the region's negotiating teams, prepares background sectoral studies to inform regional negotiating positions and runs training programmes to develop a cadre of experienced regional negotiators for the future.

The RNM has been in constant evolution and underwent some restructuring in 2001. It is now headed by a Director-General and the two main offices in the region are in Jamaica and Barbados.

Sources: *The RNM in Brief: Integrating the Caribbean on External Negotiations,* Caribbean Regional Negotiating Machinery, Bridgetown, January 2000; " 'Patterson Report' Calls for a Reshaped RNM", *Daily Gleaner* 17/09/2001; "New Structure Agreed for the Caribbean Negotiating Machinery" *CARICOM Watch,* Issue No. 6, 6/11/2001.

CARICOM's integration process has received mixed reviews over the last ten years. Intra-regional trade has expanded, with regional exports accounting for 23 per cent of total exports by 1998, up from 12 per cent in 1990. The CARICOM market has been particularly important for some of the smallest economies in the zone like Dominica, St. Vincent and the Grenadines and Barbados, who export between 30 per cent and 70 per cent of their total volume of exports there, although Trinidad dominates intra-regional exports overall (CTIR 2000). Nonetheless, the implementation of the CARICOM Single Market and Econom (CSME), first announced in 1992, has progressed extremely slowly and the negotiation and implementation of market liberalisation agreements with other countries in the Greater Caribbean has been laborious. The CSME, originally intended to precede and to pave the way for operating in a global free trade system, has been overtaken by both the WTO and FTAA processes and thus its ultimate relevance will be reduced. The differences in the sizes and structures of CARICOM economies have become more marked in a globalised age, and this has made it harder to harmonise intra-regional economic policies and to adopt common positions in their negotiations with other actors. There have been a number of disputes related to trade, border and migration issues among CARICOM countries themselves, as well as between them and countries in the Greater Caribbean during the last five years. Such disputes, in addition to the domestic political tensions experienced in several member countries, and challenges associated with establishing, funding and managing regional institutions have led to calls for more effective regional governance mechanisms in CARICOM.

In addition to this burst of regional institution-building, a number of countries in the Pan-Caribbean zone have reoriented their foreign relations substantially as part of their adjustment strategies to globalisation and economic liberalisation. One example is Mexico, which in the late 1980s embarked on an ambitious North–South process of regional integration with the USA and Canada. Cuba and the Dominican Republic are two other countries, traditionally isolated from wider regional developments, which have sought new directions. In the mid-1980s, as its economy underwent a major restructuring process, the Dominican Republic began to diversify its economic and political links away from its former exclusive focus on the USA. It explored closer relationships with CARICOM and the Central American Community, eventually seeking in 1998 to become a bridge country and form a strategic alliance between the two sub-regions. It became a member of the ACP group in 1990 and expanded its trade and development relationship with the EU. It participated in a number of functional co-operation activities with CARICOM including the Regional Negotiating Machinery until 2002, but has now opted to again negotiate individually in hemispheric trade talks (Ceara Hatton and Girvan 1998; Lewis 1995). To some extent, this mirrors the approach adopted by Costa Rica, which has held itself aloof from Central American integration initiatives in the 1990s, choosing to pursue an individual strategy of negotiating trade agreements and forging alliances.

Cuba has focused on reintegration into the Caribbean and Latin America since the demise of the Soviet Union and COMECON in the early 1990s. It has had to circumvent the obstacles posed by continued US restrictions on relations with the country and rules governing participation in the Inter-American System and the FTAA which exclude Cuba from membership under its present system of government. The Cuban response has been to conclude a web of trade, economic and cultural co-operation agreements with as many countries in the hemisphere as possible and to use active regional diplomacy to counteract US attempts to impose hemispheric isolation. Canada, Mexico and Venezuela are important economic partners, Cuba and CARICOM have deepened their socio-economic and political co-operation and Cuba has participated actively in the ACS co-operation agenda. It also gained admission to the ACP group since it has been exploring a co-operation agreement with the EU (Byron 2000).

These developments of the last decade have resulted in a heightened rate of transnational activity throughout the Pan-Caribbean zone. While the numerous bilateral and multilateral trade agreements have generated only a gradual increase in the volume of trade flows outside of the traditional subregional groupings, there has been a significant increase in the intersocietal linkages across the region, growth of civil society movements and investment-generated business networks (see Plate 4.2 which shows Caribbean adaptations to new technologies which can aid such interconnections).

Additionally, circum-Caribbean migration occurs as a result of numerous factors. Environmental disasters, most notably the volcanic eruptions in Montserrat since 1995, have

Plate 4.2 *Traditional Caribbean architecture is combined with new technology, Port of Spain, Trinidad*
© Tracey Skelton

caused the resettlement of populations either outside the region or in neighbouring territories. An increase in student movements and academic exchanges is taking place among the secondary and tertiary institutions of the region, across the linguistic divides, with Cuba, for example, providing over 1500 scholarships to CARICOM nationals in the 1990s, while, with the support of the ACS, the EU and a network of Caribbean universities, a number of academic exchange and joint graduate programmes have materialised among Spanish, French and English-speaking institutions. Since the mid-1980s, labour migration flows within the Caribbean have been in response to low growth rates and poor socio-economic conditions in some larger Caribbean territories like Guyana, Jamaica and Haiti in contrast to the more buoyant economic conditions in smaller territories like Anguilla, the Cayman Islands, Turks and Caicos Islands, Antigua or St. Kitts and Nevis. To a limited extent, people have also responded to CARICOM measures to encourage the movement of skilled labour among its member states. Cuba has concluded several bilateral agreements with CARICOM states allowing for Cuban professionals, particularly in the health sector, to work for contractual periods in those countries. Also, there is considerable movement between the Dominican Republic and English-speaking islands in the Eastern Caribbean based on ancestral origins, citizenship entitlements and perceptions of employment opportunities. All these movements will undoubtedly transform regional consciousness and identity perceptions during the decades to come, in addition to increasingly influencing regional and national politics and policy debates (see Chapter Six for more information about migration).

Conclusion

The recent waves of globalisation have made a profound impact on Caribbean economic, social and political life. The effects are not uniform but highly differentiated, depending on the size of the country, its resource endowments, previous mode of insertion into the international political economy and levels of economic and human development. The region shows increased fragmentation in terms of international responses, yet paradoxically, there is greater interconnectedness at the regional level. One common denominator which characterises all actors, is a deepening and growing complexity in their relations with the USA, hub of a North American and possibly an eventual hemispheric economy.

While most Caribbean populations will certainly adapt to globalisation and maximise their access to the continental economic and social space in which they are located, the Caribbean state has been subjected to much stress in the new global environment. We conclude with Norman Girvan:

> If the Caribbean was an invention of the 20th century, it seems certain to be reinterpreted and perhaps transcended in the 21st. The Caribbean of tomorrow will not be an exclusively Anglophone and Hispanic conception … not tied exclusively to geographical space or definition … it is by no means clear that all … of these societies will survive as viable entities- units that provide for the basic social, economic and community needs of a collection of defined citizens and with some capacity for autonomous action. Some may become just places to reside in for a while, to visit, to holiday in and to retire to … (Girvan 2001).

Notes

[1] The Caribbean is diverse in its language groups and colonial histories, and contains both independent states and several European and US dependent territories. Among the archipelagic territories, Cuba, the Dominican Republic and the US Commonwealth of Puerto Rico are Spanish-speaking, there are the Dutch islands of the Netherlands Antilles, the French *Départements d'Outre Mer* and the British Overseas Territories of Montserrat, the Cayman Islands, Anguilla, the British Virgin Islands and the Turks and Caicos Islands, as well as the United States Virgin Islands. There is the sub-regional grouping of countries known as the Caribbean Community (CARICOM), which encompasses thirteen Commonwealth Caribbean countries with a legacy of British colonialism as well as two more recent members, Suriname and Haiti. There are two other sub-regional groups in the Caribbean Basin area, namely the Group of Three (Mexico, Colombia and Venezuela) and the Central American Community, which includes Costa Rica, Nicaragua, Honduras, El Salvador and Guatemala. Panama, Belize and the Dominican Republic are linked to this latter grouping either as associate members or observers. Only one regional entity in the Caribbean Basin, the Association of Caribbean States, seeks to incorporate all these diverse actors. It promotes co-operation of a political, socio-cultural, economic and environmental nature.

[2] These banana producers can be divided into four main groups: EU producers who include the French *Départements d'Outre Mer* (DOMs); traditional suppliers from the Windward Islands, Jamaica and Suriname, who are members of the African Caribbean and Pacific group of countries (ACP), who have benefited from preferential access to the EU market since 1975 under the Banana Protocols to the Lomé Conventions; non-traditional ACP suppliers, such as the Dominican Republic, recently acceded to the Lomé Convention and not a party to the Banana Protocol; Latin American producers, also described as 'dollar banana producers' who account for 75 per cent of world banana exports and 60 per cent of the EU market share. For more information, see W. Sandiford, K. Nurse, *Windward Islands Bananas: Challenges and Options under the European Single Market*, Friedrich Ebert Stiftung, Kingston 1995, and P. Sutton, 'The Banana Regime of the European Union, the Caribbean and Latin America' *Journal of Inter-American Studies and World Affairs* Vol. 39, No. 2, Summer 1997, pp. 5–36.

[3] It should be noted that one of these firms, Chiquita Brands, allegedly made large financial contributions to both the Republican and the Democratic parties in 1993–94 and lobbied prominent Congressmen to impose sanctions against Colombia and Costa Rica, two Latin American countries that had been willing to reach an earlier settlement with the EU. See P. Sutton, *Op.Cit.*

[4] Phase One would come into effect by July 1, 2001 with the EU's adoption of a new licensing system; Phase Two would increase the tariff quota by 100,000 tons in January 2002 with access provided for Latin American bananas and US distributors; Phase Three would start in January 2006 when the EU would switch to a tariff only regime for banana imports. See *Tradewatch*, the electronic newsletter of the Caribbean Export Agency, July 4, 2001.

[5] P. Lewis, 'A Future for Windward Island Bananas? Challenge and Prospect', *Commonwealth and Comparative Politics*, Vol. 38, No. 2, July 2000, p. 68, explains 'the Fair Trade label ... is based on enlightened European consumers paying higher prices which reflect more accurately the cost of production and are thus more likely to provide a living wage for producers'.

[6] For details, see D. Jessop, 'This Week in Europe', Oct. 27 2000, www.oneworld.org/euforic/cce/2000oct27.htm.

[7] Material for this section relies partially on material drawn from J. Byron 2001.

[8] Some Caribbean countries, notably those in CARICOM, have expressed dissatisfaction with the inadequacy of current Special and Differential Treatment and have lobbied consistently for the extension of the principle of special measures to counteract vulnerability to other countries, such as small economies. In the WTO Trade Ministerial Meeting in Doha, Qatar, November 2001, it was agreed that a Working Group would be set up to make recommendations to the next WTO Ministerial Conference. See *ECLAC Issue Brief* No. 8, December 2001, 'The Doha Ministerial and its Implications for Caribbean Economies'.

[9] The Caribbean Basin Initiative was started in 1984 by the Reagan Administration in the USA. It involved granting one-way duty-free market access to the USA for a number of non-traditional exports from countries in the Caribbean Basin i.e. countries in Central America, Guyana, Suriname and the island Caribbean. A number of political and economic conditionalities applied which meant that some countries, notably Cuba, have been excluded from participation in the CBI. Although textiles were not included in the original list of products granted access under the CBI, ironically, the CBI has had its greatest impact on stimulating growth and investment in the textiles and apparel

industry in Caribbean export processing zones. NAFTA Parity means treatment for the CBI products equivalent to that granted to Mexican products under NAFTA.

[10] The Caribbean members of the ACP Group are all the CARICOM countries and the Dominican Republic. Although Cuba participated as an observer in the Cotonou negotiations, it withdrew its application for accession to the Treaty in May 2000.

[11] This had to be approved by the WTO. The latter granted the necessary waiver at the Trade Ministerial Meeting in Doha in November 2001.

[12] Costa Rica mainly accounts for Central America's trade flows with the EU. See data contained in Inter-American Development Bank, *Integration and Trade in the Americas: Special Issue on Latin America and Caribbean Economic Relations with the European Union,* IADB, Department of Integration and Regional Programs, Washington D.C., May 2002, pp. 18–19.

[13] Such an accord focuses not only on tariff and non-tariff barriers to trade, but also on government procurement, intellectual property rights, services, competition policy, investment provisions and dispute settlement procedures.

[14] A major case in point is the fact that no US territory has joined the ACS because Cuba is a member state.

References

Amin, S. 1997: *Capitalism in the Age of Globalization.* London: Zed Books.

Basch, L., Glick Schiller, N. and Szanton-Blanc, C. 1994: *Nations Unbound: Transnational Projects, Post-Colonial Predicaments and Deterritorialized Nation-States.* Amsterdam: Gordon and Breach Publishers.

Benn, D. 2000 'Globalisation and the North-South divide: power asymmetries in contemporary international economic relations'. In D. Benn, K. Hall (eds.) *Globalisation: A Calculas of Inequality,* Kingston: Ian Randle Publishers, pp. 295–325.

Benn, D. and Hall, K. (eds.) 2000a: *Globalization: A Calculus of Inequality, Perspectives from the South.* Kingston: Ian Randle Publishers.

Benn, D. and Hall, K. (eds.) 2000b: *Contending with Destiny: The Caribbean in the 21st Century.* Kingston: Ian Randle Publishers.

Bernal, R. 1998: 'The integration of smaller economies in the Free Trade Area of the Americas'. Paper presented at UWI LACC/IIR and AGCI Workshop *Economic Integration and Free Trade in the Americas: Chilean and CARICOM Perspectives.* February 4–6.

Bernal, R. 2000 'The Caribbean in the international system: outlook for the first 20 years of the 21st century'. In D. Benn, K. Hall (eds.) *Contentding with destiny: The Caribbean in the 21st Century.* Kingston: Ian Randall Publishers, pp. 295–325.

Bryan, A. (ed.) 1995: *The Caribbean: New Dynamics in Trade and Political Economy.* Miami: North-South Centre Press, University of Miami.

Bryan, A. and Serbin, A. (eds.) 1996: *Distant Cousins: The Caribbean-Latin American Relationship.* Miami: North-South Centre Press, University of Miami.

Byron, J. 1998: 'The Association of Caribbean States: growing pains of a new regionalism?' *Pensamiento Propio* No. 7, May–August.

Byron, J. 2000: 'Square dance diplomacy: Cuba and CARIFORUM, the European Union and the United States. *European Review of Latin American and Caribbean Studies.* No. 68, April.

Byron, J. 2001: 'The CARICOM/CARIFORUM sub-region in 1999–2000: towards new models of regional governance?' In Jacoue, F., Romero, A. and Jerbin, A. (eds.) *Anuario de la Integacion Regional en el Gran Caribe,* No. 2 Caracas: Nueva Sociedad. pp 113–139.

Caribbean Council for Europe Newsletter, 200, 27th October.

Caribbean Reference Group (CRG), *Promoting Regional Hemispheric Integration in the Fight to Reduce Poverty in the Americas.* Initial advocacy position prepared by the CRG under the co-ordination of the Caribbean Policy Development Centre, Bridgetown, Barbados, *circa* November 2000.

Caribbean Tracle and Investment Report, 2000: 52–55.

CARICOM Secretariat, 2001: *Caribbean Trade and Investment Report 2000: The Dynamic Interface of Regionalism and Globalization*. Kingston: Ian Randle Publishers in collaboration with the CARICOM Secretariat.

Ceara Hatton, M. and Girvan, N. 1998: *CARICOM, Central America and the FTAA*. Kingston: Friedrich Ebert Stiftung.

Commonwealth Advisory Group. 1997: *A Future for Small States: Overcoming Vulnerability*. London: Commonwealth Secretariat.

Commonwealth Secretariat/World Bank. 2000: *Small States: Meeting Challenges in the Global Economy*. London: Joint Commonwealth Secretariat/World Bank Taskforce Report. April.

Devlin, R., Estevadeordal, A. and Jorge Garay, L. 1999: *The FTAA: Some Longer Term Issues*, INTAL/ITD Occasional Paper No. 5, August. Washington D.C.: Inter-American Development Bank.

ECLAC Issue Brief, No. 7, June 2001: 'The Implications of the EU's EBA for the Caribbean.'

ECLAC Issue Brief, No. 8, December 2001: 'The Doha Ministerial and Implications for Caribbean Economies'.

Economic Intelligence & Policy Unit, CARICOM Secretariat 2000, *CARICOM Trade and Investment Report 2000: Dynamic Interface of Regionalism and Globalisation*. Kingston: Ian Randle Publishers.

Friedman, T. L. 2000: *The Lexus and the Olive Tree*. New York: Anchor Books.

Fog Olwig, K. 1993: *Global Culture, Island Identity: Continuity and Change in the Afro-Caribbean Community of Nevis*. Chur, Switzerland: Harwood Academic Publishers.

Gamble, A. and Payne, A. 1996: *Regionalism and World Order*. London: Macmillan.

Gill, H. 1996 'Widening the relationship? The Association of Caribbean States' in A. Bryan, A. Serbin (eds.) *Distant Cousins: The Caribbean-Latin American Relationship*. University of Miami, Coral Gables: North-South Centre Press, pp. 97–118.

Girvan, N. 2001 'Reinterpreting the Caribbean.' In Mecks, B. & Lindahl, F. (eds.) *New Caribbean Thought: A Reader*. Kingston: UNI Press.

Grugel, J. and Hout, W. (eds.) 1999: *Regionalism across the North-South Divide*. London: Routledge.

Held, D. 1997: Democracy and Globalization. *Global Governance*. 3, 3 September–December.

Held, D. and McGrew, A. (eds.) 1999: *The Global Transformations Reader: An Introduction to the Globalization Debate*. Cambridge: Polity Press.

Held, D. and McGrew, A. (eds.) 2000: The great globalization debate: an introduction' in D. Held, A. McGrew (eds.) *The Global Transformations Reader: An Introduction to the globalization Debate*. Cambridge: Polity Press, pp. 1–45.

Hettne, B., Inotai, A. and Sunkel, O. (eds.) 1999: *Globalism and the New Regionalism*. London: Macmillan Press.

Hoogvelt, A. 1997: *Globalization and the Post-Colonial World: The New Political Economy of Development*. Baltimore MD: John Hopkins University Press.

Hurrell, A. and Woods, N. (eds.) 1999: *Inequality, Globalization and World Politics*. Oxford: Oxford University Press.

Institute Europe, 1999: Caribbean Council for Europe Weekly Newsletter, No. 25, March 23. I,D.

Inter-American Development Bank, Department of Integration and Regional Programs, 1999 *Integration and Trade in the Americas: Special Issue on Latin American and Caribbean Economic Relations with the European Union*. Washington D.C.: IDB. May.

Inter-American Development Bank, Department of Integration and Regional Programs. 2000: *Integration and Trade in the Americas: Periodic Note.* Washington D.C.: IDB. December.

Jacome, F., Romero, A. and Serbin, A. (eds.) 2001: *Anuario de la Integracion Regional en el Gran Caribe.* Caracas: Nueva Sociedad.

Jessop, D. 'This Week in Europe', 23/3/1999, www.oneworld.org/euforic/cce/1999mar23.htm.

Jessop, D. 'This Week in Europe', 27/10/2000, www.oneworld.org/euforic/cce/2000oct27.htm.

Klak, T. (ed.) 1998: *Globalization and Neoliberalism: The Caribbean Context.* Lanham, MD: Rowman and Littlefield Pubs.

Lewis, D. 1995 'Intra-Caribbean relations: a review and projections' In A. Bryan (ed.) *The Carribbean: New Dynamics In Trade and Political Economy.* Miami: North-South Centre Press, pp. 75–100.

Lewis, P. 2000: 'A future for Windward Islands bananas? Capital challenge and prospect'. *Journal of Commonwealth and Comparative Politics.* 38, 2: July.

Lopez-Cordova, J. E. 2001: *NAFTA and the Mexican Economy: Analytical Issues and Lessons for the FTAA,* INTAL/ITD Occasional Paper. Washington D.C.: IDB.

Maingot, A. 1994: *The US and the Caribbean.* London: Macmillan Press.

Meeks, B. and Lindahl, F. (eds.) 2001: *New Caribbean Thought: A Reader.* Kingston: UWI Press.

Miller, S. 2002: 'Deputy US Trade representative shares U.S. perspectives on free trade in the Americas'. *Washington File.* September 20.

Mittelman, J. (ed.) 1997: *Globalization: Critical Reflections.* Boulder, CO: Lynne Rienner Publishers.

Nicholls, S., Birchwood, A., Colthrust, P. and Boodoo, E. 2000: 'The state of and prospects for the deepening and widening of Caribbean integration'. *The World Economy.* 23, 9.

Nurse, K. and Sandiford, W. 1995: *Windward Islands Bananas: Challenges and Options under the European Single Market.* Kingston: Friedrich Ebert Stiftung.

Payne, A. 1994: 'U.S. hegemony and the reconfiguration of the Caribbean'. *Review of International Studies.* 20.

Salazar, J. Manuel, 2001: *Towards Free Trade in the Americas.* Washington D.C.: OAS/Brookings.

Scholte, J.A. 2000: *Globalization: A Critical Introduction:* London: Macmillan Press.

Sen, A. 2000: 'Globalization and its discontent'. Paper presented at World Bank Annual Conference on Development Economics *Development Thinking at the Millennium.* Paris, 26/06/2000.

Solis, L., Solano, P. 2001: 'Central America: The difficult road towards integration and the role of Canada'. *FOCAL Policy Paper* FPP-01-07, Ottawa, May.

Sutton, P. 1997: 'The banana regime of the European Union, the Caribbean and Latin America'. *Journal of Interamerican Studies and World Affairs.* 39, 2, Summer.

Tradewatch, 4/7/2001, electronic bulletin distributed by the Caribbean Export Promotion Agency.

Thomas, C. Y. 1988: *The Poor and the Powerless: Economic Policy and Change in the Caribbean.* London: Latin American Bureau.

Thomas, C. Y. 1998: 'Globalization, structural adjustment and security: the collapse of the post-colonial developmental state in the Caribbean'. *Global Development Studies.* Vol. 1, Nos. 1–2, Winter/Spring.

5
Caribbean tourism: trouble in paradise?

Beverley Mullings

Introduction

The visitor's book at Bluff House, Green Turtle Cay, on the Bahamian island of Abaco is filled with passionate thank-you's from guests, penned as they leave their holiday haven for the journey back home. The messages read: 'This surely must be paradise. Can't wait to come back'. And 'Another day in paradise for two weeks. Glorious holiday. Kind and friendly people'. And, simply 'Heaven on Earth'. (Patullo 1996, p. 141).

Patullo's observation of the way that tourists to the Caribbean, imagine and experience the islands gets to the heart of an indisputable contradiction. Most tourists travel to exotic and far away places like the Caribbean in order to experience the extraordinary encounters that before travel can only lie in the realm of the imagination. But particularly in 'Third World' locales the reality of such places may often be quite the opposite of the fantasy and in order to attract the economic resources of tourists, exotic locales must therefore actively produce the fantasy. Therein lies the contradiction, that by their very presence, tourists transform the landscapes that they visit, creating paradise in the midst of crisis and immiseration. The Caribbean, in the collective European and North American imagination, has always been a paradise, a place for exotic and laid-back encounters, yet the reality is that 40 years of tourism has threatened the social and environmental foundations upon which these fantasies have been built.

Today scholars (Britton 1991; Cater 1995; Urry 1990; Urry 1995) argue that tourism is a force that arises from, and gives rise to, geographical unevenness and social inequality. Indeed, despite the fact that tourism is now considered the most important source of international trade, (accounting for 13 per cent of world exports and 8 per cent of employment in 1999 (WTTC, 2001), many writers today remain ambivalent about the expansion of this industry (Butler 1998; Hall and Lew 1998; Mowforth and Munt 1997). Many argue that particularly in the 'Third World', tourism is more likely to benefit multinational corporations and tourists primarily from the industrialised world, and the rich within the local economy. Tourism is also increasingly viewed as having a negative effect on the cultures and environments of 'Third World' countries, transforming societies and economies in ways that benefit tourists and the companies that transport and house them rather than the local people who live there. Given these opposing views of the value of tourism, it is important to examine in more detail the applicability of these claims to the Caribbean and the validity of current concerns regarding the future of this industry. This chapter explores the factors that have created trouble in paradise. It examines the history, production and consumption of Caribbean tourism over the last 40 years. Then, focusing on recent changes in the nature of the consumption and production of international tourism services, this chapter will examine the prospects for the future of tourism in the region.

Tourism in the history of the Caribbean

In 1969, Michael Peters, one of the most comprehensive writers on the subject of international tourism noted the potential benefits of tourism to the 'developing areas' of the world. As he noted then:

> The economic gap between rich and poor countries has widened over the last ten years. But to create new industries and to transform rural life in Asian, African and Latin American countries is a gigantic task. The relevance of tourism to this situation is that income from international travel can bring the foreign exchange essential for major investment (Peters 1969).

Tourism as viewed by Peters and other industry proponents, was seen as a primarily economic solution to the poverty and inequalities that beset regions like the Caribbean. Proponents of the industry like Peters, argued that tourism was an important source of foreign exchange earnings and given its labour-intensive nature, employment. Particularly for 'Third World' economies whose position in the Old International Division of Labour[1] made them over-reliant on the production of

Plate 5.1 *Havana Cathedral, Cuba and tourist stalls. This UNESCO site represents the way Cuba is trying to develop tourism but also tread a difficult path between earning foreign capital and minimising social and development costs.*

© David Howard

agricultural commodities, tourism was viewed as a welcomed opportunity for economic diversification. Significant in these early analyses of the role of tourism in the development process was the scant regard that was given to the social and economic costs of tourism that host countries had to bear (Plate 5.1).

Certainly over the last 40 years the image of the Caribbean as the world's sugar and banana producer has changed and now the islands are popularly viewed as the quintessential tourist's tropical paradise. Yet the transformation of the islands into principal sites of tourist consumption is a historically recent phenomena. While tourism was always an important industry to the region, its contribution to the Gross Domestic Product was smaller than that of agriculture and mining activities and services were largely oriented towards Europe's and North America's wealthiest. Even as technology reduced the cost of travel, permitting larger numbers to engage in tourism pursuits, state officials remained cautious about encouraging major expansion of this industry. So how did the Caribbean come to be viewed as synonymous with tourism? How did tourism come to be the primary and, in some cases, virtually only source of foreign exchange earned by these islands today?

Up until the 1960s, all of the islands, with the exception of Haiti[2] were economically, politically and socially linked to British, Spanish, French, Dutch and American colonial powers. As colonies, most islands were geared primarily towards the production of agricultural goods and mineral resources for colonial markets. Tourism up until this point was small and primarily geared towards famous and rich Americans and Europeans such as Noel Coward, Errol Flynn, Ernest Hemingway and the Rockefellers, all of whom developed extensive ties to particular islands. The development of tourism as an industry really occurred after the 1960s and rapidly expanded with the growth of mass international jet travel and the granting of full independence to a number of the territories in the region. Newly independent islands like Jamaica, Barbados and Trinidad and Tobago in an effort to modernise their economies encouraged the development of mass tourism through the construction of hotels and the provision of financial incentive programmes for prospective investors. While most heads of government in the Caribbean recognised the benefits that could accrue from the development of a more mass-oriented form of tourism, many preferred to rely upon other industrial sectors such as manufacturing and mineral extraction to be the primary engines of growth. The manufacturing industry in particular was viewed as more likely to generate the backward and forward linkages so necessary for long term development, and was seen as less likely to be deeply affected by changes in demand. Tourism, on the other hand, was viewed with ambivalence because of its ability to be seriously affected by rapid changes in demand and the potentially negative impact of this sort of service on a population recovering from the historical legacy of slavery and colonial rule. As Patullo (1996) points out in her erudite examination of the costs of tourism in the region, in the 1970s tourism was viewed as a demeaning industry that was too reminiscent of the region's recent colonial past. To understand the reticence with which leaders endorsed the tourism industry, it is necessary to examine the structure and style of tourism that evolved as the industry expanded during the 1970s through 1990s.

Foreign corporations and tourism development

It was recognised very early on that, because the islands could not finance tourism projects without diverting resources away from the other sectors that were also being developed, governments would have to rely upon exogenous investment in order to construct the hotels and infrastructure necessary to attract international tourists. It was also realised that, in order to create a market, links would also need to be made with foreign airlines and tour operators. In a flurry of competition many of the islands sought to attract foreign investors to their tourism industries during the 1960s and 1970s. Most islands, for example, offered hotel incentives that reduced an investor's liability for import duties and income taxes. Such incentives usually included provisions for the duty free importation of raw materials and equipment as well as income tax relief and relief on hotel profits and dividends. While the incentives were successful in attracting international hoteliers, tour operators and airlines to the islands, it quickly became clear that the tourism industry was likely to be of greater financial benefit to the foreign investors than the host countries that subsidised their presence. Given the importance of airlines, tour operators, travel agents and hoteliers to the flow of tourists into and out of the islands, the policies, practices and interests of these four groups had tremendous influence over the growth of Caribbean tourism.

By the early 1970s a number of studies were beginning to document the high proportion of foreign ownership of hotels on the islands (Bryden 1973; HMSO Department of Employment 1971). While foreign ownership levels were lower on the larger islands (in 1968 approximately 55.6 per cent of hotel capacity in Jamaica was owned by foreign interests) (Jefferson 1972), on the smaller islands this percentage was much higher. Bryden (1973), for example, states that 89 per cent of all hotels and guest houses in Antigua in 1968 were foreign owned. By 1984 the industry was dominated by multi-national companies with 13 Holiday Inns, 9 Hiltons, 9 Sheratons, 8 Trust House Fortes, 7 Club Méditeranée de Paris and 5 Grand Metropolitan Inter-Continental Hotels operating in the region (Thomas 1988).

While the idea of hotel ownership by foreigners was not considered to be problematic, it became very clear by the 1970s that few of the large multinational hotel chains in the region would create the types of linkages to stimulate local development as originally envisaged. While these hotels did contribute to the provision of local employment, much of the employment generated was in highly labour intensive, relatively low paid jobs such as housekeeping and food preparation. The earnings that accrued to host governments through these forms of employment was minuscule compared with the potential earnings that were lost through the repatriation of the profits and wages of expatriate managerial staff and the high levels of imports acquired by most hotels under centralised purchasing systems. In Jamaica, for example, Jefferson states that in 1968 approximately 70 per cent of the food consumed in the sector was imported (1972, p. 177).

By the 1970s the high levels of foreign exchange leakage also became a dominant characteristic of the relationship between island governments and air transport and tour operators. Up until the 1960s tourist travel to the islands had been largely restricted to sea travel, with popular stories of visitors arriving on boats designed to transport bananas to the USA. With the introduction of the jet airplane in the 1960s a number of airlines carriers began to establish routes in the region. Carriers from the dominant colonial interests such as KLM (Dutch), BOAC (British), Air France and others like Pan Am from the USA, accounted for the majority of tourists who chose the islands as a vacation spot. Yet, as many of the region's governments noted, the reliance on these large carriers made the industry vulnerable. Through their marketing and stop over decisions these large corporations wielded undue influence over the viability of a specific destination. In response, a number of the islands established national carriers. National carriers like British West Indian Airways (BWIA) founded in 1940 and based in Trinidad and Tobago, Air Jamaica[3] and the Leeward Islands Air Transport Company (LIAT) founded in 1956, however, never managed to compete effectively with these large and powerful airlines[4]. Most of the national carriers accounted for only a fraction of the tourists to the islands, as most travellers tended to choose the larger airlines as part of tour packages offered by tour companies and travel agencies many of which were integrated with the airline companies. Given the high cost of air transportation equipment, the large loans secured mainly from developed countries to finance these costs and the inability to directly access the tourist-generating markets, it is not surprising that most of the national airlines quickly became debt-ridden loss-making enterprises that earned little or no returns. While some countries abandoned these loss-making entities e.g. Air Barbados, others like Air Jamaica would continue to act as a drain on the public resources for the next 20 years.

The role of mass tourism in Caribbean development

In theorising why the tourism industry in the Caribbean made so small a contribution to local regional development, one would need to examine the compatibility of the forms of tourism production with the forms of tourism consumption that evolved in the region. One would also need to examine the extent to which the structure of industry that evolved on the islands was the product of some larger scale relationship between these recently de-colonised countries and the industrialised world. John Urry (1990) argues that the boom in tourism in the 1960s and 1970s relied upon a particular mode of tourism production and consumption. The so-called 'mass tourism' of the post-war years relied upon the mass transportation of individuals with greater disposable income and leisure time than before to places previously preserved for the rich. In this period, profits to industry accrued primarily through the economies of scale derived from the standardisation of tourism goods and services. Like the manufacturing industry, the profitability of tourism depended on the mass provision of standardised transport, accommodation and leisure services. This standardisation of tourism services was viewed as crucial to attracting tourists to places that were by all accounts impoverished. Thus as Erick Cohen surmised in 1978 a tourist infrastructure of facilities based on western standards needed to be created even in the poorest of countries because such infrastructure would provide mass tourists with an 'ecological bubble' reminiscent of the environments they were accustomed to. While the social and economic structures and institutions that most governments inherited after independence were suited to the provision of the small, customised guest houses and villas frequented by the wealthy, they were not compatible with the structures and institutions needed for large-scale mass tourism. Combined with the relations of dependency that resulted from 400 years of colonial rule, the structures of tourism were destined to reproduce the region as a place that existed primarily to satisfy the holiday consumption needs of the more developed industrial economies.

The mass forms of tourism that developed in the 1960s and 1970s were not only ill-suited to the post-colonial economic structures and institutions in existence on the islands, they were also incompatible with the region's physical environment and social institutions. In relation to the region's social institutions, though tourism was a source of employment for large numbers of unskilled and primarily women workers, it provided very few avenues for occupational mobility. In addition the hospitality requirements of housekeeping, waiting or grounds-keeping were often too reminiscent of requirements for service during slavery. Few islanders were happy to engage in performances as the 'friendly local' even though these performances were as important to attracting European and American tourists as the beaches and hotel amenities. The importance of local people to the creation of a holiday in tropical paradise can be seen in the way that the islands were marketed in the late 1960s and early 1970s. Images of white tourists being served by black waiters and housekeepers were important components of the fantasies that were created in order to market the region. As one 1969 Jamaica Tourist Board advertisement entitled 'The Life You Wish You Led' promised:

> The villas come equipped with gentle people named Ivy or Maud or Malcolm who will cook, tend, mend and launder for you. Who will 'Mister Peter, please' you all day long, pamper you with homemade coconut pie … weep when you leave (cited in Patullo 1996, p. 151).

Yet the images of Maud or Malcolm created by the Tourist Board were very out of step with the growing nationalist sentiments that marked the 1970s. Independence combined with the a growing solidarity with the civil rights movement in the USA created new nationalist sentiments on many of the islands. Many of these sentiments were tied to the emergence of black Caribbean identities that were diametrically opposite to the images of servility and deference promulgated in tourism promotional material. By the mid 1970s tourism was popularly regarded as an industry that not only degraded local populations but threatened local cultures. Many felt that tourists brought with them practices that ran counter to local cultural values and notions of decorum. For example, topless sun bathing on local beaches or the wearing of swimming costumes in public places other than the beach, while viewed by many islanders as a vulgar practice, had to be tolerated by workers and communities living in popular tourism spots. The influence that the lifestyles of tourists had on the aspirations and values of young people was also a source of concern to many policy makers and communities. Tourists brought with them a continual reminder of the relative impoverishment of the islands. Their consumption habits and lack of sensitivity to local customs helped to fuel among the young in particular, aspirations for the seemingly luxurious and indulgent lifestyles enjoyed by these visitors that were pursued at any cost.

The lost development decade and the rise of tourism as a primary source of foreign exchange earnings

The growing sense of national pride and a desire for self-reliance in the 1970s became the driving force behind the large loans taken out by island governments to finance the infrastructure: roads and airports, and the infant industries: food processing and light manufacturing needed to stimulate the process of industrialisation. On many islands governments also invested heavily in health and education projects in an effort to overcome the lack of investment in the island populations during the colonial period. These strategies were part of a general strategy of import substitution designed to create self-sufficiency in the production of basic goods and services. The policies of import substitution, however, did not stimulate the development process as envisaged. Few of these state-created industries served international markets, and only a few, regional ones. Given the size of the islands, domestic markets were not large enough to keep local industries like cement manufacture or textiles viable. Thus the combination of inefficient production systems, the oil price crisis, increasing debt and the slowing down of growth (that stimulated large rises in interest rates and failing levels of demand) in the developed world led to the beginning of a period of economic crisis that many islands in the region have not yet recovered from (see Chapter Three for more discussion of issues of debt).

During the 1970s the rate of growth of tourism in traditional destinations like Jamaica and Puerto Rico declined, while new entrants to the industry like Antigua, Dominica and the Dominican Republic recorded the fastest rates of growth (see Plate 5.2). In traditional destinations like Jamaica, the long period of economic and social turmoil that accelerated after the 1974 oil crisis, combined with international press reports critical of Michael Manley's programme of democratic socialism, reduced the pace of growth in visitor arrivals (Stephens and Stephens 1986). In non-traditional destinations, the expansion of tourism represented attempts to diversify economies already in crisis. What became clear, by the mid 1980s, as foreign exchange earnings from agriculture and manufacturing continued to decline, was the increasing importance of tourism to the economic survival of almost all of the islands.

Plate 5.2 *Las Terranas beach in northern Dominican Republic is typical of the scene which attracts tourists*

© David Howard

In response to the crisis facing their economies during this period many islands were obliged to implement Structural Adjustment Programs (SAPs) in order to receive financial assistance from international banks and lending agencies like the World Bank and International Monetary Fund (IMF). Under the SAPs most of the governments in the region implemented policies to create new forms of export-oriented industry (Deere, Antrobus, Bolles, Meléndez, Phillips, Rivera and Safa 1990; McAfee 1991). While the World Bank never encouraged island governments to become more reliant on tourism, the stringent austerity measures of the IMF, combined with the World Bank's narrow focus on liberalisation and deregulation strategies, left the region's governments with few alternative globally competitive exports (Klak 1998; Klak and Myers 1996). The growing reliance on tourism across all of the islands during the late 1970s and 1980s should therefore be viewed as a consequence of economic crisis and the inability of governments to develop other globally competitive exports.

Caribbean governments throughout the late 1970s and early 1980s employed a number of strategies to boost tourism. In Barbados, the state sought to encourage greater local involvement in tourism by building hotels that were subsequently leased to foreign interests. Governments in Jamaica and Curaçao also bought a number of hotels but these purchases were made to 'rescue' private sector firms that had run into financial difficulties (Adam, Cavendish and Mistry 1992; Manley 1982). Manley (1982) states:

> We acquired nearly half the number of major hotels in Jamaica. Again this was not difficult at the time, presumably because a number of foreign operations decided to quit Jamaica after the world economic debacle dealt its blow to international tourism in 1974 and 1975 (Manley 1982, p. 93).

In addition to the acquisition of hotels, many Caribbean governments tried to increase arrivals by opening their tourist markets to the cruise-ship sector and supporting private sector initiatives to develop niche markets. In Jamaica, for example, the state engaged in vigorous advertising and marketing campaigns to boost falling tourist numbers. In one such campaign, visitors were encouraged to explore the island's rich heritage and varied landscape under the slogan, 'we're more than a beach, we're a country'. As the foreign exchange earnings from the agricultural and manufacturing industries declined throughout the 1980s governments worked harder at encouraging larger and larger numbers of tourists to visit their islands, with little regard for the environmental and social costs that many of the tourism strategies imposed.

Finding niches in the global market: cruises and all-inclusives

Of the various strategies embarked upon during the late 1970s and 1980s, two, the cruise destination initiative and the all-inclusive initiative, had a significant impact on the structure, size and growth of tourism in the region. The cruise destination initiative became a significant component of Caribbean tourism in the 1980s (see Plate 5. 3). Currently the region accounts for 46 per cent of the international cruise industry (Kai Guth 1999), with over 20 cruise lines currently in operation. The growth of the cruise industry in the region has been spectacular. Patullo (1996), for example, noted that between 1986 and 1994 the number of cruise-ship arrivals recorded in St. Lucia increased from 58,000 to 173,538, an increase of 199 per cent. Many of the region's governments welcome and promote the cruise market largely because of the income that they derive from port charges and the head taxes that cruise passengers pay. A number of writers, however, (Dickinson 1993; Pattullo 1996) have questioned the extent to which this segment of the industry has made a significant contribution to the region's development. Many of these skeptics argue cruise lines contribute even less to employment and develop even fewer linkages with local economies than land-based hotels. Because they are not located in any one national territory these 'placeless' floating hotels are neither obliged to employ Caribbean nationals in their fleets nor pay many of the taxes levied by governments on land-based hotels.

Overall, of the expenditures by the cruise lines on fuel, chemicals, port services and food, and by passengers on taxes and duty free items, very few are on items produced in the region. Based on figures published in a 1993 study conducted by the Florida-Caribbean Cruise Association (FCCA) (Price Waterhouse 1994), Patullo estimates that cruise ships spent only US$6 per passenger on food and drink produced in the Caribbean. In a 1994 study of the economic impact of tourism in the Caribbean, it was estimated that the average cruise ship passenger spent US$154 at each port stop. It was also estimated that of this amount, 45 per cent was spent on duty-free shopping, 17 per cent on tours and attractions and 8 per cent on food. Given the fact that the majority of duty-free goods in the Caribbean are not locally produced the figures suggest that almost half of the estimated expenditures are not linked to local economies in the region. A number of writers have argued that the figures in this Price Waterhouse study are inflated, and have suggested that the more conservative estimate of US$52 per person per port-stop calculated by the Organization of American States for Jamaica in 1992, might be more accurate (Pattullo 1996).

The extent to which the cruise industry represents a net drain on the island economies becomes clearer when the environmental impacts of the cruise industry are considered. As cruise ships have become larger, issues of waste control have become of serious concern to many environmental policy makers. The FCCA estimates that the average cruise ship (2,000 passengers and crew) generates five tons (4,535 kg) of garbage and waste products *a day*. The storage and disposal of waste during long ocean crossings or while stopping at ports without the infrastructure for disposal is an expensive engineering feat. Recent cases brought before the US federal government indicate that in order to reduce costs some cruise lines have simply dumped their waste products at sea. A report recently released by the US General Accounting Office (US GAO, 2000) found that, from 1993 to 1998 alone, cruise ships were involved in 104 confirmed cases of illegal dumping, and have paid more than $30 million in fines. In 1999

Plate 5.3 *A cruise ship docked at Redcliffe Quay, Antigua beside the Jolly Roger tourist boat. The vessels represent the ultra-modern and fake history, both designed for tourists' pleasure.*

© David Howard

one company, Royal Caribbean Cruises, pleaded guilty to 21 felony counts and agreed to pay $18 million in fines for illegally dumping oily waste water and hazardous wastes in six US jurisdictions, lying to the Coast Guard and falsifying waste discharge records. While the report focused on the problem of illegal dumping only in waters under US jurisdiction, note was made of 17 other alleged incidents occurring outside US waters. While there have been no legal cases brought against a cruiseline in the Caribbean, anecdotal accounts suggest that the region has not been exempt from these practices. The limited contribution of the cruise industry combined with its weak level of integration in the region mirrors that of the many other transnational corporations in the region. In 2000 Princess Cruise, the third largest cruise line in the world, transferred its services from Jamaica to Costa Myer in Mexico because, according to industry sources, it had been offered better incentives (Davis and Roxborough, 2000). Similar disinvestments occurred in St. Lucia in 1992 when CARICOM, the regional economic community agreed to increase the head-tax levied on all cruise passengers to US$10 over a three-year period.

The all-inclusive strategy has been heralded as the most successful of regional attempts to create niche markets in the global industry (Poon, 1988, Poon, 1989). The all-inclusive concept pioneered by the Jamaican-owned Superclubs group, offers tourists the opportunity to have a 'cash-free' vacation. Each resort caters to a particular segment of the tourism market (families, hedonists and heterosexual couples) and at a prepaid price, vacationers are entitled to the unlimited consumption of the hotel's goods and services. The all-inclusive concept has been an enormously economically successful strategy that has become truly Pan-Caribbean in scope. In Jamaica, the all-inclusive sector made the largest contribution to GDP ($J1,604m or US$70m) in 1992 and contributed approximately $J4,623m (US$20m) in direct revenue to the Jamaican government (OAS 1994). This tax contribution represented just over a fifth of the revenue received by the state from the entire tourism industry. It is therefore not surprising that the state assisted the expansion of the two locally-owned resort chains, Sandals and the Superclubs Group. The hotels in these groups expanded from 2 in 1983 providing accommodation for 9.5 per cent of the visitors to Jamaica to 21 in 2001 accounting for over half of all tourists to the island. In 2001 the all-inclusive concept has come to symbolise the Caribbean tourism experience, with hotels in Antigua, Aruba, the Bahamas, Martinique, the Dominican Republic, Guadeloupe, the Turks and Caicos Islands, St. Lucia and the US Virgin Islands, offering these types of holidays.

While the all-inclusive hotels have been described as the solution to tourist fears of crime and harassment (The Economist 2000); others remain ambivalent about their contribution to local economic development (Mullings 1999; Pattullo 1996; The Gleaner January 26 1998). Because all expenses are pre-paid, few tourists in these packaged holidays ever venture outside of the hotel complexes to directly purchase goods or services from locals in the surrounding communities. Indeed, tourists in these hotels are routinely reminded that even small expenditures such as tips are unnecessary, thus effectively closing-off even this opportunity for money to leak into the local community. While all-inclusives have made a significant contribution to government coffers in terms of tax revenue, their contribution to the creation of linkages with local economies has been even more limited than the traditional European Plan hotels. In a 1992 assessment of the economic impact of tourism in Jamaica conducted by the Organization of American States (OAS), for example, it was found that while the eleven all-inclusive hotels in their sample generated the largest amount of revenue, their impact on the economy was smaller than other hotels because they imported more goods and services and employed fewer people, per dollar of revenue (OAS 1994).

It would appear that the success of the all-inclusive holiday strategy has resulted in a growing concentration of foreign exchange earnings into the hands of a few hoteliers. Small hoteliers, for example, complain that they are being squeezed out of the industry by lack of government marketing support that has been largely diverted towards the already successful all-inclusive hotels. Small hotels also complain that the high rates of interest on loans make it difficult for them to provide tourism services that can compete with the all-inclusives (Gayle 1993). Other service providers, primarily those indirectly involved in tourism (taxi drivers, vendors and local restaurant owners) also claim that opportunities to export their services to tourists have declined.

Many local people protest against the enclave nature of all-inclusive hotels and their tendency to privatise and restrict access to prime stretches of beach that legally should be considered public space. On islands like Barbados and Jamaica by law all land and sea below the high-water mark is public property but many beaches can only be accessed by crossing private land and the charges levied by many all-inclusives can be as high as $US200. Much of the discourse used by all-inclusive hotels to justify their exclusionary practices tends to focus on their desire to safeguard tourists from crime and harassment by locals. But in reality their actions routinely alienate local people many of whom must submit to stringent security checks in order even to enter the hotel complexes. The negative social impact of all-inclusives can be seen in the various songs of protest that reflect local hostilities, as the lyrics of the winning 1994 St. Lucia Calypso King Song in **Box 5.1** demonstrates.

■ Box 5.1 Excerpted lyrics from the winning 1994 St. Lucia Carnival King song

Alien

All-inclusive tax elusives
And the truth is
They're sucking up we juices

Buying up every strip of beach
Every treasured spot they reach.

Some put on Sandals
Exclusive vandals
It's a scandal the way they operate
Building brick walls and barricades
Like a state within a state.

For Lucians to enter
For lunch or dinner
We need reservations, passport and visa
And if you sell near the hotel
I wish you well,
They will yell and kick you out to hell

Chorus:

Like an alien
In we own land
I feel like a stranger
And I sensing danger
We can't sell out the whole country
To please the foreign lobby
What's the progress
Is it really success
If we gain ten billion
But lose the land we live on?

Sung by Mighty Pep, lyrics by Rowan Seon.

Source: cited in Patullo 1996: pp. 80–81

These cruise ship and all-inclusive tourism strategies of the 1980s can be considered successful if success is defined in terms of increasing visitor arrivals and government tax revenues. By 1999, travel and tourism services in the Caribbean accounted for 16 per cent of the region's Gross Domestic Product (GDP), 22 per cent of its exports, and 15 per cent of all employment (WTTC 2001). If success, however, is defined in terms of sustainability[5], these strategies did not achieve these goals. While tourism promotion throughout the 1980s expanded Caribbean tourism to islands not traditionally viewed as Caribbean destinations, very little regard was given to the impact of these forms of mass tourism on the social and physical environments in these places.

The environmental and social impacts of mass tourism development in the 1980s

The environmental impact of mass tourism in the Caribbean has only recently begun to be acknowledged (de Albuquerque 1991; Lorah 1995; Nurse 1990; Pattullo 1996; World Bank 1992). While the tourism industry has always been recognised as a heavy consumer of water resources[6] many of the island's policy-makers are now beginning to measure the extent to which site and infrastructure development for tourism has contributed to land consumption, habitat loss and disturbance to ecosystems in the region. A number of studies have argued that the environment in many Caribbean islands has been degraded by activities linked to tourism promotion. For example, coastal areas on most of the islands continue to be threatened from the increased sedimentation that occurs as beach and sand dunes are destroyed to make way for the construction of beachfront hotels. Historically the major forms of destruction were the result of land clearance during the construction of hotels and roads and to artificially create wide stretches of beach. Land clearance of this kind has damaged coral reefs and destroyed valuable coastal habitats such as the wetland environments in St. Maarten and Jamaica. Recently water pollution has become an even greater destructive agent to the ecosystems of the islands. A recent report by UNEP also identified the sewage and solid waste disposal practices in major tourism areas as the most serious threats to coastal zones in the region. While some hotels in the region are connected to central sewage systems, many dispose of sewage effluent through sub-surface means. There is evidence that certain areas of the coastline are periodically contaminated by sewage that poses environmental and health risks. If hotel wastewater plants are operating below optimal capacity sewage effluent is often directly discharged into the sea, resulting in immediate contamination of the marine environment. Combined with pollution from the synthetic organic chemicals, oil, and pathogens discharged by cruise-ships, jet skis and speed boats, eutrophication and deterioration of water quality have become real threats to much of the region's coastal ecosystems and their living resources.

Although scholars and policy-makers have always been wary of the potentially negative social costs of Caribbean tourism, many are beginning to document the extent to which local cultures and social relationships have been transformed by the growing reliance of the islands on the tourism dollar (Hobson, Perry and Dietrich 1994; Kempadoo 1999; McKay 1993; Pattullo 1996). The expansion of tourism across the region during the 1980s, combined with declining rates of economic growth and the austerity programs of reform that many islands have had to implement, has transformed the tourist into a valued and lucrative commodity. Particularly on those islands most affected by economic decline, tourists have complained of being continuously hustled and harassed by locals intent on selling every type of product and service, from local crafts to hair plaiting and sunburn rubs. While the all-inclusive hotels were designed to 'protect' tourists from such 'unwelcome' intrusions, their inability to create significant backward linkages with local economies have only served to increase the need by locals to gain access to the tourist dollar as a form of income generation. Without access to income-generation opportunities in the formal tourism sector, many local people have turned to the informal and underground economy in order to support their households. It is in the informal sector that the most negative social costs associated with tourism can be found.

In a pioneering exploration of the growth of sex tourism in the Caribbean, a number of scholars have explored the relationships of power, the exploitation and public health costs of this growing sector within the region's tourism service (Kempadoo 1999). In case studies drawn from the Anglophone, Francophone, Spanish and Dutch Caribbean, authors point repeatedly to the fact that both Caribbean men and women increasingly become commodities for the consumption of tourists from Europe and North America in particular. It is argued that while demand for this latest aspect of Caribbean tourism is based heavily upon racial and gender stereotypes, it is often because of the unequal economic positions occupied by providers and suppliers that these sexual fantasies are realised. The growth of sex tourism throughout the Caribbean has heightened social tensions within local communities. While the incomes of many sex workers currently sustain households that would otherwise have been destitute (Codrescu 1998; Fusco 1998; Kempadoo 1999), this contribution is rarely recognised. Instead, workers are stigmatised, routinely harassed by police and government officials and abused, with little access to the protections offered to workers in other sectors. Government rhetoric regarding the threat to tourism that sex workers pose, often seems contradictory given the fact that the marketing of the region's tourism relies heavily upon images that promise exotic, sexual encounters (Bolles 1992; Mullings 2001). While sex worker organisations have been established in Suriname and the Dominican Republic, most Caribbean governments continue to take a punitive rather than protective attitude to workers, further driving sex work underground and heightening the violence, exploitation and public health risks that are associated with this type of work.

A sustainable future? Re-defining paradise and Caribbean tourism

Governments in the region recently initiated a formal commitment to the principles of sustainable tourism. Sustainable tourism, with its commitment to maintaining the long-term viability of the economies, societies and environments of regions that export tourism services, a concept whose meaning continues to be debated (Mowforth and Munt 1997; Hall and Lew 1998; Simpson 2001). Butler (1998), for example, argues that when the costs of implementing sustainable tourism policies result in a reduction in tourism development the concept is rarely enthusiastically supported. Thus in places where sustainable tourism practices have been adopted, acceptance has tended to occur when economic benefits are not threatened, or when there has been extensive public relations and marketing of the sustainability principles. In the case of the Caribbean, the factors influencing tourism providers and policy-makers to adopt sustainable tourism practices mirror those observed by Butler. The nature of current commitment to the principles of sustainability in the provision of Caribbean tourism is reflected in the decision by the Association of Caribbean States (ACS) to market the region as a single destination and to monitor the extent to which member countries meet agreed quantifiable sustainability criteria. Once ratified by member-states, the agreement will allow for the marketing of the region internationally as the first sustainable tourism zone in the world. While the notion of sustainability has been a major component of the current rhetoric used to market the region, much of the discussion has focused on ways of expanding tourism markets rather than reducing tourism development. For example, much of the discussion has focused on increasing intra-regional travel. That sustainability as currently outlined in the regional tourism concept embraces economic over non-economic forms of sustainability is understandable, especially given the fact that, in the current global economy with its emphasis on neo-liberal free trade, the region has fewer and fewer options for foreign exchange earnings. Yet it is possible that some strategies, despite their minimal contribution to foreign exchange earnings, could in the long term contribute more to the region's development and the quality of life of its people than current tourism forms.

Changing forms of tourism consumption

A number of scholars have argued that the nature of tourism consumption has been transformed by the emergence of a new, relatively small but wealthy category of tourists since the late 1970s (Mowforth and Munt 1997; Shaw and Williams 1994; Urry 1990, 1994 and 1995). These 'new' tourists, it is argued, are quite different from the traditional mass tourist because they derive satisfaction from travel not only because of the break that tourism creates from the routine of everyday life but also because of the superior cultural and class status that particular types of travel confer. The symbolic capital that certain forms of tourism consumption represent, has created a new class of traveller whose demand for 'non-mass' forms of tourism may encourage the future development of more environmentally, socially and economically sustainable forms of Caribbean tourism. It is argued that 'new' tourists seek travel experiences that convey to others their appreciation of cultural and ecological diversity and their financial ability to pay for such holidays. While many writers rightly warn that the motivations behind certain forms of 'new' tourism may objectify and exploit the landscapes and people that are being 'appreciated' (Mowforth and Munt 1997; Mullings 2001; Munt 1994), these new forms of consumption may also create forms of tourism that are lucrative and spread the tourist dollar beyond the large hotels, airlines and tour operators.

Two such forms of 'new' tourism, eco-tourism and community tourism, are potentially better suited to the region's economic and social structures, institutions and environmental landscapes than the segmented mass tourism of the last 10 years. Eco-tourism with its commitment to nature-based travel that contributes to the conservation of local environments and the well being of local people has been praised by many policy-makers in the region. Projects in Bonaire, the Turks and Caicos Islands and Dominica represent some of the best examples of attempts to encourage this form of tourism. In Bonaire, an island that was never a traditional mass tourism destination, for example, attempts to promote underwater tourism have gone hand in hand with the creation of a self-financing conservation park (see Box 5.2). While tourists are encouraged to explore the island's rich marine flora and fauna and extensive coral formations, they must comply with rigidly enforced regulations. For example, no anchoring is permitted (there is a series of mooring buoys instead), spearfishing is banned and divers are warned not to touch the coral or even to photograph it with a close-up lens. Visiting boats are not allowed to dump their ballast water either – one recent violator was promptly caught and fined. Such attention to detail won Bonaire the *Islands* magazine 'Ecotourism Award' in 1994 (see Box 5.2).

■ Box 5.2 Ecotourism in the Bonaire Marine Park

The Bonaire Marine Park surrounds the islands of Bonaire and Klein Bonaire and extends from the high water mark to the 200' depth contour. The area of the Park is an estimated 2700 hectares.

It was first established in 1979, but due to financial difficulties was not actively managed from 1984 until 1991 when it was revitalized utilizing Dutch Government foreign aid grant funding. Comprehensive legislation exists and is enforced on island.

The major use of the park is for recreational diving and snorkelling with some subsistence fishing by local people and other water sports. The goal of the Marine Park is to protect and preserve the island's marine resources i.e. coral reefs, seagrasses and mangroves, whilst maximizing returns from both recreation and commerce. The Bonaire Marine Park in the Dutch Antilles is one of the first protected marine areas in the Caribbean to have become entirely self-financing through levying admission fees to scuba divers. Fees support the on-going active management of the park's coral reef, sea grass and mangrove ecosystems, as well as educational activities and orientation sessions for divers, who are the largest users of the park.

The government of Bonaire ceded management of the Marine Park to a local non-governmental, not for profit foundation called STINAPA, Bonaire. STINAPA Bonaire has recently undergone a radical restructuring whereby the various user groups (hoteliers, dive operators, fishermen, tourist office) now have a seat on the Board of STINAPA.

The system has been an unqualified success since it was introduced in 1992. Recent studies by Dr. Callum Roberts and the volunteer group REEF have shown that Bonaire's fish population is the most diverse in the Caribbean and ranks among the best in the world.

Source: www.bmp.org/html

Community tourism on the other hand, aims to include and benefit local communities, particularly indigenous peoples and villagers. For instance, local people might host tourists in their communities, managing the scheme communally and sharing the profits. There are many types of community tourism projects, including some where the 'community' works with a commercial tour operator, but all community tourism projects should give local people a fair share of the benefits/profits and a say in deciding how incoming tourism is managed. A number of islands have started to explore the possibilities for community-based forms of tourism. In Jamaica, for example, the Tourism Product Development Company (TPDCo), is currently involved in a community development in the Accompong Maroon settlement, a community whose traditions today still strongly reflect the history of struggle and resistance against slavery. As part of the project it is hoped that tourists will stay in the homes of the residents, and share in the experiences of their everyday lives. As the acting director of TPDCo states: 'visitors will come and stay in the homes of the residents, eat from the same pot, and immerse themselves in the culture of the area'. Similarly, Cuba, in Las Terrazas situated in the biosphere reserve of Sierra del Rosario,[7] the government and the community formed a tourism co-operative to preserve the region's cultural and ecological value, in ways that benefit the local community and environment. The community of Las Terrazas was formed in 1971 and subsidised by the state to regenerate the forest, severely damaged by centuries of deforestation due to the coffee and tobacco farming and ranching. While tourism provides more than a million dollars in income each year, the scale and pace of expansion is regulated by the community who have the power to limit the number of visitors given access to the area.

While plans to support community tourism in Accompong and in Las Terrazas may direct much needed income to these areas, it is crucial that decisions over the scale, pace or even implementation of this project be made by the majority of the members of this community rather than external tourism managers and community elites. It remains to be seen whether current and future efforts to develop sustainable forms of tourism, will be successful. While it is clear that tourism will continue to be the major source of economic survival for all the islands in the immediate future, without the creation of true links that empower local communities and foster linkages with other sectors in Caribbean economies, the future of 'paradise' will continue to be in jeopardy.

Notes

[1] A global system of production where third world countries functioned as the primary producers of the agricultural and mineral raw materials used by first world countries to their production of manufactured goods.

[2] After a massive slave uprising in 1791 and a two-year war that started in 1802, the black inhabitants of the French colony Saint-Domingue proclaimed, on January 1, 1804, their independence from France and the birth of Haiti, the second republic in the Americas and the first free black republic in the world.

[3] Air Jamaica began as a venture between Air Canada and the Jamaican Government in 1969 using the name of a former airline that, in association with the British Overseas Airways Corporation (BOAC) and BWIA, operated an international service in the early 1960s. In 1994

Air Jamaica was privatised as part of islands structural adjustment program and is currently chaired by Gordon 'Butch' Stewart owner of the Sandals 'all-inclusive' Resorts Group.

[4] The presidential summary of the annual report for British West Indies Airways states that between 1998 and 2000 BWIA was the only regional based airline that was in profit (British West Indies Airways, 2003).

[5] For the purposes of this chapter, sustainable tourism is defined as tourism that is viewed at various levels as socially and morally appropriate as well as environmentally suitable.

[6] Consumption by tourists may be up to ten times more per head than the local community, especially in hot climates, where swimming pool, showers, golf courses and baths are heavily used (WTTC, 1995).

[7] Sierra del Rosario was designated a Biosphere Reserve by the United Nations Education, Scientific and Cultural Organisation (UNESCO) in 1985. 'La Terrazas community was conceived as a miniature city, with basic facilities for its urban functioning and an architectural style whose key element is the harmonization of buildings with the landscape and the relief ... [the] infrastructure aims to integrate tourism into the community' (www.dtcuba.com/eng/buscar_reportajes.asp?cod=48.)

References

Adam, C., Cavendish, W. and Mistry, P. 1992: *Adjusting Privatization Case Studies from Developing Countries*. London: Heinemann.

Bolles, L. 1992: 'Sand, sea and the forbidden'. *Transforming Anthropology*, 3 (1), pp. 30–34.

Britton, S. G. 1991. 'Tourism, capital and place: towards a critical geography of tourism'. *Environment and Planning D. Society and Space*, 9 (4), pp. 451–478.

Bryden, I. 1973: *Tourism and Development: a Case Study of the Commonwealth Caribbean*. Cambridge: Cambridge University Press.

Butler, R. 1998: 'Sustainable tourism – looking backwards in order to progress?' In Hall, M. and Lew, A. (eds.) *Sustainable Tourism: A Geographical Perspective*. Harlow, Essex: Addison Wesley Longman. pp. 25–34

British West Indies Airways 2003: CEO's corner. *Caribbean Beat Travel Magazine*, January/February http://www.bwee.com/about/ceojan03.htm.

Cater, E. 1995: 'Consuming places: global tourism'. In Allen, J. and Hamnett, C. (eds.) *A Shrinking World: Global Unevenness and Inequality*. New York: Oxford University Press. pp. 183–232.

Codrescu, A. 1998 'Picking the flowers of the revolution'. *The New York Times Magazine*. February 1, pp. 32–35.

Davis, G. and Roxborough, P. 2000 'Jamaica to lose $400m in cruise ship fallout'. *Jamaica Gleaner Online*: Kingston.

de Albuquerque, K. 1991: 'Conflicting claims on Antigua coastal resources: the case of the McKinnons and Jolly Hill salt ponds'. In Girvan, N. and Simmons, D. (eds.) *Caribbean Ecology and Economics*. Barbadas: Caribbean Conservation Association. pp. 195–205.

Deere, C., Antrobus, P., Bolles, L., Melédridez, E., Phillips, P., Rivera, M. and Safa, H. 1990: *In the Shadows of the Sun: Caribbean Development Alternatives and US Policy*. Oxford: Westview Press.

Dickinson, R. 1993: 'Cruise industry outlook in the Caribbean'. In Gayle, D. and Goodrich, J. (eds.) *Tourism Marketing and Management in the Caribbean*. London: Routledge. pp. 113–121.

Fusco, C. 1998: 'Hustling for dollars: Jineterismo in Cuba'. In Kempadoo, K. and Doezema, J. (eds.). *Global Sex Workers: Rights, Resistance and Redefinition*. New York: Routledge. pp. 151–166.

Gayle, D. 1993: 'The Jamaican tourist industry: domestic economic growth and development'. In Gayle, D. and Goodrich, J. (eds.) *Tourism Marketing and Management in the Caribbean*. London: Routledge pp. 41–57.

Hall, C. M. and Lew, A. 1998: *Sustainable Tourism: a Geographical Perspective*. Harlow, Essex: Longmans.

HMSO Department of Employment 1971: *Manpower Studies No. 10 Hotels*. London: HMSO.

Hobson, J, Perry, S. and Dietrich, U. 1994: 'Tourism, health and quality of life: challenging the responsibility of using the traditional tenets of sun, sand, sea, and sex in tourism marketing'. *Journal of Travel and Tourism Marketing*. 3 (4): pp. 21–38.

Jefferson, O. 1972: *The Post War Economic Development of Jamaica*. Kingston: Institute of Social and Economic Research.

Kai Guth, H. 1999: 'Cruise industry proves mixed blessing for economies of Caribbean island. *Environment Hawaii* 9 (11).

Kempadoo, K. (ed.) 1999: *Sun, Gold and Sex: Tourism and Sex Work in the Caribbean*. Boulder: Rowman Littlefield.

Klak, T. (ed.) 1998: *Globalization and Neoliberalism: The Caribbean Context*. Boulder, Co: Rowman & Littlefield Publishers.

Klak, T. and Myers, G. 1996: *Industrialization-By-Invitation in the 1990s: the Discursive Tactics of Neoliberal Development*. Publisher unknown.

Lorah, P. 1995: An unsustainable path: tourism's vulnerability to environmental decline in Antigua. *Caribbean Geography.*, 6 (1), pp. 28–39.

Manley, M. 1982: *Struggle in the Periphery*. London: Writers and Readers Publishing.

McAfee, K. 1991: *Storm Signals: Structural Adjustment and Development Alternatives in the Caribbean*. London: Zed Books.

McKay, L. 1993: 'Women's contribution to tourism in Negril, Jamaica'. In Momsen, J. (ed.) *Women and Change in the Caribbean: Pan Caribbean Perspective*. Bloomington: Indiana University Press.

Mowforth, M. and Munt, I. 1997: *Tourism and Sustainability: New Tourism in the Third World*. New York: Routledge.

Mullings, B. 1999: 'Globalization, flexible tourism and the international sex trade in Jamaica'. In Kempadoo, K. (ed.) *Sun, Sex and Gold: Tourism and Sex Work in the Caribbean*. Boulder, Co: Rowman & Littlefield Publishers.

Mullings, B. 2001: 'Fantasy tours: exploring the global consumption of Caribbean sex tourism'. In Gottdiener, M. (ed.) *New Forms of Consumption: Consumers, Culture and Commodification*. Boulder, Co: Rowman & Littlefield Publishers. pp. 227–250.

Munt, I. 1994: 'Eco-tourism or ego-tourism?' *Race and Class*. 36 (July/Sept.) pp. 49–60.

Nurse, L. 1990: 'The deterioration of Caribbean coastal zones: a recurring issue in regional development'. In Cox, J. and Embree, C. (eds.) *Sustainable Development in the Caribbean*. Halifax: The Institute for Research on Public Policy.

OAS 1994: *Economic Analysis of Tourism in Jamaica. Unpublished technical report of the OAS in co-operation with the Jamaica Tourist Board and the Ministry of Industry, Tourism and Commerce*. Washington D.C.: Organization of American States.

Olsen, B. 1997: 'Environmentally sustainable development and tourism: lessons for Negril, Jamaica'. *Human Organization* 56.3. 290.

Pattullo, P. 1996: *Last Resorts: The Cost of Tourism in the Caribbean*. London: Cassell.

Peters, M. 1969: *International Tourism*. London: Hutchinson.

Poon 1988: 'Innovation and the future of Caribbean tourism'. *Tourism Management*. 9 (3). pp. 213–220.

Poon, A. 1989: 'Competitive strategies for a "new tourism"'. In Cooper, C. (ed.) *Progress in Tourism, Recreation and Hospitality Management*. Vol. 1. London: Belhaven Press. pp. 91–102.

Price Waterhouse 1994: *The Economic Impact of the Passenger Cruise Industry on the Caribbean*. Florida: Florida-Caribbean Cruise Association.

Shaw, G. and Williams, A. 1994: *Critical Issues in Tourism: a Geographical Perspective*. Cambridge, Massachusetts: Blackwell Publishers.

Simpson, L. 2001: 'Carib could be world's first "sustainable tourism zone"'. *The Jamaica Gleaner*. Kingston.

Stephens, E. and Stephens, J. 1986: *Democratic Socialism in Jamaica: The Political Movement and Social Transformation in Dependent Capitalism*. London: Macmillan.

The Economist. 'Local ambivalence about Caribbean tourism is damaging the industry'. 2000.

The Gleaner January 26 1998: 'Only Big Man benefiting from Tourists Safety'.

Thomas, C. 1988: *The Poor and the Powerless: Economic Policy and Change in the Caribbean*. London: Latin American Bureau.

US GAO 2000: Marine pollution: progress made to reduce marine pollution by cruise ships but important issues remain. Gao/RCED-00-48.

Urry, J. 1990: *The Tourist Gaze*. London: Sage.

Urry, J. 1994: 'Cultural change and contemporary tourism'. *Leisure Studies*. 14 (4). pp. 233–238.

Urry, J. 1995: *Consuming Places*. New York: Routledge.

World Bank 1992: *Caribbean Region: Current Economic Situation, Regional Issues and Capital Flows, 1992*. Washington D.C.: The World Bank.

WTTC 2001: *Tourism Satellite Accounting Research Caribbean*. London: World Travel and Tourism Council.

6
Contexts of migration and diasporic identities

Laurence Brown

Introduction

Across the Caribbean archipelago, migration has been one of the most significant forces defining and shaping its island societies. The movements of Amerindian settlement across the region were transformed from the sixteenth century by European colonisation and the forced migration of enslaved Africans (see Chapter Eight). The abolition of the trans-Atlantic slave trade in the nineteenth century was followed by new waves of indentured immigrants from Asia, Africa and Europe. These population movements have not only made the Caribbean a unique intersection of diasporas, but have also entwined its heterogeneous communities with each other. Migration has therefore been both a unifying force in the region – with movements of peoples extending across political or linguistic borders – as well as exacerbating the diversity within each society.

Migration's dual impact of fuelling commonality and diversity, which is so visible in histories of immigration *into* the region, is even more striking in the waves of emigration *from* Caribbean territories. This chapter focuses on the nineteenth and twentieth century movements of Caribbean peoples, and particularly how the dimensions, destinations and character of these migratory currents have changed over this period. The flows of migrants across and outside the Caribbean have profoundly affected the societies which they leave behind (however temporarily), from the nature of family life, the character of local economies, to the mental worlds of their home islands. A second concern of the chapter is to map the nature of the communities and cultures which Caribbean migrants have constructed in a range of differing destinations. These diasporic identities powerfully link migrants to home and have often provided the very basis for them to challenge the obstacles of their new environments (see Plate 6.1). This diversity of experiences and identities is perhaps the core defining element of the Caribbean diaspora (Chamberlain 1998; Foner 2001; Levine 1987)

Migrant labour, post-emancipation society and the sugar economy

At the opening of the nineteenth century, the European colonies of the Caribbean were dependent on both the complex networks of regional movements between the

Plate 6.1 *Dominican Republic political electioneering in Washington Heights, New York, USA*
© David Howard

island territories and on the constant trans-Atlantic traffic of imported slave labour and the export of agricultural staples, especially sugar, tobacco and coffee. The high prices for such tropical produce meant that slave societies were overwhelmingly focused on export production and therefore dependent on sea-borne supplies for their subsistence. Shipping routes through the region also carried a regular flow of colonial officials, planters, merchants, overseers, skilled slaves, domestic servants and field slaves both within and between the different European empires. Such currents of free and forced migration were central to both the plantation economies of the larger territories, and the sea-based commerce of the marginal smaller islands.

Despite common connections to imperial trade and to neighbouring territories, each colonial society was shaped by its own distinctive demography and geography. From the early 1600s, the British islands of the eastern Caribbean – Barbados, Antigua, St. Kitts, Nevis, Montserrat – had their small surface areas almost completely monopolised by intensive sugar cultivation. The environmental strains caused by plantation agriculture made them dependent on extremely high populations of slave labour to maintain production levels. During the nineteenth century, the focus of economic activity in the Caribbean shifted from these 'old islands' to new areas whose fertile soils promised higher yields and greater profits. Trinidad and British Guiana (now Guyana), which were claimed as British colonies at the turn of the 1800s, were joined by the Spanish colonies of Cuba and Puerto Rico as the new centres for sugar production in the region. In all four territories, the creation of large centralised plantations and investment in new processing technology allowed for economies of scale which dramatically expanded sugar exports. With the abolition of the Atlantic slave trade and then of slavery itself during the nineteenth century, this transformation in the regional economy demanded a search for migrant labour.

For British Guiana and Trinidad, the British abolition of the Atlantic slave trade in 1807 threatened their expanding plantations with economic collapse, as both colonies were dependent on constant shipments of African slaves to even maintain their population levels. This labour shortage was worsened with the abolition of slavery in the British Caribbean between 1834 and 1838. Legal emancipation sparked a period of intense debate and uncertainty over whether colonial export economies could be maintained by free labour. As those who had been slaves and their former masters began to negotiate the basis for a new social order, the process of transformation differed markedly across the British territories. The rugged environments of Trinidad, Jamaica, British Guiana and the Windward Islands had preserved unclaimed physical spaces outside of plantation or government control. These highlands had been important sites of slave resistance and with emancipation were rapidly taken up by those keen to construct their own freedom (see Chapter Two). Therefore, in those British territories not completely monopolised by plantation production, access to land fuelled internal migration as freed peoples asserted their independence from the plantations.

In the older British colonies of Barbados and the Leewards Islands, the dimensions of this flight from the estates were considerably constrained. With access to land controlled by the estates, planters sought to make their workforces completely dependent on plantation employment by keeping their former slaves on the edge of subsistence. In response, the latter sought to use wage labour, peasant farming and mobility to neighbouring estates, towns or territories to claim an alternative life. With fewer opportunities for internal migration, the islanders of the Leewards and Barbados viewed temporary or permanent external migration as an important form of economic advancement and political resistance (Richardson 1983).

Unlike the subsistence wages offered on the 'old' islands, the substantial exodus of ex-slaves from the estates in Trinidad and British Guiana had caused southern planters to offer considerably higher wages through a task-work system. Such conditions and the opportunity of land settlement all represented a substantial degree of worker autonomy which was of crucial importance for those who had lived through chattel slavery. These terms were an important part of the recruiting efforts of Guyanese and Trinidadian planters who sought to use both privately chartered shipping and public funds to transport migrant labour from the old British islands. The use of immigration agents to provide the passage for potential migrants, or the offer to ship's captains of a bounty for each labourer transported, were seen by the colonial elites in the other British colonies as a direct threat to their own interests.

Between 1838 and 1839, the planter-dominated legislatures of Barbados and the Leeward Islands swiftly enacted a series of laws to prevent the feared departure of their workers to the southern colonies. Despite the façade of paternalism in the new legislation against 'unscrupulous' immigration agents and to 'protect' the junior *and* elderly dependents of migrants from abandonment, such laws had an obvious economic intent (Richardson 1983, pp. 82–3). Such constraints failed to prevent an estimated 20,000 migrants from the British islands of the Eastern Caribbean travelling to British Guiana and Trinidad in the decade following 1838. While contemporaries described this movement as overwhelmingly composed of male field labourers, it also comprised significant numbers of women and children (partly due to British regulations requiring gender balance in immigration schemes funded by colonial governments).

The British state ultimately banned the bounty systems of recruitment as causing dangerous tensions between its West Indian colonies, but more significant in stifling the flow of movement south was the economic depression of 1846 that resulted from the British removal of protective tariffs on sugar. The collapse of sugar prices fuelled a major economic and social crisis across the British Caribbean, as planters severely cut wages and the size of their workforces to compensate for its failing value. Unwilling to pay the relatively high wages which had previously attracted regional migrants, planters in Trinidad and British Guiana increasingly relied on indentured immigration from India, West Africa, Madeira and China. While in the short-term the depression ended organised labour recruitment from the British islands, its long-term impact was to reinforce the changing character of migrant labour in the region.

The recruitment of this new multi-ethnic indentured workforce was heavily subsidised by loans from the imperial and colonial governments. Planters not only avoided much of the direct economic costs of the new immigration, but also gained more control over their workforce. The indentureship contracts of the new arrivals created a range of legislative restrictions which limited the immigrants to estate labour. This shift away from the regional migration of free labour to the importation of indentured workers from outside the region became the model which was also adopted in the French Antilles following the French abolition of slavery in 1848. In Martinique and Guadeloupe, colonial elites claimed that the experience of the British colonies showed that economic production could only be continued through the importation of a replacement workforce from Africa and Asia. Significantly, French planters did not look to recruit migrants from the neighbouring British colonies until the early 1860s, when they faced increasing difficulties in recruiting indentured labour from outside the region (Brown 2002).

During the 1860s, the expansion of sugar production in the British West Indies was fuelled by the continuing arrival of Indian immigrants under long-term indenture, and the development of seasonal migration by workers from within the region. The need for labour was heightened by the expansion of sugar production in Trinidad and British Guiana during the second half of the nineteenth century. British capital in the two territories focused on the creation of large central refining factories equipped with modern vacuum pans and centrifuges to increase the amounts of sugar extracted from the cane. Such modernisation considerably intensified the production process, making harvesting more concentrated and intensive. While Asian indentured immigrants who were legally tied to the estates became the main workforce for planting and cultivating, the intensified labour needs of harvest meant that outside gangs of cane cutters were recruited from local villages or from the distant islands. The seasonal arrivals of Barbadians and Leeward Islanders to British Guiana were 'seasoned agricultural labourers – fully capable of strenuous physical exertion and of performing the skilled task of cane-cutting' (Rodney 1981, p. 48). Labour specialisation and social segregation kept these two immigrant workforces distinct but interlinked, as sugar exports from Trinidad and British Guiana reached record levels in the 1870s.

The collapse of sugar prices in the mid-1880s due to competition from European subsidised beet-sugar, not only caused a substantial decrease in seasonal migration for harvest, but also marked the shifting focus of sugar production from the British to the Spanish Caribbean. Cuba had been economically and socially transformed from the late eighteenth century by its entry into the global sugar market. By 1860 Cuba produced almost a third of the world's sugar, but its massive dependence on slave labour was ended only in 1886 as part of the struggle for national independence. Paralleling the abolition of slavery, the Cuban sugar industry had increasingly concentrated production through large centralised sugar mills (or *centrales*) whose economies of scale generated increased demands for harvest labour.

The modernisation caused by the expansion of the *centrales* in Cuba and the Dominican Republic was fundamentally shaped by increasing US economic investment, political hegemony and privileged access to US markets. This conjuncture was perhaps most strikingly exemplified by the US military occupation of Haiti and the Dominican Republic during the First World War. During the occupation an estimated half a million Haitian peasants became seasonal migrants in the sugar harvests of the Dominican Republic or Cuba, a process deliberately encouraged by the US authorities (Lundahl 1982). At the same time thousands of migrants from Jamaica, the Leeward and Windward Islands, Barbados and Dutch Curaçao either migrated seasonally or settled in the two countries. Perhaps as many as half a million Afro-Caribbean migrants travelled legally and illegally to Cuba and the Dominican Republic in the wake of the First World War when soaring sugar prices caused dramatic economic growth in the two countries.

In Cuba, there were significant differences between these streams of migration as the Haitian migrants were more likely to be male fieldworkers who lived in barracks for the harvest while Jamaican migrants were almost equally divided between men and women, with the latter working in domestic service or as seamstresses. For the English-speaking migrants, sharing a common language with their American employers not only gave women opportunities as domestics, but also enabled some men to claim skilled work in the sugar factories (Knight 1985). Within the hierarchy of sugar production, language and their previous experience in the industry helped a few British West

Indians establish permanent positions in the *centrales*, however, while their experiences differed from the Haitian migrants, they both faced the common obstacles of racial discrimination and intensifying harassment.

Throughout the early 1900s, Cuban and Dominican authorities were consistently hostile to non-white immigration. While during the brief boom that followed 1918, the sugar industry had been able to assert its own needs for migrant labour against public opinion, by the mid-1920s there were intensifying demands in both countries for an end to immigration. Migrants who left the sugar estates or remained after harvest were frequently subjected to police harassment or violence. Increasingly, Cuban quarantine regulations were zealously enforced to deter immigrants while those without employment were rapidly repatriated, which particularly threatened seasonal workers. By 1933 legislation restricted employment of foreigners, all of which tightly constricted the lives of those who remained in Cuba. In the Dominican Republic, the antagonism against Haitian workers reached a more bloody conclusion, as under the dictatorship of Truffillo in 1937, troops massacred an estimated 20,000 migrants. Across the Hispanic Caribbean during the 1930s, nationalist opposition to US economic and political hegemony increasingly focused on the forced repatriation of black West Indian migrants.

From gold rush to silver men: migration across the Caribbean Basin

Whilst the main movements of population within the Caribbean were linked to the seasonal rhythms and economic shifts of the sugar industry, there were always other currents of migration which became increasingly important by the end of the nineteenth century. From the mid-1800s, Barbadians were recruited to work in Brazil and the Congo while the lure of gold drew small numbers of Jamaicans to the shores of California and Australia. The 1870s sugar boom in Trinidad created a wide range of employment opportunities for migrants from construction work, domestic service and policing (Johnson 1973). Many Barbadians shifted into urban occupations in Trinidad, while other migrants moved on to the gold fields of Venezuela in 1870s and 1880s. The Venezuelan gold rushes powerfully impacted on Dominica, which had been relatively isolated from the earlier post-emancipation migration currents. Equally, in Bermuda in the early 1900s, the construction of naval docks provided employment opportunities for those in the northern Leeward Islands (Richardson 1983, pp. 111–22).

Still other West Indians travelled to Panama at the turn of the century in a mass migration which fundamentally transformed not only the Isthmus itself, but also their home societies across the Caribbean. The linking of the Pacific and Atlantic oceans took four efforts from 1850 to 1914, each of which was heavily reliant on West Indian labour. The gold rush to California was the spur to the 1850 construction of a railway across Panama that would considerably speed travel between the Americas' two coasts. Construction of the 48-mile railway across the Isthmus was completed in 1855 with an estimated labour force of 5,000 West Indians (Newton 1984, p. 30). These were mostly

Jamaicans, recruited by a company agent or ship's captains working on commission who arranged free transportation to Panama similar to the schemes used by sugar plantations in Trinidad and British Guiana.

From 1879, immigrant labour re-emerged as central to a second attempt to traverse the Isthmus when French entrepreneur Ferdinand de Lesseps championed the construction of a sea canal linking the Atlantic and the Pacific. Faced with the deadly obstacles of malaria and yellow-fever, the sponsors of the *Compagnie Universelle du Canal Interoceanique* wrongly claimed that black workers were immune from such tropical dangers. In March 1881 the French company put up posters in Jamaica promising wages of a dollar a day on the project, while they also established recruiting offices in Barbados, St. Lucia and Martinique that drew migrants from almost all of the eastern islands. Its estimated that as many as 50,000 West Indians worked on the French canal during the 1880s, almost half of whom were Jamaican (Newton 1984, p. 23). With the ever-present threat of disease, it is not surprising that West Indians would move through the country seeking to negotiate better wages and conditions on the different sites of canal-work..

In late 1888 the grand project of the sea canal was halted, when the *Compagnie Universelle* was declared bankrupt. Only two-fifths of the canal had been completed, while its West Indian workforce was left stranded on the Isthmus. As British subjects, large numbers sought aid from the British consul for repatriation who in turn called on their respective island governments. In Jamaica, St. Lucia, St. Kitts and Barbados, the local assemblies were strongly opposed to paying for the repatriation of such large numbers, especially given their antipathy to the initial migration to Panama in the first place. In 1889 the Jamaican government reluctantly spent a total of £4,409 on repatriating 7,522 of its citizens. Its hostility to repatriation was reflected in the instructions to port officials to keep the belongings of the returnees until the full costs had been repaid. In Barbados funds for repatriation were only granted due to repeated pressure from the British Colonial Secretary, while some authorities suggested that stranded Barbadians should only be assisted to migrate to other counties rather than return to their crowded home (Newton 1984, p. 57).

These debates over repatriation in the British West Indies strongly shaped the later efforts to complete the construction of the Canal with migrant labour. In 1892, French construction was renewed by a *Compagnie Nouvelle du Canal de Panama*, although the British colonies were now only willing to allow the recruitment of workers if there was a contract assuring repatriation or deposits paid to their colonial treasuries. Faced with such restrictions, the new company mobilised the large numbers of West Indians who had remained in Panama after the collapse of the *Compagnie Universelle*. In early 1904 construction was taken over by the USA which months earlier had encouraged Panama to declare its independence from Columbia. A Canal Zone which was 10 miles wide and 45 miles long was directly controlled by the US military through the Isthmian Canal Commission (ICC).

Following its predecessors, the ICC immediately sought to organise the recruitment of Jamaican labourers. However, failed negotiations with the Governor of Jamaica, meant that the ICC turned instead to Barbados whose concerns about overpopulation made it more amenable to their demands. The transportation of over 30,000 workers from across the Eastern Caribbean was therefore directed through Barbados and Martinique between 1904 and 1913 (Newton 1984, p. 41). Recruited workers signed service contract for 500 days of labour at a $1 per 10 hour day, which also guaranteed quarters, medical attention and return passage (Richardson 1985, p. 118). The total number of migrants from the Eastern Caribbean to Panama should probably be doubled as many of these recruited workers either sent back passage money for family members, or were followed by others who paid their own passage. Paralleling this organised recruitment, the ICC also encouraged the spontaneous migration of thousands of Jamaicans to Panama by giving them preference in employment and preventing the Panamanian government from enforcing its restrictive immigration legislation. Facing underemployment and low wages at home, for most British West Indians the canal seem a window of opportunity.

The initial focus of the ICC's workforce was on the building of housing and improvement of sanitation in the Canal Zone, particularly combating malaria and yellow-fever. While the dangers of these diseases were eventually minimised, the constantly wet working conditions of labourers on the canal put them at risk of pneumonia and typhoid. Significantly, white American ICC employees received considerably better housing and medical care than the Afro-Caribbean migrants. Reflecting the segregation of the US military, the entire project's workforce, their levels of payment and conditions were divided by race. This racial division was symbolised by the ICC pay roll in which whites were paid in gold US dollars and blacks paid in silver Panamanian dollars.

The phrase 'silver men', used to describe West Indian returnees from Panama, therefore embodied both the promise of economic advancement through migration, and the second class treatment which these workers received on the canal. The phrase also hints at the demographic and economic impact that this migration had on the small islands of the Eastern Caribbean as their resident populations became increasingly female and Panama money transformed their societies. The remittances and savings of the migrants caused not only a fundamental improvement in material living conditions for many, but also encouraged the creation of a cash economy and a move away from the plantations. Bonham Richardson estimates that at least one million pounds reached Barbados from Panama, which revolutionised the lives of the Barbadian working class through the acquisition of small land holdings and the creation of small businesses and friendly societies (Richardson 1985).

Just as Caribbean migrants had played a vital role in the transformation of the landscape and society of Panama, so they had a similar impact on the west coast of neighbouring Costa Rica. In 1874 construction began to link the inland with the natural port of Limon by rail. The construction of the railway laid the basis for creation of an export-orientated banana industry that was dominated by US capital (Harpelle 2001). The high mortality caused by malaria and yellow-fever on the railway meant that West Indians, particularly Jamaicans, formed the bulk of the immigrant labour force. Due to the higher wages of the Canal Zone, the railway was forced to offer land concessions to keep its West Indian workers from deserting across the border to Panama (Chomsky 1996, pp. 27–8).

On its completion the railway became the key conduit in transporting all exports to Limon, which gave considerable power to its US-owner the United Fruit Company. As in Panama, the company imposed US segregation between whites and blacks through its gold and silver payrolls which extended to housing, health services, recreation and social life. West Indians responded to such racism by stressing their British citizenship to demand racial equality and by preserving their distinctive identities. The United Fruit Company also sought to use ethnic differences to maximise its control over its employees. West Indians and Costa Ricans were treated as two separate workforces – the United Fruit Company directly hired West Indians to whom it was willing to pay more and supplied basic housing and services, while locals were employed through subcontractors. Racial antagonisms between the two groups, as in Panama, could then be used to undermine strikes and labour unions (for further discussion of issues of race and ethnicity see Chapter Seven).

Fuelled by the railway, banana exports from Costa Rica rose until the early 1910s when plant disease caused a decline until the dramatic collapse of the Great Depression. In 1927 there were an estimated 20,000 West Indians resident in the country (Harpelle 2001, p. 70). Many were small land holders who were suffering from the United Fruit Company's monopoly of the railroad and its refusal to allow them to turn to subsistence farming as banana prices collapsed. They also faced the hostility of the Costa Rican government which, during the 1930s, sought to forbid West Indians from employment outside the Atlantic coast. Similarly in Panama, the Depression of the 1930s fuelled government attempts at mobilising nationalist racism by excluding West Indians from citizenship. Despite persecution, or perhaps in reaction to it, permanent West Indian communities were formed in both countries, each seeking to preserve their island cultures within a commitment to a new nation (Chomsky 1996).

One significant exception to the increasing restriction of migration across the Caribbean during the 1930s, were the Dutch islands of Curaçao and Aruba that after the First World War emerged as important oil refining centres. The recruitment of several thousand British West Indians stretched into the 1950s when modernisation and automation led to a cut in the foreign workforce. Refinery workers were housed in company barracks, which like those in the Hispanic Caribbean, Panama and Costa Rica isolated them from the local population. Many eventually returned home where their 'Curaçao' or 'Aruba' houses built of concrete rather than wood acted as symbols of migrant success stretching from Grenada to Montserrat (Philpott 1973, pp. 28, 75).

During the Second World War, American military bases provided temporary employment for large numbers of regional migrants in Trinidad, Antigua, St. Thomas and the Bahamas. The conflict also caused thousands of refugees to flee the Vichy-controlled French Antilles for the neighbouring British islands. Following the war, construction and tourism emerged as key economic industries in the region, attracting both legal and illegal migrant workers to the Virgin Islands, Bahamas and Barbados (Marshal 1979). While these old sugar islands had been marked in the nineteenth century by large outflows of their population, with the economic opportunities of tourism they have increasingly become 'receiving' as well as 'sending' societies. Attracting migrants from Haiti, Jamaica, Guyana the Leeward and Windward Islands, they are often used as stepping stones for re-migration on to North America or Europe.

Sojourners or settlers in the 'mother country': West Indians in Europe

Though migration within the Caribbean basin was shaped by the sugar economy and the impact of foreign capital and politics, West Indian emigration to Europe has been formed out of the changing relationship of colonialism. In moving across the Caribbean, migrants often crossed the borders of empire, however, in Europe, their movements overwhelmingly followed the ties of the 'mother country'. The imperial relationship gave migrants a common culture with the old world of Europe, however their colonial status set limits to their integration in that society. During the nineteenth century, the majority of migrants to England, France and the Netherlands were members of their island's ruling elite. Education abroad or simply experience of the 'mother country' was an important symbol of social status when they returned home. Elite migration to Europe therefore reinforced colonial hierarchies of race and class in the Caribbean.

The Second World War marked a fundamental change in the character of Caribbean migration to Europe and in the nature of their colonial relationships. From the British West Indies, 8,000 volunteers travelled to Britain to participate in the war effort (see Chapter Two for more discussion). Stationed across the country as service personnel or skilled workers, their experiences overseas and economic stagnation at home encouraged them to re-migrate back to Britain after the end of the war. In June 1948, the former troopship *SS Empire Windrush* docked in Britain carrying 492 West Indians, half of whom had seen war duty in Britain (Harris 1993). Their arrival symbolised the new wave of working class Afro-Caribbean migrants who, despite the labour shortage in post-war Britain, were immediately defined as a social problem by authorities and the media (Byron 1995; Carter et al 1993). In 1948 the subjects of Britain's remaining colonies had been conferred UK citizenship in the belief that most migrants to the 'mother country' would come from the white Commonwealth rather than from the Caribbean or Indian sub-continent. With public debate focused on the arrival of black immigration, British moves to decolonisation in the Caribbean during 1962 directly paralleled the removal of West Indian's right of entry into the former 'mother country' (Hansen, 2000).

The flow of Caribbean migrants to Britain during the mid-1950s numbered 25,000 annually, however the rush to beat the new immigration restrictions resulted in 107,000 arrivals from the region in 1961 and 1962. The Commonwealth Immigration Act of 1962 substantially limited subsequent Caribbean immigration to either specific categories of worker (such as nurses) or dependents. This closure of free movement was to significantly re-define both the flow of migrants and the communities they formed in Britain. During the 1950s, 92 per cent of Jamaica's migrants to Britain had been adults, many of whom left children in the care of family while they sought short-term employment overseas. In the five years after 1962, children represented 60 per cent of West Indian migrants to the UK before further legislation limited the immigration of dependents (Hall 1988, pp. 273, 281). The redefining of citizenship in 1962 therefore encouraged those West Indians who had initially intended to work temporarily in Britain to become permanent residents.

The end of the Second World War also marked a political and social turning point for the French colonies of Martinique and Guadeloupe, which were legally incorporated into the mainland as Departments of France. Despite the formal end of colonial status, both islands in the 1950s faced the almost complete collapse of their sugar economies at the same time as their populations dramatically expanded. Mass migration to the métropole was deliberately sponsored by the French State as the solution to the economic and demographic problems of its Caribbean territories. The movement of young workers to France was intended to reduce population growth, combat unemployment, reinforce political stability and encourage the cultural assimilation of Martinique and Guadeloupe as French soil. However, the Afro-Caribbean emigration to France was paralleled by increasing immigration into the islands by white French citizens, leading Martiniquais poet and politician Aimé Césaire in 1977 to label the state policy of sponsored migration as 'genocide par substitution' (Constant 1987, p. 13).

The importance of the French State in shaping the character and dimensions of migration from Martinique and Guadeloupe to the métropole was due to the creation in 1963 of the Bureau for Migration from the Overseas Departments (BUMIDOM). The Bureau aimed to provide information to potential migrants, to assist in their transport and place them in appropriate employment. In its 20 years of existence it assisted 84,600 migrants, which represented just under half of the Caribbean immigration into France during the period. More fundamentally, the Bureau actively encouraged family migration and tended to channel workers into particular sections of the French economy. Throughout the post-war migration, the main employment for West Indians resident in France was the public sector, in which they were heavily concentrated in the lower levels of the health services, post-telecommunications (or PTT) and public transport (Anselin 1995). This strongly contrasts to the experiences of West Indians in Britain who were concentrated in manufacturing and the private sector despite the recruitment by the London Transport board and the National Health Service of several thousand migrants during the 1950s. Citizenship, state policy and the continuing movements between the métropole and the Antilles created a *troisiéme Île* in France, of Caribbean families with strong connections to Martinique and Guadeloupe.

The ties between the Netherlands and its Caribbean possessions differed from the deliberate French policy of sponsored migration. Rather than strengthening the colonial bonds, migration to the Netherlands had the opposite result, substantially contributing to the rise of nationalist politics in Suriname. At the same time national independence fundamentally changed the shape of immigration from the Dutch Caribbean to Europe. During the 1950s Surinamese migrants created a range of student, nationalist and cultural organisations in Holland, for as Gert Oostindie argued:

> It was precisely in the metropolis that topics such as colonialism and the relevance of Dutch culture for a West Indian society could easily be discussed. In the metropolis, the young Surinamers were far away from an often suffocating social control at home (Oostindie 1990, p. 248).

These migrants returned home to lead the nationalist movement that triumphed in 1975 when Suriname became an independent republic. However, independence intensified ethnic tensions within the Suriname's heterogeneous population, resulting in 50,000 migrants arriving in the Netherlands during 1974–5. These were largely drawn from Javanese and East Indian Surinamers who feared political exclusion within the new nation. In 1979–80, political instability provoked a second wave of a further 30,000 migrants. This massive influx of migrants, who were so culturally different from Dutch norms, strained race relations, which were worsened with the onset of economic recession in the 1970s.

Perhaps what was most striking for Caribbean migrants to Europe was the unexpected nature of European racism. Arriving on the *SS Empire Windrush* in 1948, Trinidad Calypsonian, Lord Kitchener, composed '*London is the Place for me*' expressing the belief of many migrants that they would be welcome in the 'mother country'. Exactly a decade later, race riots in Notting Hill and Nottingham convinced many that the graffiti to '*Keep Britain White*' was true. Equally in France, Antillians who were legally defined as French citizens, experienced both direct public harassment and indirect racial discrimination in employment. Economic crisis made black immigrants the easy scapegoats for national woes during the 1970s in the Netherlands and 1980s in Thatcherite Britain. Yet, such victimisation occurred despite the fact that Caribbean migrants were always outnumbered by other larger immigrant groups of Europeans, North Africans or Asians. The rise of racist politics in Britain, France and the Netherlands revealed the empty pretensions of the mythic 'mother country'.

Significantly, at the same time that conditions in Europe were most adverse, many of these migrants were constructing permanent communities. These were shaped not only by racism but also by the strong ties of island and kin. Despite the difficulties British West Indians faced in seeking private rental accommodation from hostile landlords, they also relied on each other through sharing rooms, sub-letting and sending remittances home to fund the migration of others (see Plate 6.2). Family and friends

Plate 6.2 *Early morning, Charlestown, Nevis. Nevis is an island particularly dependent on remittances from Nevisians living overseas.*

© Tracey Skelton

were crucial in helping newcomers find housing and employment, creating West Indian clusters in London, Birmingham, Leeds, Leicester and other cities. As Ceri Peach writes of Caribbean communities in London.

> Chain migration from islands produced distinctive clusters so that, north of the river, there is a kind of archipelago of Windward and Leeward Island colonies from Dominicans around Paddington to Montseratians [sic] around Finsbury Park (Peach 1998, p. 210).

French Antillians were equally concentrated in Paris, although over time large numbers shifted to the suburban communes of Seine-Saint-Denis and Val de Marne through public housing provided by their state employers. Some of these communities, like others in Britain and the Netherlands, were racialised as ghettos by government and media drawing on images from America. As Nancy Foner points out, these images missed the reality that in Europe there was no larger black community for Caribbean migrants to join:

> While West Indians in London are constantly in the public eye as a social problem or threat to the English way of life, in New York they are, as blacks, largely invisible as immigrants to the white population (Foner 1985, p. 716).

The creation of Caribbean communities in Europe was therefore shaped by domestic cultures of race relations which were fundamentally different from those encountered by migrants to North America.

Island diasporas in North America

Jutting into the Caribbean basin, Florida was uniquely affected by migrants from the nearby islands of the Bahamas and Cuba during the late nineteenth century. The development of Miami, Tampa and Key West as thriving urban centres owed much to these permanent and temporary Caribbean residents. In the early 1900s there were over 3,500 Cubans in Tampa and a similar number of British West Indians in Miami, where they comprised three fifths of the city's black population. Cuban migration to Tampa and Key West was fuelled by rise of the tobacco industry, which required skilled artisans for the manufacture of cigars. However, economic development also fuelled the intensification of formal segregation in Florida during the early 1900s, dividing the Cuban community by race and spurring re-migration to New York (James 1988).

To the north, Caribbean migrants faced another set of racial norms, which may have been less coercive than the segregationist South but were no less absolute. The large Caribbean communities concentrated on the North-Eastern Seaboard developed out of the port cities of their arrival, particularly in New York where they mixed with the masses of African-Americans who had migrated from the southern states. These two migrant groups came together, particularly in Harlem, which during the early 1900s emerged as a 'Negro Metropolis' in the north of Manhattan numbering an estimated 200,000 residents. The initial move to Harlem by New York's black community had been intended as a form of empowerment, and its almost self-contained character certainly created economic, political, social and cultural opportunities for the West Indian newcomers. However, migrant success in Harlem during the 1920s was also a reflection of their exclusion elsewhere in American society, such as the denial of skilled employment to blacks, that encouraged many migrants to become entrepreneurs or professionals for their own community. New York's clearly defined black community was fundamental for the social networks and economic success which Afro-Caribbean migrants created, although it also marked the limits of their integration into American society (Watkins-Owen 1996).

At the same time as the emergence of Harlem as America's leading black community, other African-American communities across the US were threatened by lynch mobs and race riots in the summers of 1917 and 1919. The violence against blacks during the Red Summer of 1919 inspired a migrant from rural Jamaica, Claude McKay, to pen the powerful poem 'If We Must Die' which concluded:

Like men we'll face the murderous, cowardly pack;

Pressed to the wall, dying, but fighting back!

McKay's radicalism was echoed by many prominent West Indian migrants through a range of political and cultural organisations, led by the Universal Negro Improvement Association (UNIA). The UNIA was founded in Jamaica by Marcus Garvey in 1914 and brought to the US two years later (see Chapter Two for a discussion of Garveyism). Garvey had travelled through Costa Rica, Panama and Britain and this shaped his vision of black empowerment through self reliance and racial pride. Garveyism was a product of migration not only in its ideology, but also through its global organisation whose strongholds included the West Indian communities of Cuba, Panama and Costa Rica. The

UNIA, however, was not simply a movement of Caribbean immigrants, as its black and white American critics claimed, for its core constituency drew on black migrants from the American south as well as West Indians. The debates surrounding the rapid rise and fall of Garveyism in the mid-1920s clearly show both the tensions between Americans and immigrants within the black community and the divisions between different groups of Caribbean migrants. In reaction to the fires of racism in the early 1920s, it is significant that it was Caribbean newcomers who were often at the forefront of the political and cultural demands for change in US race relations (James 1988).

Changing immigration laws and then the Great Depression restricted Caribbean migration into North America from the mid-1920s, although during the Second World War the US goverment sought to temporarily import thousands of agricultural and factory workers from Jamaica and Barbados. In 1965 a new Immigration and Nationality Act replaced the highly restrictive McCarran-Walter Act of 1952 giving migrants from across the Caribbean greater access to the USA. Two years later Canada also shifted its immigration policies to an emphasis on economic skills and education rather than racial discrimination. These new policies only opened national borders selectively as they gave a disproportionate recognition to middle class and professional migrants and specific groups such as domestic servants, seasonal agricultural workers or nurses (Thomas-Hope 1992, p. 44). Despite divergent experiences, both middle class and working class migrants often used their initial entry into North America to fund the chain migration of other family members from the Caribbean.

Chain migration was also central to the flow of migrants between Puerto Rico and the USA. In 1917, Puerto Ricans had received US citizenship and during the inter-war years over 50,000 workers travelled to the USA where they were concentrated in construction, manufacturing and the service industry. Movement between Puerto Rico and the mainland was transformed in the 1950s by the US government's Operation Bootstrap which sought to industrialise the island and use migration as a safety valve for those who were excluded in the new economy. Following four decades of mass migration to the mainland, Puerto Ricans in the USA numbered over 2.6 million in 1990 (Sánchez Korrol 1994, pp. 216–7). However, the privileged right of entry as citizens did not spare the Puerto Ricans from discrimination in employment and housing, and their socio-economic experiences were strikingly similar to other Caribbean migrant communities in the USA.

The 1965 changes in US and Canadian immigration policy, as well as postwar developments within the Caribbean created increasingly heterogeneous migrant communities. Whereas earlier migrants lived within wider black, West Indian or Hispanic communities, the greater numbers of these 'new immigrants' from the mid-1960s meant that they formed more self-contained ethnic groups. From the late 1960s, economic crisis and political instability in the Northern Caribbean has sparked a series of population flows to the USA and Canada. The changing nature of these movements is reflected in Table 6.1. Though the images of refugee boats from Cuba and Haiti

Country	1951–60	1961–70	1971–80	1981–90
Cuba	78,948	208,536	264,863	144,578
Dominican Rep.	9,897	93,292	148,135	252,035
Guyana	NA	NA	NA	88,631
Haiti	4,442	34,499	56,335	138,379
Jamaica	8,869	74,906	137,577	208,148
Other Caribbean	20,935	58,980	134,216	128,911
Caribbean	123,091	470,213	741,126	872,051

TABLE 6.1 *Migration from the Caribbean to the US by decade 1951–90*
Source: Thomas-Hope 1999, p. 259.

arriving in Florida has been the focus for media attention, there has also been significant flows by middle class and ethnic groups from countries such as Guyana, Trinidad and Jamaica. Importantly, arrivals from Communist Cuba were much more likely to be recognised as political refugees in the USA than exiles from Haiti whose dictatorship was actively supported by the US administration.

Conclusion

Over the past two centuries, the character and destinations of Caribbean migration has continually changed in response to developments within and outside the region. In the wake of the abolition of slavery within the British West Indies, migratory movements were focused within the region and followed the seasonal rhythms of the sugar economy. In contrast, the mass migrations of the 1950s and 1960s to Europe, and 1960s and 1970s to North America, tended to be increasingly permanent movements that were strongly shaped by legal, political and economic forces outside and within the Caribbean. During the twentieth century, migrants tended to be equally divided between men and women, while during the preceding period, migrants tended to be overwhelmingly identified as male (although female migration was probably substantially under-recorded). Importantly, family histories have emphasised how these different currents of movement have often been fuelled across generations, with the migration of parents to Panama or Cuba enabling their children to later travel from the Caribbean to Europe or North America (Chamberlain 1997).

Caribbean migration is marked not by a single source, but rather by the range and complexity of migrant experiences. It has changed due to the economic transformation of the region, in which the migrants themselves played a major role. Migrant labour transformed the Caribbean landscape, helping to create the massive plantations of British Guiana and Trinidad, the *centrales* of Cuba and the Dominican Republic, the Panama Canal, the oil refineries of the Dutch Antilles and the new tourist economies.

Migratory currents were also transformed by international forces, particularly by North American investment in the region and the changing policies of European empires. The diasporic identities of these Caribbean migrants have been continually refashioned by new movements from the islands and by the changing (physical, economic, cultural and emotional) connections to the region for immigrant parents and their native-born children.

References

Anselin, A. 1995: 'West Indians in France'. In Burton, R.D.E. and Reno, F. (eds.) *French and West Indian: Martinique, Guadeloupe and French Guiana Today* London: Macmillan. pp. 112–118.

Brown, L. 2002: 'The three faces of post-emancipation migration in Martinique, 1848–1865'. *Journal of Caribbean History*, 36, 2, pp. 310–335.

Byron, M. 1995: *Post-War Caribbean Migration to Britain.* Aldershot: Avebury.

Carter, B., Harris, C. and Shirley J. 1993: 'The 1951–55, Conservative government and the racialization of black immigration'. In Winston James and Clive Harris (eds.) *Inside Babylon: The Caribbean Diaspora in Britain.* London: Verso. pp. 55–71.

Chamberlain, M. 1997: *Narratives of Exile and Return.* London: Macmillan.

Chamberlain. M. (ed.) 1998: *Caribbean Migration: Globalised Identities.* London: Routledge.

Constant, F. 1987: 'La politique française de l'immigration antillaise de 1946 á 1987'. *Revue Européenne des Migrations Internationales* 3 (3). pp. 9–29.

Chomsky, A. 1996: *West Indian Workers and the United Fruit Company in Costa Rica 1870–1940.* Baton Rouge: Louisiana University Press.

Foner, N. 1985: 'Race and Color: Jamaican Migrants in London and New York'. *International Migrant Review* 19 (4). pp. 708–27.

Foner, N. (ed.) 2001: *Islands in the City: West Indian Migration to New York.* Berkeley: University of California Press.

Hall, S. 1988: 'Migration from the English-Speaking Caribbean to the United Kingdom, 1950–80'. In Appleyard, R.T. (ed.) *International Migration Today.* Vol. 1, Paris: UNESCO.

Hansen, R. 2000: *Citizenship and Immigration in Post-War Britain: The Institutional Origins of a Multicultural Nation.* Oxford: Oxford University Press.

Harris, C. 1993: 'Postwar migration and the industrial research army'. In James, W. and Harris, C. (eds.) *Inside Babylon: The Caribbean Diaspora in Britain.* London: Verso. pp. 9–54.

Harpelle, R. 2001: *The West Indians of Costa Rica: Race, Class and the Integration of an Ethnic Minority.* Kingston, Jamaica: Ian Randle Publishers.

James, W. 1988: *Holding Aloft the Banner of Ethiopia: Caribbean Radicalism in Early Twentieth Century.* London: Verso.

Johnson, H. 1973: 'Barbadian immigrants in Trinidad, 1870–1897'. *Caribbean Studies.* 13 (3). pp. 5–30.

Knight, F. W. 1985: 'Jamaican migrants and the Cuban sugar industry, 1900–1934'. In Moreno Franginals, M., Moya Pons, F. and Engerman, S. L. (eds.) *Between Slavery and Free Labor: The Spanish-Speaking Caribbean in the Nineteenth Century.* Baltimore: John Hopkins University Press.

Levine, B. (ed.) 1987: *The Caribbean Exodus.* New York: Prager.

Lundahl, M. 1982 'A note on Haitian migration to Cuba, 1890–1934'. *Cuban Studies.* 12 (2). pp. 21–36.

Marshall, D. 1979: *The Haitian Problem: Illegal Migration to the Bahamas.* Mona: University of the West Indies.

Newton, V. 1984: *The Silvermen: West Indian Labour Migration to Panama 1850–1914*. Mona: University of the West Indies.

Oostinde, G. 1990: 'Preludes to the exodus: Surinamers in the Netherlands'. In Brana-Shute, G. (ed.) *Resistance & Rebellion in Suriname: Old & New*. Williamsburg: College of William and Mary.

Peach, C. 1998: 'Trends in levels of Caribbean segregation, Great Britain, 1961–91'. In Chamberlain, M. (ed.) *Caribbean Migration: Globalised Identities*. London: Routledge.

Philpott, S. B. 1973: *West Indian Migration: The Montserrat Case*. London: University of London.

Richardson, B.C. 1983: *Caribbean Migrants, Environment and Human Survival on St. Kitts and Nevis*. Knoxville: University of Tennessee Press.

Richardson, B.C. 1985: *Panama Money in Barbados, 1900–1920*. Knoxville: University of Tennessee Press.

Rodney, W. 1981: *A History of the Guyanese Working People, 1881–1905*. Baltimore: John Hopkins University Press.

Sanchez Korrol, V. 1994: *From Colonia to Community: The History of Puerto Ricans in New York City*. Berkeley: University of California Press.

Thomas-Hope, E.M. 1992: *Explanation in Caribbean Migration*. London: Macmillan.

Thomas-Hope, E. 1999: 'Emigration dynamics in the Anglophone Caribbean'. In Appleyard, R. (ed.) Emigration Dynamics in Developing Countries, Vol. 3. Aldershot: Ashgate.

Watkins-Owens, I. 1996: *Blood Relations: Caribbean Immigrants and the Harlem Community, 1900–1930*. Bloomington: Indiana University Press.

Waters, M.C. 1999: *Black Identities: West Indian Immigrant Dreams & American Realities*. New York: Russell Sage.

7

Caribbean social perspectives

David Howard

I looked at the regiment
of rum bottles,
at the vivid labels,
and saw two cane-cutters
carrying bundles
on most of them,
and heard:
"Massa, we workin';
we still workin' 'ard for you!"
I thought of black shoulders
under cutting lashes
instead of black faces
grinning on rum bottles.

Salkey (1973, p. 60) 'Saturday in Kingston'.

Social legacies

The legacies of the past shape societies today. 'Saturday in Kingston', by the Jamaican writer Andrew Salkey, reflects the historical role of slavery and the plantation economy on present gender, ethnic and labour relations. In the Caribbean, the shadows of previous systems, governments and people have been cast largely since the fifteenth century, albeit within the penumbra of remaining real and imagined links to indigenous communities who inhabited the territories before European invasion.

Systems of slavery and forced labour, since their widespread introduction to the region in the sixteenth century, dramatically upturned demographic and social structures, promoting the plantation system as the dominant form of production in most societies. At least four million people were forced to the Caribbean from western Africa by the beginning of the nineteenth century. Between 1701 and 1810, the British, French, Spanish and Dutch colonial powers had transplanted respectively 1.4 million, 1.3 million, 580,000 and 460,000 slaves to the Caribbean (Knight 1990, p. 112). The abolition of slavery in British territories by 1838 marked an important stage in its ultimate formal eradication towards the end of the nineteenth century. Extended endeavours were undertaken to import labour on a contract basis. Some of this indentured labour originated from Europe and Africa, but the vast majority came from Asia. These workers, often operating in material conditions similar to those under slavery, numbered over half a million Indians, approximately 135,000 Chinese and 33,000 indentured labourers from Indonesia (Mintz 1974, p. 313). Many were contracted to plantations in Trinidad, Suriname and Guyana, and remained to form significant sections of these societies (see Chapter Six for more detail about migration).

Systems of forced labour have not only shaped economies, but dramatically forged new social structures and institutions which continue to mould Caribbean societies today (Levitt and Best 1993). Theories of dependency, elaborated particularly during the 1960s and 1970s, have focused on the failure of imperial and post-colonial economic and social structures to permit the development of independent primary or manufacturing industries in the Caribbean states. Domestic production has continued to be largely foreign-owned, despite the decline of formal colonial relations (Payne 1984). The lack of ability to generate economic interdependence or autonomy, it is argued, has curtailed the material and social development of many societies in the Caribbean, where their relative small size and influence on world markets leaves them dependent on external actors, in a situation of 'persistent poverty' (Beckford 1972) (see Chapter Three on Pan-Caribbean development).

The pursuit of profits from the sugar plantations was the driving force behind the slave trade, but arguably also led to its demise throughout the region by the end of the nineteenth century (Williams 1944). Under slavery: 'It was necessary for the reproduction of the economic substructure that human beings be treated as commodities, it had to brutalise them to perpetuate itself' (Post 1978, p. 18). An early historian of the Caribbean, Edward Long, tallied the 'importation of Negroes' in much the same manner as mules, horses and cattle – commodities necessary to maintain the colony. In 1774, he unashamedly wrote of the direct link between slavery and British manufacturing:

> The Negroe slaves are purchased in Africa, by the British merchants, with a great variety of woollen goods; a cheap sort of fire-arms from Birmingham, Sheffield, and other places; powder,

Plate 7.1 *Old sugar mill, Montserrat. Ruins of sugar mills dot the Caribbean landscape as a reminder of the importance of sugar in Caribbean history, both socially and economically.*
© Tracey Skelton

bullets, iron bars, copper bars, brass pans, malt spirits, tallow, tobacco pipes, Manchester goods, glass beads; some particular kind of linens, ironmongery and cutlery ware; certain toys, some East Indian goods; but, in the main, with very little that is not of British growth, or manufacture ... on the winding-up of the account therefore, as the sale of the Negroes centers in the West Indies, so the profit arising upon them, and every other accession of gain, from whatever article of our African commerce it is produced, centers ultimately with, and becomes the property of, the inhabitants of Britain (Long 1970, p. 491).

Slaves were bluntly treated as commodities, but ones who required basic maintenance. The costs of maintaining this labour system, combined with revolt, liberal opposition and declining sugar prices, meant that slavery as a mode of production was officially abolished in British territories between 1834–38. When slavery became unprofitable, it ceased to warrant a place in the capitalist system, giving way to subsequent contracts of indentureship and today's flexible hire-and-fire policies. Typical of many economies, 'Jamaican capitalism wanted labour power only at the cheapest possible price and for irregular periods' (Post 1978, p. 42).

External dependency, insularity and shared colonial labour histories arguably link many of the region's states from a social perspective. In the context of the former territories of the British Caribbean, Clarke (1996, p. 182) concurs:

British West Indian societies were entirely creations of empire, and more especially of the systems of forced labour that had been deployed during the seventeenth, eighteenth and nineteenth centuries to operate the sugar plantations. Local political elites, increasingly elected after 1945, had been socialized to treasure Pax Britannica, and to appreciate and imitate British institutions and values.

While embroiled in less rigorous, or at least less extensive, colonial frameworks, Spanish, Dutch and French territories in the Caribbean have experienced similar imprints of metropolitan culture.

The following sections analyse the broad influence of these shared social and cultural factors. Unsurprisingly for a region of over fifty political entities and thirty-five million residents, similarities and differences abound. Benítez Rojo (1992, p. 11), analysing form and chaos throughout the Caribbean, views the region as ultimately 'a culture of the meta-archipelago: a chaos that returns, a detour without a purpose, a continual flow of paradoxes'. He develops the concept of cultural hybridities, proposing that the chaotic mixture and evolution of identities in the region, nevertheless evoke a Caribbeanness, or as he puts it, a 'soup of signs' (Benitez Rojo 1992, p. 2). It is into this soup we shall now leap.

Defining terms – Caribbean identities

Any attempt to find cohesion lies open to rebuke or dismissal in the face of evident or perceived pluralities. Nevertheless, a broad typology of Caribbean societies may be of merit when attempting to understand the regional impact of slavery, colonialism and nationalist movements. A fourfold classification of Caribbean societies has been devised which outlines ethnic and social cleavages by adopting frameworks of stratified or segmented pluralism, class stratification and folk communities (Clarke 1991). Ethnic affiliation here relates to a sense of belonging which people feel, or to which they are attributed according to kinship, race, language, religion and gender-related characteristics. Plural-stratified societies include Jamaica, the Leeward Islands and the French and Dutch Antilles in which the major socio-economic divisions are deemed to correspond with ethnic affiliation. During slavery, the racialised classifications of white, mulatto and black corresponded to the legalised strata of citizens, freed former slaves and enslaved labourers.

Plural-segmented societies within this typology constitute the broadly differentiated Creole-East Indian sectors of the Trinidadian, Guyanese and Surinamese populations and the Creole-*mestizo/a* divisions in Belize. The generalised vertical cleavages in these societies stem from the significant contribution of indentured labour to the formerly slave-based societies (Cross 1980). Hispanic territories are further categorised as class-stratified societies, since socio-economic differentiation is considered to be dominant over ethnic division. Cuba, Puerto Rico and the Dominican Republic developed under the influence of Spanish colonialism along a different time scale from much of the region. These countries experienced two key periods of sugar production, during the sixteenth and nineteenth centuries. The development of sugar plantation economies during the latter century and the higher incidences of European immigration or conditions of free labour meant that these societies evolved with a relatively less extensive system of slavery. Finally, folk societies encompass the smallest island populations who have traditionally relied on peasant agriculture and subsistence activities.

In adopting a Pan-Caribbean approach, there is a clear danger of hiding difference to forge dubious unities, particularly at the level of personal identities or belonging. As Accaria Zavala (2000, pp. 232–233) succinctly notes, 'The fact is that we are each alone and isolated from each other within our exotic shores, misunderstood by our neighbours and misrepresented by the rest of the world'. These misconceptions are generated within and outwith the region's homes, communities and national groupings. Perhaps most accessible to the majority, such suggested identities are often disseminated through the visual images of the screen or advertising billboard. Continuing her cautionary account of image projection, Accaria Zavala (2000, p. 227) charts the ills of cultural misrepresentation within Hollywood cinema:

> ... one easily sees that throughout the decades of mainstream cinema production the silver screen comes alight once more with images of Caribbeaners immersed in the stereotypically tropical: heated sex, heated arguments, knife-fighting, gun-fighting or revolutionary fighting but always fighting, thieving, copulating or dancing, always dancing, tapping feet or drums, conforming the image, performing the perfect role of the flamboyant or slimy, harmlessly irresponsible, fun-loving tropical bunny (or should I say tropical snake).

Similar inaccuracies lead us back to the themes of Andrew Salkey's opening verse. The Barcardi rum company markets one of its popular products through an advertising campaign which allures consumers with images that state, 'There's Latin spirit in everyone'. The promotion arguably portrays the Hispanic Caribbean as a happy flow of salsa, sun and boundless opportunities for fun. In a similar vein, the Malibu rum website advertises the delights of Barbados under the title of 'Bump 'n' Grind' time:

> Nights are **hot** on the island. Get washed away with the **happy** vibes and heavy **soca** beats on the dance floor.
> (www.malibu-rum.com accessed Sept. 2002)

Such advertising images and rhetoric are easy to criticise from a variety of perspectives, but they endure regardless – or as long as they feed consumer imagination and continue to sell the product.

Myths and representations play an important part in the way societies and individuals are perceived and distinguish themselves. The myth of racial democracy jostles with the uncomfortable reality of ethnic prejudice and discrimination in Caribbean societies. Given the varied ethnic composition of the region's population, an emphasis on social consensus might suggest that racism does not and cannot dominate. Conversely, authors such as Furnivall (1945, p. 164) have argued that diverse or plural societies inherently lack shared values or 'common will', being 'held together only by the pressure exerted from outside by the colonial power'. This viewpoint modelled the colonial system as a social pressure cooker, holding diverse peoples together by social and legal strictures that might explode into conflict when the lid or containing forces are removed. The most salient perspective today may be to address the sanitisation of racism (Blaut 1992). General consensus recognises that racism abounds, yet few people are confronted as racists in societies which celebrate perennially tentative national mottoes such as 'All o' we are one' (Jamaica) and 'Out of many, one people' (Guyana).

Race and ethnicity are critical factors in the attempt to understand Caribbean societies at large or at the individual level. An ethnic group relates to a collectivity of people who are conscious of having common origins, interests and shared experiences. Ideas of race, included within the concept of ethnicity, focus more specifically on subjective aesthetics and perceived ancestries. Contemporary debates highlighting race clearly recognise that races do not exist as scientific entities, but are formed subjectively by the rendering of appearance into allegedly objective systems of differentiation (Gilroy 1987). The potency and danger of race thus lies in its embeddedness as a perceived natural phenomenon which is manipulated to fuel prejudice and discrimination in society.

The significance of ethnicity is matched only by its complexity. Zenga Longmore (1989, p. 252), returning to her home in Brixton after a tour of the Caribbean, remarks on the subtle, and not so subtle, multiple identities bestowed upon her:

In every island I was a different person. 'High' in Jamaica, 'Mestizo' in the Dominican Republic, 'Mulatto' in Haiti, 'Black' in Dominica and St. Lucia, 'Mulâtre' in Martinique and Guadeloupe, and in Trinidad I was none other than a 'red skin nigger.' Such is life, and such is the unhealthy obsession with race, a colonial legacy that brutalises the Caribbean from top to toe.

Ethnic identity varies in context and outcome. Louise Bennett addresses this potential for adaptability and confusion (which may lead to positive or negative consequences) in her poem 'Pass fe white'. Written in 1949, the verse wryly recounts the experience of Miss Jane's Jamaican daughter studying in the USA where she 'passes' as white, thus gaining privileged access to 'white society' (Bennett 1966, p. 212):

Miss Jane jus hear from 'Merica,
Her daughta proudly write
Fe say she fail her exam, but
She passin' dere fe wite!

Succinctly summarised by Mintz (1974, p. 320), perspectives on race are highly dependent on individual location and person: 'Thus, in order to make any real sense of the place of "race" in Caribbean national life and politics, we need to learn about local codes of perception, about the history of the societies in question, and about the relevance of physical distinctions to the workings of political life.' Inclusive to these considerations should be gendered concepts of identity and social interaction.

Engendering Caribbean identities

Ethnicity and gender act as simultaneous and reciprocal elements of social relations, guiding the form and impact of people's access to resources and participation in society. Slavery and indentureship laid the basis not only for the ethnic composition of many Caribbean societies, but also were arguably significant factors in the development of gender relations and identities in the region. Men and women enduring systems of forced labour adapted to and resisted the constraints which framed their working day: 'Concepts of gender and race were central to how persons interfaced by the relations of slavery, established meaning that determined social order and shaped everyday life' (Beckles 1999, p. xxiii).

Patriarchal relations of power were pivotal for the superstructure of the slave system. Despite the evident ethnic differentiation of slave from plantation owner, there is no principal reason to privilege race above gender within the matrix of slave-based societies and their historical derivatives:

Certainly, the slaveowner whose legal and ideological superstructure empowered him for unrestricted socio-sexual access to the slave women as an expected return on capital, and at the same time imposed sexual constraints and curfews upon white women, interpreted this authority as having its roots in sex, gender, and race differences (Beckles 1999, p. xxiii).

The following open letter published in a Jamaican newspaper in the 1870s reveals firstly, the prevalent chauvinism and treatment of women as wholly unequal partners;

and secondly, the ultimate will of the commodified subject to reject oppression and to escape as the runaway slaves had done in a previous era:

> Caution – Whereas my wife, S. R., having left my care and protection, and is gone home to her parents (refusing any longer to serve me, and thus ceasing to be my wife), this is to give notice that if I find her in my provision ground from and after date – which she is in the habit of destroying – I shall proceed against her as a trespasser, according to law – P.R.
> (Cited in Rampini 1873, p. 31).

Patriarchal constraints notwithstanding, the development of female autonomy was arguably supported by their shared work roles with men on the plantations. The end of slavery in the Caribbean further strengthened the role of women as traders of domestic produce in the emerging markets and promoted gendered divisions of free labour (Mintz 1993, p. 238). Women's engagement with and resistance to inequalities in the productive and reproductive spheres has a long tradition. Indentured labour, argues Reddock (1990), was perceived by many women as an opportunity for economic improvement. In Trinidad, two thirds of women arriving from India during the latter half of the nineteenth century were unmarried and actively resisted traditional arranged marriages in order to develop their own economic and political independence. Momsen similarly highlights the positive correlation between contemporary economic development and the gradual reduction of gender disparities or discrimination:

> Development in the Caribbean is accompanied by the increased economic activity of women. Higher levels of education, declining fertility rates, improvements in household facilities and structural transformation of economies are facilitating women's access to paid work (1993, p. 243).

Women's participation in the labour force continues to be relatively high, with at least 60 per cent of women over fifteen years old being economically active in the larger Caribbean economies such as Jamaica and Barbados. High levels of women- headed households further manifest a tradition of women's economic autonomy. In the Eastern Caribbean, 35 per cent of households have women as household heads (Momsen 1993, p. 232). Edith Clarke's pioneering work, *My Mother Who Fathered Me* (1957), first highlighted the central significance of women's contributions to Jamaican social and economic systems. Despite the ongoing gender prejudice which informally denies women full access to employment and political representation, their role in households, societies and communities as producers, reproducers and shapers of personal and community relations has gained greater recognition (Moser 1993). Nevertheless, many of the texts confronting gender inequalities written up to four decades ago are as depressingly relevant today as they were when first published (Plate 7.2).

The focus for gender equality and parity of access to resources highlights the distribution of power, namely 'the control and autonomy individuals and groups can exercise over their own destiny and over their social environment – people, institutions, ideologies and practices' (Dagenais 1993, p. 85). In her research on labour markets in Guadeloupe (where a third of Guadeloupe's households are women-headed

Plate 7.2 *These young sisters in the Dominican Republic may experience better gender equality than their mother, but it is a fragile equality in the face of poverty and limited social and economic development*

© David Howard

compared with a fifth in France), Dagenais recognises that since official statistics account for only 48 per cent of women as economically active, there remains a clear necessity for domestic-based labour to be acknowledged fully.

Developing the politics of empowerment and allowing women to organise independently, with full access to information and services, are key components of promoting strategic gender interests (Peake and Trotz 2001). Red Thread, a Guyanese women's organisation, confronts these issues by addressing the fact that 70 per cent of women are in unskilled jobs, and by actively advancing more varied and skilled employment. The problems faced by Red Thread are primarily those of class and gender discrimination:

> A dual sector economy, high levels of unemployment and lack of training opportunities encourage the persistence of a sexual division of labour, sex-segregated occupations and the view that women's jobs should be less well paid and valued. (Peake 1993, p. 123)

Social status

Gender and ethnicity form fundamental building blocks for the construction of social status and help to define or measure the hierarchy in which these prescribed attributes are ranked. *The Children of Sisyphus* recounts the story of Dinah who daily confronts the boundaries of ethnicity and class, while working as a domestic servant in an affluent suburb of Kingston. The novel is situated on the eve of Jamaican independence in 1962, but the blunt sentiments of social and cultural differentiation between a wealthy 'uptown' and impoverished 'downtown' remain today:

> By four o'clock all five ladies had arrived. To Dinah the remarkable thing about them was that they all looked so much like each other. Their dresses were all of silk in some drab floral colour and they were draped up in the same odd places. They all walked alike, they all held their tea-cups alike, they all talked alike. They were all very light-skinned, except for the one called Mrs Brooks, and one of them, Lady something or other, she thought she heard them say, was obviously of pure white stock (Patterson 1964, pp. 134–135).

Visiting the island several years later following independence, a commentator could claim, 'In Jamaica, prosperity still has a light skin, however varied in shade; poverty – almost always – has a black one' (Glass 1989, p. 212).

A prevalent bias towards lighter aesthetics, whether advertising consumables or fronting television shows, remains a feature of many Caribbean societies. Written in the 1950s, a largely ethnically and gender-insensitive description of Jamaican society could claim, 'Hairdressers in Jamaica also help women to achieve a fairer complexion. They use a pack made up of peroxide, clay, and fuller's earth, which is worked into a paste and coated on the face. It is left on for about a quarter of an hour. The effect is supposed to be that of a light smooth skin' (Henriques 1953, p. 129). The same blunt and sadly still salient account, added:

> One's place in the scheme of things in Jamaica is thus largely determined by how you look in relation to the European. But that is not the whole story. The respectability of your family name, your profession, the type of marriage you make, and perhaps most important of all how much money you have, all help to advance or hinder your 'colour' (Henriques 1953, p. 129).

A recent article in the UK edition of a popular magazine provided a graphic account of the skin bleaching process and its ongoing prevalence in Jamaica today (Williams 2001). The skin-lightening creams contain 4 per cent hydroquinone – a harsh chemical that bleaches the outer layer of skin, but nevertheless was deemed preferable among the women interviewed to the alleged alternative homemade lotion of toilet bleach and toothpaste. The preference for lighter colouring may be overemphasised as a hangover from slavery when lighter aesthetics could increase the possibilities of possible freedom or privilege. It could also be maintained to an extent by current advertising strategies. The key criterion rests on the significance of appearance, and the subsequent provocation of prejudice.

■ Box 7.1 Social discrimination

The following extracts from Orlando Patterson's novel *The Children of Sisyphus* (1964, pp. 126 and 127) highlight the social frustrations and resistance expressed by many Jamaicans in the late 1950s, on the eve of independence and the formal ending of colonial status in 1962. Dinah, who lives in a low-income neighbourhood of Kingston, travels uptown to start work as a domestic worker in a typically middle-class residential area:

'She got off the bus at the Hope Road in front of the Royal Botanical Gardens and walked across the newly built housing estate. Her eyes roamed over the bright new concrete walls – blue, light green, black, pink and white; oh, the white one was so pretty – completely white outside except for two black clay pots with the long, slender green ferns in them. And the housewives with their brown and olive-skinned legs pouring out of their Bermuda shorts and their gardener boys with their black torsos gleaming in the sun. Such domestic bliss. Her with her little spade, he with his shear, both intent on manicuring pretty green lawns.

For a long time Dinah forgot herself as she walked across the broad, clean roads of the estate, peering into each of the little units of peace ... Round, closely clipped willows. Fat little dogs always sleeping; strange, she always thought dogs ran around and sniffed at other dead dogs ... now it was wonderfully different; when they weren't sleeping they were chasing the canaries and the grass squits, it was so strange to see a dog not chasing crows ... look at the fat, smiling little brown babies being pushed in the prams. Nice baby, powdered baby, happy, little, pretty, brown baby. Look at the women in their stiffly starched drills pushing the prams.

... Staring, now at herself. Her feelings were too intense for rage. Somehow in those past few minutes she seemed to have seethed herself out of anger. Only a numbness trapped her. She pulled herself together, and walked to the southern end of, the estate ... The numbness had. sunk to somewhere in the depths of her and there it lingered. She could forget it. Somehow it didn't seem to matter. For a moment nothing seemed to matter any more.

[Dinah finds the house of her new employer, Mrs Watkins, and knocks on the front door.]

There was a brisk walking inside, the door opened and Mrs Watkins, a tall, very pale woman with her wavy hair combed in a bun that rested conspicuously on top of her head, stared blankly at her.

"Yes, what do you want?" she began, then, recognizing Dinah: "Oh, you are the new girl"

"Yes", Dinah said, hesitantly.

"A bit late, aren't you, it's after eight-thirty ... you should be here by at least eight."

"Yes, ma'm, but the bus – "

"Oh, don't you start on me with that already. I know very well that the buses are always late, but that's no business of mine. Anyway, be that as it is, you'd better come to the kitchen and let me tell you what you are to do."

She walked away from the door, half closing it. Dinah pushed it open and went inside after her. Mrs Watkins was just about to enter the kitchen when she heard Dinah's footsteps behind her. She spun round and gaped at Dinah with astonishment. Dinah, suspecting that already she has made some great blunder, stopped where she was.

"I beg your pardon!" Mrs Watkins exclaimed, a questioning frown of amazement on her brows. Dinah was at a loss what to say or do. The only thing she could think of was to retreat to the door, hoping that whatever it was she had done wrong would be undone in the process. But she couldn't help from asking falteringly.

"What is it ma'm?"

"What is it? You dare to ask me what it is? I can see that the chances of you staying here for any length of time are very slim. Will you kindly walk around to the back entrance. And if you don't mind I'd be happy if you used that entrance in the future."

Lyrics of the Jamaican musician Buju Banton interlace many of the worst aspects of racial, gender and sexual prejudice. His popular song, 'Love mi browning', celebrated the beauty of lighter aesthetics above darker skin colours among women, while 'Boom, bye, bye' was an explicit and violent attack on homosexuality (Skelton 1995). Homophobia, condemned but also frequently advocated, continues to gain a significant airing via the region's media and cultural outlets (Wilkinson 1999).

Fear and ignorance ultimately underpin all expressions of prejudice or deeds of discrimination. Following the slave-led Haitian revolution and declaration of independence as the first black republic in the Western Hemisphere in 1804, fears of 'another Haiti' haunted much of the elite's governance of the Caribbean colonies. As Hurston (1939, p. 4) recounts during her visit to Jamaica, parallel fears were roused as late as the 1930s: 'There is a frantic stampede whiteward to escape from Jamaica's black mass'. She elucidates the importance that many light-skinned Jamaicans placed on guarding their social and political privileges by separating themselves from the majority of the population via their 'status' as white:

I was told that John Hope, the late president of Atlanta University, precipitated a panic in Kingston on his visit there in 1935, a few months before his death. He was quite white in appearance, and when he landed and visited the Rockefeller Institute in Kingston and was honoured by them, the 'census white' Jamaicans assumed that he was of pure white blood. A great banquet was given him at the Myrtle Bank Hotel, which is the last word in swank in Jamaica. All went well until John Hope was called to respond to a toast. He began his reply with: 'We negroes … 'Several people nearly collapsed. John Hope was whiter than any of the mulattoes there who had had themselves ruled white. So that if a man as white as that called himself a negro, what about them? Consternation struck the banquet like a blight (Hurston 1939, p. 4).

Despite frequent and significant slave revolts throughout the Caribbean, the Haitian revolution remains a unique example of statehood having been established as an outcome of anti-white insurrection. Over a decade of rebellion, which resulted in the establishment of the new Haitian republic, was centred on the strategic alliance between the *anciens libres* and the *nouveau libres* (Nicholls 1996, p. 37). The former were largely *mulâtre* property owners; the latter were black plantation workers, more recently liberated by the abolition of slavery in 1793. Within the broader unifying structure of statehood, racial and class tensions continued to cause rivalry between the successful revolutionary factions. Notwithstanding the constitutional declaration that all Haitians were to be recognised as black following the revolution, regardless of skin colour, the more affluent *mulâtre* population benefited from greater social and economic access to resources. Racialised sentiment remained as much a cause of division, as it served as a source of strength for the victorious revolutionaries.

The nationalist, and subsequently socialist, Cuban revolution of 1959 was the second most significant Caribbean uprising to have global political resonance. An earlier civil conflict, however, also had the potential to restructure Cuban society and reshape regional histories. At the start of the twentieth century, the evolution of the *Partido Independiente de Color* (Independent Party of Colour) in Cuba, an all black political party, sparked the flames of black rebellion. The subsequent murderous repression by a government-sponsored massacre of 5,000 black Cubans in 1912, broke the silence of black Cubans in national discourse and imagery (Helg 1995). Their voices recorded the racist sentiment which Afro-Cubans had suffered. The nationalist leader, José Marti, however, called for unity and the rejection of racial identities: 'the act of hiding and silencing individuals of African descent within a racially inclusive notion of nationhood was not only a purely ideological exercise ... blacks and blackness were attacked through a program of state-encouraged immigration that sought to dilute them in a torrent of white blood' (de la Fuente 1998, p. 47).

Between 1902 and 1931, 780,000 Spanish workers came to Cuba, but fewer than 250,000 remained beyond the sugar harvests as permanent residents. Despite 'whites' making up 72 per cent of the population according to census returns in the 1920s and 1930s, the whitening policy failed. The booming Cuban sugar sector had simultaneously recruited over 300,000 black workers between 1912 and 1931, mainly from Haiti, Jamaica and Barbados. These workers confronted high levels of racial antagonism from white Cubans, but their presence helped to reinforce the futility of any form of whitening policy. By the 1930s, Cubanness was reworked in official and literary discourse to recognise African influences and celebrate *mestizaje* or so called racial mixing. The revolutionary government declared racism to be a hangover of colonialism, a form of discrimination that had already been eradicated by new socialist policies. The failure to confront racial discrimination in an effective manner, however, extended beyond the 1959 revolution as Afro-Cubans continued to be excluded from positions of power within the government. Current government policy maintains that racial discrimination has been eliminated, but notes the need for a more equitable representation of Afro-Cubans and women in the upper strata of state politics.

Caribbean resistance – black power

Perhaps one of the most enduring legacies of colonialism is that of resistance. The Haitian revolution paved the way for ethnically aligned confrontations against a white, formerly European hegemony, which itself still exists as economic and social blocks of privilege throughout the Caribbean. Black nationalism in the early twentieth century was initially led by Marcus Garvey, a Jamaican political activist who had emigrated to the USA.

Garvey and the Universal Negro Improvement Association (UNIA), which he founded in Jamaica in 1914, provided the most significant and powerful platform for the advocacy of Pan-African awareness. The movement incorporated designs for economic and political empowerment of African peoples across the world, including plans for a voluntary re-migration to Africa. The Black Star Steamship Line was formed to assist the organisation of this return passage to the African continent. At its height during the 1920s, UNIA had branches across the Caribbean and Africa. The importance of this movement for the liberation of black nationalism still has salience today:

> The UNIA … was the most dynamic mass movement across territorial borders among African peoples this century … It is still possible to say that Garveyism occupies a central place in the struggle for democracy, dignity and social transformation (Lewis and Bryan 1988, p. 171).

Garvey died in 1940, and while never directly involved in Rastafarianism, his views on black nationalism and the return to Africa have clear religious parallels with the faith. He himself is revered by believers as a prophet of god or Jah, who worship the late King Haile Selassie of Ethiopia, crowned in 1930 as the Black Messiah and direct descendent of King Solomon. The Rastafari faith, originally established among intellectuals in Jamaica, holds that a predestined repatriation to the Promised Land of Ethiopia will lead to the redemption of all Africans exiled in the world of white oppression, or Babylon (see Chapter Eight for more discussion of Rastafarianism.) The movement has made significant cultural and social impact across much of the Caribbean and beyond, particularly highlighting the inequalities and injustices of European colonialism and contemporary capitalist systems. 'The Creed of a Ras Tafari Man', quoted in a report on the Rastafari movement in Kingston during the 1960s, bluntly outlines these popular grievances:

> Jamaica was a nice island, but the land had been polluted by centuries of crime. For 304 years, beginning in 1655, the white man and his brown ally have held the black man in slavery. During this period, countless horrible crimes have been committed daily. Jamaica is literally Hell for the black man, just as Ethiopia is literally heaven (Smith, Augier and Nettleford 1960, p. 7).

Nationalism, decolonisation and independence

Despite the strength of popular anti-colonial rhetoric and political activity, Caribbean societies in general underwent a much later period of decolonisation compared to other former colonial territories. Attempts to form a federation of British territories in 1958, which included the largest islands of Jamaica, Trinidad and Barbados, together with the Windward and Leeward isles, failed after Jamaica withdrew from the agreement and achieved independence in 1962. Subsequent moves towards independence throughout the 1960s and 1970s have left only a few small British dependent territories in the region, namely Montserrat, the British Virgin Islands, the Cayman Islands, the Turks and Caicos Islands and Anguilla (see Chapter Three for a discussion of their development status). The Caribbean, thus, while consisting of over 50 self-governing and independent states is still partly shielded, or in part smothered, by the fading blanket of European colonialism.

In 1922, the Netherlands Constitution Act promoted the status of the Dutch possessions to integrated territories, which have since combined to form the tripartite Kingdom of the Netherlands, which includes Aruba and the Netherlands Antilles of Curaçao, Bonaire, Sint Maarten, Sint Eustatius and Saba. The former Dutch colony of Suriname gained independence in 1975, but now faces what has been termed a 'crisis of nationalism' (Oostindie 1996, p. 221). In 1993, a collective of Surinamers published a manifesto urging a referendum to stimulate the revision of the country's relationship with the Netherlands. Independence, it is argued, has served to worsen, or at least failed, to stimulate a declining economic and demographic condition. Underpinned by the ongoing movement from Suriname to the Netherlands: 'The level of migration has been dramatic enough to evoke the perspective of a population actually disappearing' (Oostindie 1996, p. 212). It is estimated that there are as many Surinamers living in the country as there are resident in the Netherlands, amounting to 375,000 respectively.

Whereas Haiti and the former Spanish territories of Cuba and Santo Domingo had gained independence at the beginning and the end of the nineteenth century respectively, French territories in the Caribbean are still effectively part of the metropole. Guyane, Martinique and Guadeloupe with Saint Barthélemy and Saint Martin are *Départements d'Outre-mer*, recognised as three self-governing provinces with political representation in Paris (Burton and Reno 1995). Claims for greater autonomy are often mooted, but those seeking outright independence continue to be the minority. A similar situation exists in the case of Puerto Rico, whose population has consistently voted to remain as a Commonwealth territory of the USA, with the consequent access to the economic and political resources of the mainland.

The dominant political and economic force in the region today is evidently the USA. Three referendums during the 1990s in Puerto Rico have consistently renounced any notion of independence and only narrowly rejected the more inclusive status of statehood with the USA. Limited political interest for independence, however, is counterbalanced by vigorous expressions of nationalism that have evoked strong ethnic sentiment. 'In Puerto Rico, the symbol of the *Jíbaro* or poor rural, white or mestizo peasant served a function similar to that of *mestizaje* in Mexico, nationalizing a whitened Creole identity and symbolically erasing the troubled issues of slavery, black and white racial mixing, and the claims of blacks and mulattoes upon the nation' (Puri 1999, p. 18). *Mestizaje*, a celebration of indigenous and Spanish ancestors, resisted Spanish colonialism, but also promoted racist, anti-black sentiment.

González (1995) charts the formation of Puerto Rican identity through the layering of historical and cultural influences, employing the symbol of a four-storey house. Puerto Rican nationhood, he argued, was founded primarily on the African contribution to a popular *mestizo/a* culture, in contrast to the twentieth-century construction of a national ideal around the *Jíbaro/a* peasant of European descent. This he termed the first layer, which also incorporated indigenous and Spanish influences. The second stratum emerged during the nineteenth century as an expatriate layer of immigrants, who relocated due to the Spanish American wars of independence on the mainland. They were joined by European migrants, who reinforced the plantation economy and re-established foreign domination. Following the invasion in 1898, the third layer of US imperialism further contorted the Puerto Rican national identity, leaving the contemporary stratum of advanced capitalist investment to seal the process of 'Americanisation'.

While the flow of North American capital and culture dismantled the dominance of the Puerto Rican elite, the vacuum was filled from below by the Puerto Rican working classes (González 1995, p. 186). Popular culture and the foundation of the Puerto Rican nation has reclaimed a Caribbean identity for the island, despite the ongoing external political and economic relations of dependence. The so-called 'Taíno revival' is a contemporary reclamation of an indigenous past, celebrating and building on historical and current connections (Haslip Viera 2001) (see Chapter Eight for an examination of Taíno culture). Rather than point to the demise of Caribbean nationhood in the context of omnipotent encroachment by the USA, González (1995) emphasises the cultural strengths of the majority, the power of the popular and the natural destiny of Caribbean states to recognise a unique identity.

Paradox of resistance and dependency

Power has thus historically been perceived as imperial and racially white. The domain of control has been externalised beyond the local context in which small Caribbean states are not equipped to participate significantly on a global scale (see Chapter Four for an analysis of globalisation's impacts on the region). Lowenthal (1971) has stressed that this led ultimately to a denial of West Indian identity, a consequence of slavery and colonial legacies subduing ethnic and national self-assertion. The negation of ethnicity or social inequalities has infiltrated many Caribbean texts and consciences. Cuban poet Nicolás Guillén contests popular apathy, arguing that injustice and identities should be challenged and expressed throughout the Caribbean:

> West Indies! West Indies! West Indies!
> This is a hard-skinned people,
> Copper-coloured, many-headed and life belly-crawling
> With dry mud encrusted to the skin.
>
> This is the people who are "all right"
> when everything is real bad;
> this is the people who are "very wel"
> when nobody is well at all.
>
> Guillén (1934) West Indies LTD
> (Translated in Giménez-Saldivia 1996, p. 64.)[1]

The *pesimismo* period within Dominican literature similarly lamented the future of a country founded on slavery and impoverished connections with Europe. This inherently negative outlook was a result of a cultural affectation for European arts, combined with a clear denial of African heritage, to the extent that an indigenous past has frequently been romantically recounted in prose and poetry. Jiménes Grullón produced a celebrated text towards the end of the nineteenth century which lamented the ethnic composition of the country's population. *La República Dominicana: Una ficción* (1965) predicted an unsuccessful future for the nation following the demise of direct Spanish colonial influence in 1865. While writers such as Aimé Césaire (1956) stimulated the development of black literature throughout the twentieth-century Caribbean, African ancestries were perceived with quiet shame or disdain by many Dominicans. Coulthard (1962) has posited that literary recognition of *la négritude* was thus a Caribbean response to find a 'distinctive tonality' through the reverberations of personal, national and regional shared experiences and belonging.

> This distinctiveness of Caribbean societies is apparent from even the most cursory attempt to forge a Pan-Caribbean outlook. Clearly, Caribbean nationalisms have been characterised both by an awareness of shared identities and by a parallel or subsequent practice of particularism and insularism (Oostindie 1996, p. 227).

This recognition of broad similarities provide a means of assessing shared regional histories and social formations, to reveal a dappled mosaic of cultural and social differences that are all the more apparent when individual histories and experiences are considered.

Note

[1] Permission to quote an excerpt from the poem by Nicolás Guillén, quoted in Giménez Saldivia, L. (1996): 'Images of the "other": Caribbean society through the eyes of Cuban and West Indian writers'. in Bryan A. T. and Serbin, A. (eds.) *Distant cousins: the Caribbean-Latin American relationship*. Lynne Rienner: Boulder, was granted by the North-South Center Press at the University of Miami.

References

Accaria Zavala, D. 2000: 'Breaking the spell of our hallucinated lucidity: surveying the Caribbean self within Hollywood cinema'. In James, C and Perivolaris, J. (eds.) *The Cultures of the Hispanic Caribbean*. London: Macmillan. pp. 226–240.

Beckford, G. 1972: *Persistent Poverty: Underdevelopment in Plantation Economies of the Third World*. Oxford: Oxford University Press.

Beckles, H. McD. 1999: *Centering Women: Gender Discourses in Caribbean Slave Society*. Oxford: James Currey.

Benitez Rojo, A. 1992: *The Repeating Island: the Caribbean and the Post-modern Perspective*. London: Duke University Press.

Bennett, L. 1966: *Jamaica Labrish*. Kingston: Sangster.

Blaut, J. M. 1992: 'The theory of cultural racism'. *Antipode* 24: pp. 289–299.

Burton, R. D. E. and Reno, F. (eds.) 1995: *French and West Indian: Martinique, Guadeloupe and French Guiana Today*. London: Macmillan.

Césaire, A. 1956: *Cahier d'un Retour au Pays Natal*. Paris: Présence Africaine.

Clarke, E. 1957: *My Mother Who Fathered Me: A Study of the Family in Three Selected Communities in Jamaica*. London: Allen and Unwin.

Clarke, C. G. 1991: 'Introduction: Caribbean decolonization – new states and old societies'. In Clarke. C. G. (ed.) *Society and Politics in the Caribbean*. London: St Antony's-Macmillan. pp. 1–27.

Clarke, C. G. 1996: 'Jamaican decolonization and the development of national culture'. In Oostindie, G. (ed) *Ethnicity in the Caribbean: Essays in Honour of Harry Hoetink*. London: Macmillan. pp. 182–205.

Coulthard, G. R. 1962: *Race and Colour in Caribbean Literature*. New York: Oxford University Press.

Cross, M. 1980: *The East Indians of Guyana and Trinidad*. London: Minority Rights Group.

Dagenais, H. 1993: 'Women in Guadeloupe: the paradoxes of reality'. In Momsen, J.H. (ed.) *Women and Change in the Caribbean*. London: Turney. pp. 83–108.

de la Fuente, A. 1998: 'Race, national discourse, and politics in Cuba: an overview'. *Latin American Perspectives*. 25(3): pp. 43–69.

Furnivall, J. S. 1945: 'Some problems of the tropical economy'. In Hinden, R (ed.) *Fabian Colonial Essays*. London: Allen and Unwin. pp. 160–172.

Gilroy, P. 1987: *'There Ain't No Black in the Union Jack': The Cultural Politics of Race and Nation*. London: Routledge.

Giménez Saldivia, L. 1996: 'Images of the "other": Caribbean society through the eyes of Cuban and West Indian writers'. In Bryan A. T. and Serbin, A. (eds.) *Distant Cousins: the Caribbean-Latin American Relationship*. Boulder: Lynne Rienner. pp. 53–76.

Glass, R. 1989: *Cliches of Urban Doom*. Oxford: Basil Blackwell.

González, J. L. 1995: 'The four-storeyed house: Africans in the forging of Puerto Rico's national identity'. In Davis, D. J. (ed.) *Slavery and Beyond: The African Impact on Latin America and the Caribbean*. Wilmington: Scholarly Resources. pp. 173–193.

Haslip Viera, G. (Ed) 2001: *'Taíno Revival: Critical Perspectives on Puerto Rican Identity and Cultural Politics*. London: Markus Wiener.

Helg, A. 1995: *Our Rightful Share: the Afro-Cuban Struggle for Equality, 1886–1912*. Chapel Hill: University of North Carolina Press.

Henriques, F. 1953: *Family and Colour in Jamaica*. London: MacGibbon and Kee.

Hurston, Z. N.1939: *Voodoo Gods: An Inquiry into Native Myths and Magic in Jamaica and Haiti*. London: Dent.

Jiménes Grullón, J. I. 1965: *La República Dominicana: Una ficción*. Mérida: Talleres Graficos Universitarios.

Knight, F. W. 1990: *The Caribbean: The Genesis of a Fragmented Nationalism*. New York: Oxford University Press.

Levitt, K. and Best, L. 1993: 'Character of the Caribbean economy'. In Beckles, H. and Shepherd, V. A. (eds) *Caribbean Freedom, Economy and Society: From Emancipation to the Present*. Kingston: Ian Randle Publishers. pp. 405–420.

Lewis, R. and Bryan, P. 1998: *Garvey: His Work and Impact*. Mona: Institute of Social and Economic Research.

Long, E. 1970 (1774): *The History of Jamaica; or, General Survey of the Ancient and Modern State of that Island with Reflections on its Situations, Settlements, Inhabitants, Climate, Products, Commerce, Laws and Government*. London: Cass.

Longmore, Z. 1989: *Tap-Taps to Trinidad: A Journey Through the Caribbean*. London: Arrow.

Lowenthal, D. 1971: *West Indian Societies*. London: Oxford University Press.

Mintz, S. W. 1974: *Caribbean Transformations*. Chicago: Aldine.

Mintz, S. W. 1993: 'Black women, economic roles and cultural traditions'. In Beckles, H. and Shepherd, V. A. (eds.) *Caribbean Freedom, Economy and Society: From Emancipation to the Present*. Kingston: Ian Randle Publishers. pp. 238–244.

Momsen, J. H. 1993: 'Development and gender divisions of labour in the rural Eastern Caribbean'. In Momsen, J. H. (ed.) *Women and Change in the Caribbean*. London: Turney. pp. 232–246.

Moser, C. O. N 1993: *Gender Planning and Development: Theory, Practice and Training*. London: Routledge.

Nicholls, D. 1996: *From Dessalines to Duvalier: Race, Colour and National Dependence in Haiti*. London: Macmillan.

Oostindie, G. 1996: 'Ethnicity, nationalism and the exodus: the Dutch Caribbean predicament'. In Oostindie, G (ed.) *Ethnicity in the Caribbean: Essays in Honour of Harry Hoetink*. London: Macmillan. pp. 206–231.

Patterson, O. 1964: *The Children of Sisyphus*. London: New Authors.

Payne, A. 1984. *Dependency under Challenge: The Political Economy of the Commonwealth Caribbean*. Manchester: Manchester University Press.

Peake, L. 1993: 'The development and role of women's political organizations in Guyana'. In Momsen, J. H. (ed.) *Women and Change in the Caribbean*. London: Turney. pp. 109–131.

Peake, L. and Trotz, A. 2001: *Gender, Ethnicity and Place: Women and Identities in Guyana*. London: Routledge.

Post, K. 1978: *Arise ye Starvelings: The Jamaican Labour Rebellion of 1938 and its Aftermath*. The Hague: Martinus Nijhoff.

Puri, S. 1999: 'Canonized hybridities, resistant hybridities: chutney soca, carnival, and the politics of nationalism'. In Edmondson, B. J. (ed.) *Caribbean Romances: The Politics of Regional Representation*. Charlottesville: University Press of Virginia. pp. 12–38.

Rampini, C. 1873: *Letters from Jamaica: the Land of Streams and Woods*. Edinburgh: Edmonston and Douglas.

Reddock, R. 1990: 'The Caribbean feminist tradition'. *Women Speak!* 26–27: pp. 12–24.

Salkey, A. 1973: *Jamaica*. London: Hutchinson.

Skelton, T. 1995: 'Boom, bye, bye: Jamaican ragga and gay resistance'. In Bell, D and Valentine, G. (eds.) *Mapping Desire: Geographies of Sexualities*. London: Routledge. pp. 264–283.

Smith, M. G., Augier, R. and Nettlford, R. (eds.) 1960. *Report on the Rastafari Movement in Kingston, Jamaica*. Mona: Institute of Social and Economic Research.

Wilkinson, S. 1999: 'Homosexuality and the repression of intellectuals in *Fresa y chocolate*'. *Bulletin of Latin American Research*. 18 (1): pp. 17–34.

Williams, E. 1944: *Capitalism and Slavery*. Chapel Hill: University of North Carolina.

Williams, P. 2001: 'Would you risk your life to find a boyfriend?' *Marie Claire* (June): pp. 26–30.

8

Cultural formations in the Caribbean

Lennox Honychurch

Introduction

The culture of the Caribbean people as practised and experienced among the islands of the Caribbean Sea, that stretch from the Bahamas in the north to the mainland shores of the Guianas in the south, comprises a complex amalgam of influences gathered together over a period of some five hundred years. Caribbean anthropologists, like their colleagues in sociology, history, geography, political science, economics and even literary criticism, are increasingly expanding the frontiers of their respective disciplines to overlap and encompass previous academic boundaries in their quest to effectively represent and interpret the heterogeneity of the Caribbean experience. In his post-modernist perspective of the region, the Cuban, Antonio Benitez-Rojo considers that this eclecticism should not be regarded as a reluctant concession but rather as a considered strategy. For him, the Caribbean can be regarded as a cultural sea without boundaries. 'Who can tell us that he has travelled to the origins of Caribbeaness?' he asks. 'This is why my analysis cannot dispense with any of the paradigms, while at the same time it will not be able to legitimate itself through any one of them, but rather only in and through their nonlinear sum' (Benitez-Rojo 1992, p. 270).

Anthropology's front-runner in the Caribbean by almost two decades, Melville Herskovitz, conducted research among Afro-Caribbean populations in Suriname, Haiti and Trinidad between 1928 and 1939 (Herskovitz 1937; Herskovitz and Herskovitz 1934, 1947). His groundbreaking study on the Haitian peasantry stimulated post-war work on peasantries, sugar cane workers and social pluralism by other North American anthropologists such as Julian Steward (1956), Michael Horowitz (1967) and Eric Wolf (1966). They found, as the entire corpus of Caribbean anthropology has since confirmed, that their studies had to be read against a background of the incongruity between the traditional object of their discipline and the inescapable history of the region. In a recent review of his life's work in the Caribbean, Mintz has concluded that its people engage in a continuous and historically rooted process of refashioning the cultural material that has come their way. In its multi-racialism, this process emerged as part of the encounter of the entire non-Western world, with the West, within the Caribbean. From as early as the seventeenth century, this process represented a social and cultural modernity, which was happening in the colonies before it happened in Europe (Mintz 1996, p. 305).

Amerindian

The prehistory of the indigenous people of the Caribbean, up to and including the period of European conquest, has been a vague zone to the general reader of Caribbean culture. In history books of the region prior to the 1980s it was quickly dismissed as divided between periods dominated by 'peaceful Arawaks' and 'warlike Caribs'. The situation is far more complex. Archaeologists of the Caribbean led by members of The International Association for Caribbean Archaeology (IACA), are still in the process of tracing the patterns of migration, trade and raiding routes that existed along the island arc prior to European intervention. In his 60 years of working in the region, Irving Rouse, the *eminence gris* of Caribbean archaeology, has had to make numerous revisions to his pre-Columbian map of the region as new material has emerged (Rouse 1948 a and b; 1974; 1986; 1992). Distinct styles of pottery, divided into successive ceramic series, extend along the island chain from the mouth of the Orinoco River to the islands of the Bahamas. These have formed the basis of theories on regional systems and chronological frontiers of culture. Various groups of mainland people moved from the Orinoco delta northwards over a period of 4,500 years, from about 3000 BC to 1500 AD. They followed the course of the South Equatorial Current as it mixed with the waters of the Orinoco River and curved up into the Caribbean. Aided by the ocean currents and the close proximity of the islands to one another along the chain, waves of settlers paddled their way into the region in fleets of dugout canoes.

The earliest group of indigenous people to come up the islands was an archaic group of hunter-gatherers. They ground and chipped basic stone tools. One of their first settlements has been identified by a site at Otoire in eastern Trinidad. This is dated at *c* 4000 BC. They moved across the sea channel from Trinidad to the islands of Tobago and Grenada *c* 2000 BC. Because of their initial location at Otoire, archaeologists call these people the Otoiroid.

The Saladoid people followed these Otoiroid in *c* 250 AD. They are associated with the introduction of horticulture and ceramics into the islands. The Saladoid chronology starts *c* 2000 BC in the middle ranges of the Orinico River at a place called Saladiero. The Saladoid had migrated along the riverine route from the headwaters of the Orinoco valley to the South American coast. Here they developed a new sub-series called Cedrosian Saladoid. This they carried to the Antilles. Their horticulture was concentrated on the cultivation and processing of cassava (*Manihot esculenta*). They settled all along the islands of the Lesser Antilles and gradually peopled the Greater Antilles. Here, among the large islands of Hispaniola, Puerto Rico, Jamaica and Cuba, the Cedrosian Saladoid spread widely, extending into the scattered islands of the Bahamas. Because of this wide distribution their culture grew apart, diverging into separate series and sub-series. By the middle of the ceramic age the Caribbean had diversified into four regional lines of cultural development:

- The mainland, including the islands of Trinidad and Tobago.
- The Windward Islands.
- The Leeward and Virgin Islands.
- The rest of the Greater Antilles and the Bahamas archipelago (Rouse 1992, p. 71).

Region 4 was centred on Hispaniola, which was the base for renewed migration spreading into the Bahamas and Cuba (the Western Taino) and back into the Virgin Islands and the Leeward Islands (the Eastern Taino). The 'Classic' Taino developed on the coast and in the interior of Hispaniola and Puerto Rico (Coe, Snow & Benson 1986, p. 160; Rouse 1992, pp. 105–137).

It was a society composed of chiefdoms with ceremonial ball courts and a religion based on the worship of sacred objects carved from wood, bone, shell and stone called *zemis*, one of the earliest studies of which was carried out by De Hostos (1923). All of the above branches of the Cedrosian Saladoid have, in historic times, been covered in the literature by the appellations 'Arawak' and 'Tainos'. These were the people who Columbus met on his first voyage (Cohen 1969, p. 86). Sued Badillo (1995, p. 77) strongly rejects Rouse's earlier theory of a frontier between Puerto Rico and the Lesser Antilles (Rouse 1986: 31, pp. 144–55) and has argued that since the first continental migrations of ceramic people to the Caribbean, the Eastern Caribbean and Puerto Rico had formed a rather homogeneous cultural area. He affirms that although there were changing orientations in ceramic styles, there was no break in cultural continuity between the two areas and this permitted a two-way flow of cultural influences. At both ends of the Lesser Antilles therefore, there was significant interaction. It placed the people who occupied the centre of this route in a prime location for trading with the continent to the south and the Greater Antilles to the north, and it exposed key settlements along the chain to the cultural influences that accompanied this trade. The end of the pre-Columbian era in the Lesser Antilles has been associated with the Sauzoid series *c* 1200 AD (Rouse 1992). But this has been contested by Boomert (1995, pp. 28–29) who argues that the Cayo complex, *c* 1250 AD, found in the Windward Islands from Tobago to Dominica (Boomert 1986, 1987) 'is the only protohistoric pottery tradition from the Windward Islands meeting all the requirements needed to classify it as the Island Carib ceramic assemblage' (Boomert 1995, p. 28).

Carib prehistory and identity

At present two broad models have been proposed to account for the archaeological, linguistic, historical and ethnographic information concerning the Island Caribs, known to be the last Amerindian group in the Lesser Antilles. The more traditionally established model, ingrained into the consciousness of the entire population of the modern Caribbean through the education system over the last 50 years, can be called the 'Carib Invasion' model. Based almost entirely on seventeenth-century texts, it proposes that the 'warlike' Caribs were descended from mainland Caribs who, in the centuries shortly before European contact, had conquered some or all of the Lesser Antilles, attacking the earlier settlers, the 'peaceful Arawaks' or Taino, killing (and in some versions, eating) the men and taking the women as their wives (Davies 1666, p. 204).

In the other, more recent 'Arawakan Continuity' model, the people now called the Island Caribs, who inhabited the Lesser Antilles in 1492, were descended from the same people as the Greater Antillian Taino (Wilson 1994). However, divergent trajectories of cultural change had made them relatively distinct between AD500 and 1000. Linguistics have associated the island populations with the Arawakan group of languages widely distributed throughout the Amazon River Basin, the Guianas, the Orinoco Valley and, in Columbus's time, throughout the Caribbean as well. What has traditionally been assumed to be the victorious Carib 'men's language', separate from the conquered Arawak 'women's language', is now considered to have been a pidgin trading language used when communicating with the Karina, mainland Caribs. The structure of the Island Carib language, which the early French missionaries had called 'Carib', has now been identified as Arawakan (Taylor 1997). Such linguistic arguments have been used in support of the 'Arawak Continuity' model.

In summarising his assessment of these two models, Wilson concludes that whatever the eventual outcome, historical and archaeological evidence from the Lesser Antilles suggests that there was more cultural heterogeneity than had previously been recognised:

> Although speculative, I feel it is more likely that the prehistoric and early historic Lesser Antilles contained a complex mosaic of ethnic groups, which had considerable interaction with each other, the mainland and the Greater Antilles. As now, the individual islands and island groups would have become populous trading centres or isolated backwaters according to the abundance of their resources, the strength of their social and political ties with other centres, and their unique histories of colonisation and cultural change (Wilson 1994).

That there was a 'complex mosaic' composed of popular trading centres and isolated backwaters at the time of this immigration is supported by Allaire (1977), in his pioneering study of contrasting pre-Columbian settlements on the geologically older and younger parts of Martinique. He argues that groups who were active at the same period may have had cultural practices significantly different to each other depending on whether they occupied the older reef-bound lowlands or the steep, actively volcanic regions. Older sections incorporated geological, botanical and faunal resources, which the younger parts of islands did not. Martinique has been the most studied of the group and has provided archaeologists with examples of contrasting habitats on the same island. This has led to indications that the cultural distribution of pre-Columbian groups in this part of the Lesser Antilles was far more complex than originally thought and the island has become the focus of debate for the most recent theories on the origins of the Island Carib (Allaire & Mattioni 1983).

When such aspects of the natural environment are studied in relation to the human ecology of Amerindians and the later Creole societies, which developed after them on the islands, important resource zones may be identified across the region, which could have had equally significant implications in pre-Columbian times. By reassessing the environment of the islands through the eyes of foragers, hunter-gatherers, fisherfolk, horticulturists and cultivators, and informed by both archaeology and ethnohistory, it is possible to construct a basic resource map. This is guided by the biological archaeology of middens and refuse areas around settlements, and by studies of the geology of artefacts such as stone tools and pottery (Olson 1982).

Ethnohistorical and oral information on the ethnobotany of the Island Caribs further informs the search for surviving areas of natural vegetation where such resources would have been available or are still in existence (Multer et al 1986). Seasonal migrations, trade routes and inter-island patterns of fishing and gathering would have been developed according to the location of such resources (Wing 1968; Wing & Reitz 1983).

The culture of the indigenous people was very closely associated with the environment. The size of the islands that they occupied often determined the cultures that they developed. The Lesser Antilles, being close to the continent and being tied into the trade that was carried on with this region, was therefore much more influenced by life on the Orinoco and Guianas coastline. The Greater Antilles, being further removed, and with settlements being on large islands with more resources, developed more complex cultures. While the Southern Lesser Antilles people still had a tradition of having originated from South America, the creation myths of the Taino people of the Greater Antilles placed their beginnings in the caves of Hispaniola. The Tainos appear to have considered themselves superior to the wild 'small islanders' to the south-east, for when Columbus arrived on Hispaniola on his first voyage of 1492 he was warned about the fearful 'Other' across the waters. With preconceived notions of cannibalism and savagery picked up from the Tainos he sailed further south on his second voyage in 1493 and found a people upon whom he and his reporters placed a reputation that has survived for centuries. The earliest mention of the Caribs is that made by Columbus in his journal on 26 November 1492: 'All the people that he has found up to today, he says are very frightened of those of *caniba* or *canima*' (Hulme & Whitehead 1992, p. 19). His initial reference to the word is as a place where people were located, rather than the name of the people themselves. In other statements the Tainos may have been using the term to refer not to a specific ethnic group but to any hostile band who attacked their villages, particularly those who came from the small islands to the east of where they were in Hispaniola. They have variously been called *canima, canybal, caraibe, carebie, caribbee, charaibe* and *cribe* in other European languages (Hulme & Whitehead 1992, p. 354).

'Carib', as it is interpreted among the people of Dominica and the islands of the Eastern Caribbean today, means any of the descendants of the aboriginal people who occupied islands of the Lesser Antilles at the time of the arrival of Columbus. Also those who are associated with settlements on the central east coast of Dominica, the north east coast of St. Vincent and an area within the district Choiseul in southern St. Lucia. In Dominica particularly, there has been a cultural revival movement in progress since the 1970s as young Caribs research their past, form cultural groups, and in several ways attempt to revive traces of an indigenous culture that have been heavily mixed with European and African influences over the last 500 years. This process of admixture between Caribs, Europeans and Africans was the beginning of Creolisation, a process which became the dominant cultural dynamic in the colonisation of the region.

Creole

'Creole' was first used in the Americas to describe those persons of European descent born and brought up in the Indies, so as to differentiate them from the supposedly superior Iberian-born resident and from the supposedly inferior *mestizo*: the progeny of Spanish and Amerindian parents. It is a word of Portuguese and Spanish origin, *criuolo* in Portuguese, *criollo* in Spanish, variously interpreted in its early usage as meaning: created, nursed, brought up and domesticated. With the arrival of other European powers into the Caribbean and their seizure and partitioning of lands across the region, the word was appropriated by the Dutch, French and British. By then Creole was also being applied to the so called 'seasoned' or second generation Africans, born and brought up into the Creole ways of their respective European colonies, and speaking the relevant Creole language which had emerged from the colonial melange of cross cultural influences pouring into the Caribbean. The Oxford Dictionary of Caribbean English Usage (Allsopp 1996) takes up two pages of fine print to explain the term and its derivatives. Virginia Dominguez who has studied the changing usage of Creole in Louisiana since the eighteenth century, concludes:

> A single definition of the term creole may have been adequate for all of these societies during the early stages of European expansion. But as the creole populations of these colonies (or former colonies) established diverse social political and economic positions for themselves over the years, creole acquired diverse meanings (1986, p. 13).

The term is used in the Caribbean to apply to language, specific social groups and the inherited culture of the islands or, as Allsopp phrases it in one of the subsections of his dictionary: 'of or belonging to, or typical of, the life-style and culture of today's Black West Indians'. Later, however, under Creole White, he provides the definition: 'A Caribbean person of strongly marked European stock, with no obvious signs of African mixture'. 'Obvious signs' are the operative words here, and such questions as the interpretation and perceptions of 'purity' will eventually emerge in any discussion on the White West Indian and the Carib.

As a designation of colour and origin in its earlier sense, 'Creole' is sometimes a subtle euphemism also combining references to both colour and class, drawing attention to the fact that Caribbean people of whatever ethnic mixture are confronted daily with their past, for it colours both the observers' and the natives' understanding and handling of their present. This is so because, as one Cuban writer put it, 'every race within the region and every hybrid under the banner of its skin and its speech, carries a local history, a sociology and an economics which feature a common turbulence' (Benitez-Rojo 1992, p. 119). But used in such a context its meaning varies locally. In Jamaica and several other islands of the English-speaking Caribbean 'Creole' designates anyone of Jamaican (or respective island) parentage, except East Indians, Chinese and Maroons, or Caribs in the case of Dominica, St. Vincent and St. Lucia. As in Guyana 'Creole' does not include Amerindians, and East Indians are also classified as a separate entity. In Trinidad it primarily denotes the mainly white, 'French Creole' descendants of seventeenth- and eighteenth-century planters, but secondarily it is applied in the same manner as in Guyana. In the French Antilles, as in Trinidad, 'Creole' refers more to local born whites than to 'coloured' or black persons, although confusingly, in reference to culture, it is applied to 'the entire way of life' of the people of Martinique, Guadeloupe and its dependencies. In this respect, the term is more commonly applied in the islands of the English Caribbean, which at some time in their history had been occupied by France, namely Dominica, St. Lucia, Grenada or, in the case of Trinidad, where the dominant population had been of French extraction who were living under British and Spanish rule.

Lowenthal points out that the word was extended 'to things, habits and ideas: Plants grown, goods manufactured, and opinions expressed in the West Indies were all "Creole" ' (Lowenthal 1972, p. 32). Writing in the 1970s, Lowenthal was of the view that in the English-speaking Caribbean, 'where independence and black power now favour national and ethnic appellations, the term Creole is today considered old-fashioned, self-conscious, or "arty" ' (1972, p.33). But 30 years later there had been a post-independence resurgence of the term, particularly in the French-influenced islands mentioned above, where the *negrétude*, black power, or 'back to Africa' movements observed by Lowenthal in the late 1960s have been tried, tested and found inadequate in representing the 'Caribbean self'. As a result, *Creolité* has witnessed a revival, and even the Lesser Antillian Rastafarian movement now moulds the locally created components of Creole culture in ethnobotany, music, food and fashion, with the vision of an Ethiopian diaspora of which the late Emperor Haile Selasie I is the spiritual inspiration. This is the continuing process of creolisation identified by Brathwaite (1971) as being active in the eighteenth century. He was convinced that studying Creole society of the period was essential to an understanding of a present 'which is becoming increasingly concerned with racial and cultural identity and West Indian's place in the world'. He confirmed that the region's 'present condition and cultural orientation ... are as much a result of the process of creolisation as the slavery which provided the framework for it' (Brathwaite 1971, p. i). Lewis (1983) also sees it as the main generator of the historical evolution of Caribbean society in its ideological aspects from 1492:

> The process was that of a subtle Creolizing movement, whereby all of those modes of thought were absorbed and assimilated and were then reshaped to fit the special and unique requirements of Caribbean society as they developed from one period to the next.

The moral and intellectual baggage of Europe, this is to say, once unloaded, became indubitably Caribbean (Lewis 1983, p. 27).

But only a few, such as Gullick (1976b; 1985; 1995) in St. Vincent, have considered the creolisation process as it affected those people who were already occupants of the Caribbean at the time of the European and African arrival. In this, the most colonial of all colonial societies, where the deepest wrong was done, the effects of the process of colonisation and the creolisation, which accompanied it, have – like the subject peoples themselves – been marginalised. While others arrived with their respective cultures and contributed them to the crucible of change, or *exchange*, within the proverbial 'melting pot', the Amerindian culture was already there.

African

The majority of the people of the Caribbean are the descendants of West Africans originating from a wide range of tribal groups, whose members were captured along the West African seaboard and from the interior. They were exchanged for trade goods, enslaved and transported across the Atlantic to work on the plantations of the islands and mainland colonies of the circum-Caribbean. The cultural variation was as immense as the geographical area from which these people were drawn. It spread from present-day Senegal in the north, southwards along the Gulf of Guinea to Angola. This range included as many as 50 main cultural groups and their numerous related sub-groupings. The diversity of language reflected this complex merging of cultures as people whose origin on the coast could be as much as 2,000 miles apart were thrust together in small controlled communities in the Caribbean. Tribal languages that appear here and there in Caribbean speech range from Hausa, Kru, Ibo, Edo, Bini, Nembe, Yoruba, Ashanti, Ibibo and Ijo to Fulani, Ewe, Kikongo, Efik, Kwa, Fon and Twi and a couple of dozen others. The shreds of cultural patrimony transported in the mind across the terrifying waters of the Middle Passage were pieced together on the shores of the Caribbean into a patchwork of cultural practices, traditions and skills. Their origins became blurred, picked up and pinpointed here or there during the twentieth century by linguists, folklorists and the early anthropologists of the region.

Traces of what was Igbo, Ibo or Ibibo lingered in a word here, a song pattern there, or a character of the spirit world, whose African roots had survived but who had acquired a French or Spanish name in the process of creolisation. The destruction and re-creation of the shattered cultures of West Africa in the form of a variegated collage of influences is the main feature of the African cultural remnants in the region. For much of the 500 years, ever since the first Spanish ship transported the first boatload of Africans direct from the Guinea coast to Hispaniola in 1518, the validity of this African remnant has been rejected. For most of the nineteenth and twentieth centuries its presence was seen as a socially negative undercurrent of West Indian society that was better suppressed, covered up or denied. Only in the latter half of the twentieth century, during a period of great social and political transformation, did the African element in Caribbean culture have its renaissance, manifesting itself in the work of academics, artists, dancers, writers, cultural activists and the Rastafarian movement.

Stripped of everything but the contents of the mind, the African who arrived in the Caribbean carried only memory and skills. And yet it was from these intangible possessions that a new world was recreated, transformed and reordered. For all of its apparent confusion it was anchored by key lifelines of cultural security that helped to give stability, aid survival and make sense of a world gone mad. The plantation system and the regimen of work, mental stress and personal degradation associated with enslavement did not allow for the replication of the structured tribally determined patterns of life as had existed in Africa. Despite their condition they wove these lines of survival wherever possible into their plantation existence. Spaces of cultural opportunity were taken advantage of at every available turn. Subterfuge, sarcasm, innuendo and bitter humour became the antidotes to the circumstances in which the Africans had found themselves. In folktales, songs and dances these threads were woven, providing a pliable ever-changing mask to the reality that lay beyond. The scraps of religious beliefs, once rigidly defined from tribe to tribe became a composite. Some elements were stronger on one island than another depending on the majority of influence from one group of Africans rather than others. But there were general themes associated with a spirit world where good and evil were in contest and whose balance had to be maintained. Spiritual possession and respect for the ancestors ran through it all in spite of the variations.

The African religions and beliefs were outlawed from the earliest days of plantation slavery, not merely because they were seen to be pagan, primitive and generally unchristian but more so because the plantocracy feared these practices were a cover for revolt. Paranoia against any form of African religious spiritualism rose sharply after the Haitian revolution, during which messages and plans of insurrection were passed on during such gatherings. However, despite these restrictions certain forms of traditional religious practices survived under a blanket of secrecy. Those who professed to control spiritual powers were respected and there existed a network of shamans whose skills were called upon to cast spells, make charms and call up the spirit world. They were consulted for their knowledge of the use of herbs to cure illnesses and destroy enemies. These 'obeah' men or women were visited for help and advice and legislation survives on the islands up to today criminalising obeah and those associated with the practice.

There is a certain degree of historical continuity in the ceremonies linked to these religious beliefs. A few are still practised in the different forms of *voodoo* that survive in Haiti and in the *shango* of Trinidad and *pocomania* of Jamaica. Voodoo, for instance, originated from Dahomey, based on the worship of the good, poisonless serpent spirit, Dangbay. The priest or *voodun* communicates with this spirit and makes Dangbay's will known to others. Dances such as the *Kalenda, Chica* and *Voodoo* are part of these religious rites where spirit possession accompanied by intense drumming and chants forms the climax of worship. Transformation has taken place over time and voodoo has been exported with the Haitian Diaspora to New York, Miami and other cities in

North America. In the tourist enclaves of Haiti itself, voodoo ceremonies are presented as floorshows and as such have been stripped of all of their original meaning.

A host of tribal languages were quickly lost as people from one part of West Africa were mixed with others on the plantations. Soon slaves of each European colony were speaking their own form of English, French, Spanish or Dutch, depending from which nation their colonial masters originated. In cases where islands changed hands regularly between opposing European powers and where colonists from both Britain and France were resident, as in the case of Dominica, St. Lucia, and later Trinidad, parallel Creole languages developed in the same place. Many of the 'patois' or Creole forms of speech still exist. One can tell which island someone is from by listening to his or her accents.

Gradually the old African folk tales were remodelled and retold in these new languages. Here and there particular African words or the names of spirits and folktale characters survive. The spider hero of the Akan people, Ananse, lives on in the Anansy stories. Tales involving magic and forests and rivers were also common. But here the spirits had merged with European folklore and had Europeanised names. One hears of the River Mama or Mama D'leau, the water spirit, and the forest spirit Papa Bois. Such characters are common in the former French colonies along with the Loupgarou, a male werewolf, and La Diabless, the she-devil.

Changes in belief systems over time can be exemplified by a study of the currently used word, Jumbie or Duppy as applied to an evil spirit. The word Jumbie or Jombie originates from a branch of the Bantu language especially of the *kongo-ngola* group in which there is the good *nsambi* 'God' and the evil *nsumbi* 'Devil'. Carried across from Africa to Caribbean in various Central and West African language sub-groups, *nsumbi* became Jumbie or Jombie in its Creole form. Good and evil were under the same spiritual power constantly tussling for a balance between the two. Songs and religious practices celebrated the contest, but over time only the Jombie, the evil spirit, was remembered. In early folklore this Jombie could affect your health while you were asleep at night or wreck your good fortune. Practitioners of Obeah were supposed to be able to drive the spirit out or make it affect others. The Jombie is now largely used as a bogeyman in stories to frighten children into obedience.

Music traverses language and so it survived better than other art forms. It was also incorporated into work and periods of festivity and lamenting and so had a continuity that evolved over time from slavery into freedom and further into the twentieth century emerging in forms of reggae, calypso, zouk and soca. Holes for sugar cane planting were dug to chants and the beat of drums. There were songs of sadness, joy, worship and revolt. Later, in the post-emancipation period, hauling of boats, sawing of wood, moving of houses and gathering of fishing nets was done to song. Much of the music was accompanied by dancing, some of these like the bele and kalenda had strong African retentions whereas European dances such as quadrilles, polkas, reels and lancers were given an African transformation, speeded up and choreographed anew with a flare which transformed them into something distinctly Caribbean.

The tunes for such dances incorporated the fiddle, accordion and banjo with a variety of drums and percussion instruments, which had their roots in Africa. Flutes, rattles, 'shack-shacks', scrapers, tambourines and 'bamboo-tamous' were among them. Goatskin was stretched across hollow wooden frames carved from tree trunks and casks from the sugar factories were utilised to form drums, the tamous or 'gro kas' of the French territories. The Spanish islands of the Greater Antilles and influences from Venezuela added an Iberian flavour to African rhythms and were complimented by brass instruments and guitars and quartos. In the British Caribbean, the island of Trinidad was particularly influenced by this, transforming the back-up music for its calypsos and it is even more strongly evident in the 'parang' music of certain communities.

The times of great celebration and festivals were Christmas, Easter, Whitsun and 'Crop-over' when the last canes were brought to the mills for crushing. In the French influenced colonies, the Roman Catholics celebrated Carnival for two days before Lent (see Plate 8.1). From this there developed a lively tradition of street bands with colourful characters dancing and singing in costumes. The songs that accompanied these revelries often told of some recent scandal or some momentous event and

Plate 8.1 *Carnival celebrations in Kingstown, St. Vincent and the Grenadines in 1967. The figure at the centre is a float depicting Buddha. The building behind is the Court House, which doubled as the Legislative Council Chamber during the colonial period. It was also the scene of the outbreak of the October 1935 labour unrest.*

© Cleve McD. Scott

this custom lives on today in the calypsos which are composed and sung during these occasions.

The image of carnival and masquerade is an appropriate analogy to use when reflecting on Caribbean society in the first decades of the twentieth century. As the major cultural group, the patterns set by the African Creole working class permeated the cultural expressions of Caribbean society. This was despite the efforts of the dominant class of Europeans and the influential professional sector, made up of the descendants of 'free people of colour', to maintain the colonial status quo. It was concerned with maintaining the longstanding connections of government and commerce with the world economy and particularly with the culture of each colony's respective mother country. In effect there existed a rigid facade aimed at 'keeping up appearances' while the undercurrent of the mass culture flowed vibrantly on beneath the mask. Political and social change from the 1920s slowly tipped the balance as Caribbean nationalism and self-discovery, made manifest in the arts on several levels, gave birth to a form of cultural liberation that allowed reality to surface and reveal itself from the 1950s. In many parts of the Caribbean this cultural manifestation had been given added dimensions by the arrival of Asian and Iberian immigrants from the middle of the nineteenth century.

Post-emancipation cultures

As the prospect of full emancipation loomed before the Caribbean plantocracy in the 1830s there was concern about a shortage of labour to work the cane fields, particularly in the 'new colonies' of Trinidad and British Guiana and for the Dutch in Suriname. For a brief period in the 1840s some agents in the islands encouraged Africans from the Gambia and Sierra Leone to come over as wage labourers, but the numbers were small and their cultural impact was only really felt in parts of Trinidad where they refreshed some of the more Creolised African retentions remaining from the period of slavery.

More significantly the British first tried Portuguese labour from the island of Madeira, where European farmers of Portuguese origin were struggling with agricultural problems that were crippling the local economy. From 1835 a few hundred Madeirans escaping famine and land shortage arrived to work for wages on the plantations and were set down in the tropical equatorial climate amidst an unfamiliar and widely mixed society. As labourers they were not successful and suffered from the poor quality food, housing and medical attention. For a time they stopped coming but as a vine pest continued to wreck the grape crop in Madeira, poverty forced whole families to leave for the Caribbean, which absorbed some 40,971 Madeiran Portuguese between 1835 and 1881. Most of them soon moved into the main towns becoming shopkeepers and tradesmen and by the mid-twentieth century had established themselves as major players in the commerce and politics of mainly Trinidad, British Guiana, Antigua, and St. Vincent (for further analysis of migration see Chapter Six). Cuba was the first island to use Chinese labour early in the nineteenth century. It was not until 1835 that the first ships transporting Chinese immigrants arrived in Trinidad, British Guiana, Jamaica. Some arrived in the French colonies and in Suriname the Dutch also took in large numbers of

Javanese from their colonies in Indonesia. There was an agreement that indentured labourers would be given a passage home after their five-year period of indenture was over. Numerous Chinese took advantage of this but others remained, moving, like the Portuguese, into the towns and becoming hucksters and small shopkeepers. In all, over 17,000 Chinese came to the British West Indies between 1835 and 1884. Their cultural impact was strongest in Trinidad, Jamaica and British Guiana in terms of food and aspects of commercial activity.

In 1838, the ships *Hesperus* and *Whitby* sailed out of the Bay of Bengal and headed for Demerara, some 14,800 kilometres across the world carrying the first of many thousands of East Indians that would make the voyage in hundreds of ships until the first decade of the twentieth century. The success of East Indian labour to the economies of those colonies that received them was shown in the speedy rise in sugar production in Trinidad and Guyana after 1850. Although as a rule the East Indians were promised a free return passage to India after completing their five or ten year contracts, the majority remained saving money to rent or buy land and invest in their children's education. Their pride in their culture and their Hindu and Muslim religious heritage transformed the societies in which they settled. A visitor to Trinidad in the middle of the twentieth century was able to write:

> Wide tracts of Trinidad are now, for all visual purposes, Bengal. The same vegetation is here, the same villages, a semblance of the same clothing, and everywhere little Hindu cemeteries with headstones inscribed with Urdu characters. We came across a large temple of Vishnu standing under mango and palm trees. Little coloured flags fluttered from poles of bamboo, and the walls inside were frescoed with the figures of Shiva and Parvati and her son Katri and with outlines of Ligam and the bull of Shiva. (Fermor 1951)

In song and dance too, and in the adaptations to music, East Indian influence has made itself felt in the African Creole culture where it sunk its roots. The most popular food items were widely adopted so that today, throughout the Caribbean, versions of *roti* and *pelau* are now considered to be local dishes sold in most street side stalls and restaurants. So strong has been the growth of East Indian influence and population growth, that in Guyana and Trinidad sharp political and cultural divisions have emerged erupting from time to time into violent confrontation or at least causing underlying tensions that cut across society (Honychurch 1981).

At the end of the nineteenth century and first two decades of the twentieth century small but influential groups of minor traders from Syria and Lebanon made their way to the Caribbean. Starting at first as itinerant vendors of cloth, clothing and cheap jewellry among the scattered villages and plantations, this group rose to prominence in the business sector from the 1930s and 1940s, establishing themselves as important powerbrokers in commerce and (mainly behind the scenes) in politics. Their descendants moved into the legal services and tourism development while maintaining strong business networks not merely in their respective territories but across the region.

Taken together, these diverse cultural crosscurrents have thrown up a peculiar hybrid, a chaotic modernity anchored by strands of tradition and conservative circumspection that are rooted in a variety of historical associations. After more than a century of such interaction an observer in Trinidad could sum up the society by saying:

> A Trinidadian feels no inconsistency in being a British citizen, a Negro in appearance, a Spaniard in name, a Roman catholic at church, an obeah practitioner in private, a Hindu at lunch, a Chinese at dinner, a Portuguese at work and a coloured at the polls. (Lowenthal 1972)

Rastafarianism

In 1930 a tribal warlord from a remote corner of Ethiopia named Ras Tafari Makonen was crowned the 111th Emperor of Ethiopia in a line traced back to the union of King Solomon and Queen Makeda of Sheba. His new title was His Imperial Majesty the Conquering Lion of The Tribe of Judah, Elect of God. Tafari took a new name: Haile Selassie – 'Power of the Holy Trinity'. Several preachers in Jamaica began to pray to Haile Selassie as the living God and the hope of African redemption. Worshipers of Selassie became known as Ras Tafaris or Rastamen. The Rastas wore long hair and beards because of an order on the Old Testament that no razor shall touch the head of the faithful. They became known as Locksmen, or Dreadlocks, and in some places they were simply called Dreads.

There is no definite creed for the Rastas. Some smoke large amounts of ganja or marijuana, while others shun it. Their members are in the forefront of repeated calls on the governments of the region to decriminalise the use of marijuana which has now become a virtually uncontrollable weed in the forested zones of several islands and is claimed by all of its advocates to have valuable medicinal qualities. Most of them are vegetarians, avoiding shellfish and meat, particularly pork. Processed or salted food is suspect and they prefer 'I-tal', natural grains, fruit, roots and vegetables. Some do not work while others are fine woodcarvers artists and craftsmen. The corruption of modern society is 'Babylon' and they hope to find peace in 'Zion'.

The spread of reggae music, which was influenced by, and popularised, the Rastafari, spread from Jamaica and influenced youth elsewhere in the Caribbean especially from the early 1970s. During that decade, many of them down the islands adopted the lifestyle, rejecting the prevailing establishment value system and turning to a more 'rootsy' lifestyle living off the land. The circumspect society and traditional, even if 'socialist', political establishment of the region reacted warily to this new movement that erupted in their midst. The question of hairstyle, dress, the cries of 'down with Babylon' and the declaration of novel perceptions of the Caribbean worldview caused a tide of reaction and response which shook island communities into new directions of social transformation.

The foremost exponent of this movement that swept the Caribbean was Bob Marley, for many the embodiment of Rastafarian culture as he was the best-known ambassador of reggae to the world. By the time of his death in May 1981 he was internationally acclaimed and for many the climax of his career was his performance at the Zimbabwe Independence celebrations in April 1980. It was in this sphere that the African Diaspora in the Caribbean gave to Africa a new cultural dimension distilled in the region from numerous ingredients emerging from the colonial experience, transferring a Caribbean perception of an almost totally mythical Africa back to the 'homeland' itself. The influence of Rasta philosophy as carried in the lyrics of Bob Marley's songs has been taken up by groups as far removed from each other as urban youth on the African continent, New Agers in Europe and Aborigines in Australia.

Post-war US influence

After the Second World War the traditional European powers in the region, except for France, gradually turned their attention inward towards building a European community. This was first to form a strong western alliance as a bulwark against Soviet influence during the Cold War but later, after the fall of communism in the late 1980s, it moved towards establishing a global power group to offset the unilateral dominance of the USA. As Britain embarked on its policy of relieving itself of its colonies in the region, the USA filled the vacuum. France made its colonies overseas departments of its continental state and the Dutch gave its islands greater autonomy within a form of associated status with the Netherlands. Suriname became fully independent and the Spanish lost their last colonies in the Caribbean in 1898 (see Plate 8.2).

The close proximity of the powerful northern neighbour made itself more effectively felt from 1940, when it established military bases on several British islands. Already the agencies of US popular culture in the form of radio and the cinema were taking root on the islands. As the century progressed technology provided greater avenues for contact.

Plate 8.2 *Spanish architecture, Havana, Cuba. Although Spain was effectively forced out of the Caribbean in 1898 its legacy remains visible in architecture and audible in language.*

© Tracey Skelton

There was increased tourism from North America following the Cuban Revolution and the US embargo on visits to Cuba. This was evident as US tourism investment shifted into the Bahamas and then into the Eastern Caribbean after 1959. This was coupled with the introduction of passenger jet aircraft on Caribbean routes and the increase in the size and numbers of cruise ships touring the region (see Chapter Five). As the Cold War progressed the Caribbean became a sensitive area in the geopolitics of the 1960s to 1990s, receiving greater US attention. The Black Power and Civil Rights era from the 1960s galvanised Caribbean attention as a new generation of intellectuals was influenced by the ideas of Black Pride and Pan-Africanism first espoused by Marcus Garvey in the 1920s. The black presence in US media, sport, politics and show business provided strong feelings of shared identity between the Caribbean and the USA. This intensified as television and Internet connections became widely available by the end of the century. The media blitz emanating from North America was embraced by Caribbean people despite the pockets of resistance and the warnings coming from vocal but outnumbered advocates of 'Caribbean cultural identity'. However, for a society that had absorbed so much, that had in fact been created by the process of adopting and reworking cultures, the flood of US popular culture into the region can be viewed simply as another addition to the 'melting pot' that will be reworked in its own time. A form of Creole nationalism, which attempts to maintain national pride and cultural awareness in the face of these manifestations of globalisation, has emerged in response to these changes.

Creole nationalism

There was in all the states of the Caribbean a middle-class intelligentsia who were largely responsible for articulating the adolescent nationalism of the fledgling English-speaking territories in the early twentieth century. They regarded the accumulated Creole 'folk ways' as representative of a type of idyllic proto-nationalism, one that was less touched by the 500-year long intervention of colonialism from which the islands were emerging. Here were symbols of survival, evidence of resistance and examples of social and cultural self-determination. When the nationalist politicians of the 1960s and 1970s sought symbols for the stimulation of a nationalist identity it was to this 'folk culture' that they turned. Here were the 'roots' which provided the framework for an 'indigenous' tradition, which would be revitalised, promoted or preserved in co-operation with Departments of Culture. By Hobsbawm's definition, such programmes are classed as 'the inventing of tradition' and it is essentially a process of formalisation and ritualisation, characterised by references to the past, if only by imposing repetition:

> We should expect it to occur more frequently when a rapid transformation of society
> weakens or destroys the social patterns for which 'old' traditions had been designed, producing
> new ones to which they were not applicable, or when such old traditions and their
> institutional carriers and promulgators no longer prove sufficiently adaptable and flexible, or
> are otherwise eliminated. (Hobsbawm 1992, p. 4)

In Oostindie's view, 'The contemporary efforts of intellectuals of various ethnic backgrounds to substitute creole culture for earlier counter-discourses such as *négritude* therefore seems to address the project of bringing together the remaining "coloured" and black segments of the local population no less than the attempt to insert the local culture as a unique entity into the outside cultural world' (Oostindie 1996, p. 10). Parallels may be found in the ideas of such West Indian intellectuals as Stuart Hall and Rex Nettleford. Nigel Bolland (1992) argues that one of the reasons why the creole-society model has been so attractive in recent years is its nationalistic insistence on the validity of creole culture and its potential role in national integration in societies that have recently become independent.

To link cultural activism and identity with tourism, is becoming less of a contradiction in terms, as the small, vulnerable economies of these islands become increasingly dependent on this form of trade. 'Cultural experiences' form a major part of the commodity, while at the same time sustaining the ideological perception of some kind of unique cultural emblem, which manifests national identity in the midst of the tide of globalisation. This is the new reality. Baud (1996) has illustrated that the symbols and historical interpretations, which are chosen to bolster ethnic or national identities are not completely arbitrary, nor is their emotional appeal:

> It may be true that these symbols are distorted, exaggerated, sometimes invented, but even in this latter case, such inventions do not fall from the sky. They originate in the history or culture of a given group of people and are only accepted when they do not deviate too far from existing cultural perceptions and social memories. These memories are not necessarily true themselves, but they are social facts at the moment of their general acceptance (Baud 1996, p. 121).

Bolland emphasises this in his study of creolisation (1992), for it is a process in which the identity of each group which composes the Creole society is continually being re-examined and redefined in terms of the relevant oppositions between different social formations at various historical moments. Quite simply this has been the survival technique of Caribbean societies through the last five centuries: a continual reworking and appropriation of what comes its way. It is a form of cultural Darwinianism that is continually renewing, reordering and strengthening the resilience of its people.

References

Allaire, L. 1977: *Later prehistory in Martinique and the Island Caribs: problems in ethnic identification.* International Association for Caribbean Archaeology (IACA) Congress Report, Martinique.

Allaire, L. and Mattioni, M. 1983: 'Boutbois et le Godinot: deux gisements aceramiques de la Martinique'. In *Proceedings of Ninth International Congress for the study of Pre-Columbian Cultures in the Lesser Antilles.*

Allsopp, R. 1996: *The Oxford Dictionary of Caribbean English Usage.* Oxford: Oxford University Press.

Baud, M 1996 '"Constitutionally White": the forging of a national identity in the Dominican Republic'. In Oostindie, G. (ed.) *Ethnicity in the Caribbean.* Basingstoke: Macmillan. pp. 121–151.

Benitez-Rojo, A. 1992: *The Repeating Island: The Caribbean and the Postmodern Perspective.* Durham: Duke University Press.

Bolland, O. N. 1992: 'Creolization and creole societies: a cultural nationalist view of Caribbean social history'. In Hennessy, A. (ed.) *Intellectuals in the Twentieth-Century Caribbean,* Vol. I *Spectre of the New Class: the Commonwealth Caribbean.* Basingstoke: Macmillan.

Boomert, A. 1986: 'Cayo Complex of St. Vincent: ethnohistorical and archaeological aspects of the Island Carib problem'. *Anthropologica.* 66: pp. 3–68.

Boomert, A. 1987: 'Gifts of the Amazons: "green stone" pendants and beads as items of ceremonial exchange in Amazonia and the Caribbean'. *Anthropologica.* 67: pp. 33–54.

Boomert, A. 1995: 'Island Carib archaeology'. In Whitehead, N. (ed.) *Wolves From The Sea.* Leiden: KITLV Press.

Brathwaite, E. 1971: *The Development of Creole Society in Jamaica 1770–1820.* Oxford: Oxford University Press.

Coe, M., Snow, D. and Benson, E. 1986: *Atlas of Ancient America.* Oxford: Equinox Book, Facts on File Ltd.

Cohen J. M. 1969: *Christopher Columbus – The Four voyages.* Harmondsworth: Penguin.

Davies, J. 1666: *The History of The Charriby Islands.* London. (Transl. fr. Charles Rochefort 1665.)

Dominguez, V. 1986: *White by Definition: Social Classification in Creole Louisiana.* New Brunswick: Rutgers University Press.

Fermor, P. L. 1951: *The Traveller's Tree.* London: John Murray.

Gullick, C. J. M. R. 1976a: *Exiled from St. Vincent: The Development of Black Carib Culture in Central America up to 1945.* Malta: Progress Press.

Gullick, C. J. M. R. 1976b: 'Carib ethnicity in a semi-plural society', *New Community* Vol. 5, No. 3.

Gullick, C. J. M. R. 1985: *Myths of a Minority.* Netherlands: Van Gorcum.

Gullick, C. J. M. R. 1995: 'Communicating Caribness'. In Whitehead, N. L. (ed.), *Wolves From the Sea: Readings in the Anthropology of the Native Caribbean.* Leiden: KITLV Press. pp. 157–170.

Herskovitz, M. M. 1937: *Life in a Haitian Valley.* New York: Knopf.

Herskovitz, M. M. and Herskovitz, F. M. 1934: *Rebel Destiny: Among the Bush Negroes of Dutch Guyana.* New York: McGraw Hill.

Herskovitz, M. M. and Herskovitz, F. M. 1947: *Trinidad Village.* New York: Knopf.

Hobsbawm, E. 1992: 'Inventing traditions, Introduction'. In Hobsbawm, E. and Ranger. T. (eds.) *The Invention of Tradition.* Cambridge: Canto, University Press.

Honychurch, L. 1981: *The Caribbean People Book 3.* Walton-on-Thames, UK: Thomas Nelson & Sons.

Horowitz, M. M. 1967: *Morne Paysan: Peasant Village in Martinique.* Austin: Rinehart & Winston.

Hulme P. and Whitehead N. 1992: *Wild Majesty: Encounters with the Caribs from Columbus to the Present Day.* Oxford: Oxford University Press. International Series No. 183.

Lewis, G. 1983: *Main Currents of Caribbean Thought, the Historical Evolution of Caribbean Society in its Ideological Aspects, 1492–1900.* Kingston, Jamaica: Heinemann Educational Books (Caribbean) Ltd.

Lowenthal, D. 1972: *West Indian Societies.* Oxford: Oxford University Press.

Mintz, S. W. 1996.'Enduring substances, trying theories: the Caribbean region as *oikoumenê*'. *The Journal of the Royal Anthropological Institute.* 2 (2): pp. 289–311.

Multer H. G. *et al.* 1986: *Reefs, Rocks & Highways of History.* Antigua: LISA.

Olsen, F. (ed.) 1974: *On the Trail of The Arawaks.* Oklahoma University Press. *Perspectives*/Ed: A.R., University of Arizona Press.

Olson, S. L. 1982: 'Biological archaeology in the West Indies'. *The Florida Anthropologist* 35: pp. 162–168.

Oostindie, G. (ed.) 1996: *Ethnicity in The Caribbean.* Basingstoke: Macmillan Caribbean.

Readings in the Anthropology of the Native Caribbean. Leiden, The Netherlands: KITLV Press. pp. 61–90.

Rouse, I. 1948a: 'The Arawak'. In Steward, J. (ed.) *Handbook of South American Indians,* Vol. 4, Bulletin 143, The Circum-Caribbean Tribes, Smithsonian Institution Bureau of American Ethnology.

Rouse, I. 1948b: 'The Carib', Steward J. (ed.) *Handbook of South American Indians.* Vol. 4, Bulletin 143, The Circum-Caribbean Tribes, Smithsonian Institution Bureau of American Ethnology.

Rouse, I. 1974: 'On the meaning of the term "Arawak"'. In Olsen, F. (ed) *On the trail of the Arawaks.* Norman: University of Oklahoma Press. pp. xiii–xvi.

Rouse, I. 1986: *Migrations in Prehistory: Inferring Population Movements from Cultural Remains.* New Haven: Yale University Press.

Rouse, I. 1992: *The Tainos: Rise and Decline of the People Who Greeted Columbus.* New Haven: Yale University Press.

Steward, J. (ed.) 1948: *Handbook of South American Indians.* Smithsonian Institution Vol.4, Bulletin 143, The Circum-Caribbean Tribes, Smithsonian Institution.

Steward, J. 1956: *The People of Puerto Rico.* Urbana: University of Illinois Press.

Sued Badillo, J. 1978: *Los Caribes; Realidad o fábula.* Río Piedras: Editorial Antillas.

Sued Badillo, J. 1995.'The Island Caribs, new approaches to the question of ethnicity in the early colonial Caribbean'. In Whitehead, N. L. (ed) *Wolves From the Sea: Readings in the Anthropology of the Native Caribbean.* Leiden, The Netherlands: KITLV Press. pp. 61–90.

Taylor, D. M. 1997: *Languages of the West Indies.* New Haven: Yale University Press.

Wilson, S. M 1994: 'The cultural mosaic of the indigenous Caribbean in Europe and America'. In Bray, W. (ed) *The Meeting of Two Worlds: Europe and the Americas 1492–1650.* The British Academy 81: pp. 37–66.

Wing, E. S. 1968: *Aboriginal Fishing in the Windward Islands.* St. Ann's Garrison, Barbados: IACA Second. pp. 103–107.

Wing, E. S. and Reitz, E. 3. 1983: 'Animal exploitation by prehistoric people living on a tropical marine edge'. In Grigson, C. and Clutton-Brock, J. (eds.) *Animals and Archaeology: 2. Shell Middens, Fishes and Birds.* pp. 197–210.

Wolf, E. 1966: *Peasants.* New Jersey: Prentice Hall Inc.

Wolf, E. 1990: *Europe and the People Without History.* New Haven: University of California Press, Yale University Press.

Index